Fifty Hikes in Western New York

Genesee River Gorge in Letchworth State Park

Fifty Hikes in Western New York

Walks and Day Hikes from the
Cattaraugus Hills to
the Genesee Valley

Dr. William P. Ehling

Photographs by the author

A Fifty Hikes™ Guide

Backcounty Publications
Woodstock, Vermont

To my children, Teresa, James, and Clare, who took easily to the outdoors as children and now as adults take seriously the pleasures of hiking to a hilltop or walking next to a stream. May they always enjoy those quiet moments they find in their own outdoors.

An Invitation to the Reader

Over time trails can be rerouted and signs and landmarks altered. If you find that changes have occurred on the routes described in this book, please let us know so that corrections may be made in future editions. The author and publisher also welcome other comments and suggestions. Address all correspondence to:

Editor
Fifty Hikes™ Series
Backcountry Publications
P.O. Box 175
Woodstock, Vermont 05091

Library of Congress Cataloging in Publication Data

Ehling, Bill, 1920–
    Fifty hikes in western New York: walks and day hikes from the Cattaraugus Hills to the Genesee Valley/William P. Ehling; photographs by the author.
        p.   cm.
    "A Fifty hikes guide."
    Included bibliographical references.
    ISBN 0-88150-164-6
    1. Hiking—New York (State)—Guide-books. 2. New York (State)—
Description and travel—1981 —Guide-books. I. Title.
GV199.42.N65E38   1990
917.47—dc20   90-36522
                                                                        CIP

© 1990 by William P. Ehling
Second printing, 1991
Published by Backcountry Publications
A division of the Countryman Press, Inc.
Woodstock, Vermont 05091

Printed in the United States of America
Typesetting by NK Graphics
Series and cover design by Wladislaw Finne
Map overlays by Richard Widhu
Paste-up by Donna Wohlfarth

Acknowledgments

Searching out and writing about the trails of Western New York has put me in debt to many people—especially to those who developed the state forests, built the trails, protected the ecological heritage, and allowed the natural world to remain a place of beauty in which to walk.

I extend my personal thanks to the members of the Niagara Frontier Chapter of the Adirondack Mountain Club, whose contributions in walking trails and in providing written reports of them were invaluable. A special thanks to Wilma Cipolla, who acted as liaison and organized this special effort, and to Richard Broussard, Michael Fedor, Peter Gillespie, Michael Hopkins, Sue Kalafut, Amy Kopp, Marie Palermo, and Sue Petherick, who served so ably as reporters.

A special thanks to my editor Sarah Spiers; I am especially grateful for her diligence in seeing that the copy adheres to grammatical rules and is factually correct, and I sincerely appreciate her concern for the many details required before a book like this can become a reality. My thanks also go to Chris Lloyd and Carl Taylor of Backcountry Publications, who provided the support that puts this book into the hands of the reader.

I am particularly grateful to all those in Region 9 of the state's Department of Environmental Conservation who took the time to provide information about the history, locations, and vital features of the state forests and wildlife areas in Western New York; a special thanks goes to James A. Beil, regional forester, and Charles P. Mowatt, associate forester, who provided maps, pamphlets, and other aids that made data collection so much easier.

A heartfelt thanks goes to Olga, who always appreciated the importance of the time that researching and writing this book required. She willingly hiked with me the many trails in all kinds of weather and greeted the sights and sounds of the outdoors on each trip with the kind of enthusiasm that makes the whole effort of putting together a manuscript worthwhile.

To the many other people whose assistance in so many ways made possible the collection of information and writing of copy, I express my sincerest thanks.

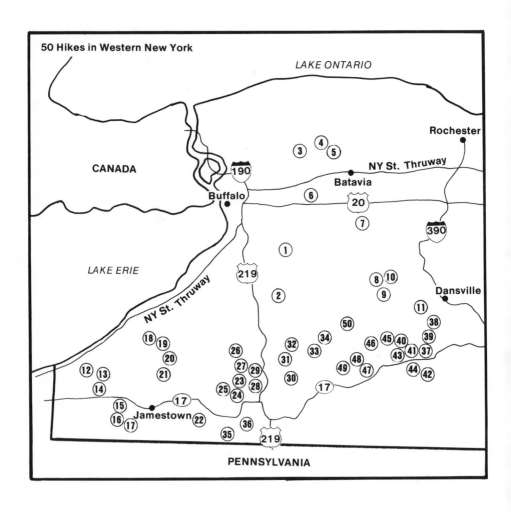

Contents

Introduction

Westward, Ho! Dedicated and seasoned hikers in Western New York know the many assets this part of the state holds for the foot traveler, but not everyone has either the time or the luck to experience its many scenic pleasures first-hand. This guide invites you to look farther afield, to become acquainted with the region's richly diverse landscapes, and to experience the excitement of finding new hiking areas. The fifty hikes in this book provide fifty inducements to get to know one of the best-kept hiking secrets—Western New York.

This part of New York has characteristics and charm that set it apart from other regions of the state. It touches two of the Great Lakes, Lake Erie and Lake Ontario. It boasts a rich intellectual and cultural tradition associated with the Chautauqua Institution on Chautauqua Lake and a long fishing tradition associated with the large muskellunge fish caught in that lake. Thousands of visitors come every year to see one of nature's wonders, Niagara Falls, a geological and glacial phenomenon. After the Ice Age more than 11,000 years ago, when the mile-high glacier receded, the Niagara River was diverted northward over a high escarpment, which switched its direction to its present course that joins Lake Erie to Lake Ontario.

Western New York is a land of ethnic diversity as well, ranging from its first inhabitants, the American indians, to its most recent, the Amish, who moved into Cattaraugus County from Pennsylvania and Ohio in 1849. The Seneca Nation, one of six tribes making up the Iroquois Confederacy, owns three reservations in Western New York and the only U.S. city, Salamanca, wholly located on an Indian reservation.

The area has large metropolitan areas, Buffalo and Niagara Falls, and smaller cities like Olean and Jamestown. It also has tree-shaded villages, quiet hamlets, and prosperous farms. It is a region, to paraphrase Noel Perrin's title, *First Person, Rural,* that has personal significance for those who seek out scenic landscapes in rural America.

What Western New York also has in great abundance, however, are farmlands and forestlands, wetlands and brushlands, lakes and ponds of various sizes, and fish-filled creeks and rivers, like the Genesee River and Cattaraugus Creek, which run through some of the most impressive gorges in the Northeast.

Most important, this region is a place where you can walk in quiet solitude amid the natural sights and sounds of a glen or gorge, marshland or forest, or walk a simple footpath that crosses a field or passes next to a stream. It is a place made for walking, whether in the form of a day hike or a week-long trek.

How to Use This Book

At the top of the page that introduces you to a hike, you'll find the official name of the site (usually a state forest), the hiking distance, the hiking time, the vertical rise, and the name of the topographical map(s) of the hiking area.

Hiking Distance is the distance, measured in miles, of the recommended hike as set forth on the topographic map(s). It always includes a round-trip trek—that is, the distance going and returning. Generally, the hiking distances are under six miles. Most people in fair shape and good health can walk from four to six miles without difficulty or discomfort and, someone in good hiking condition can manage from six to ten miles. The average hiker should be able to do any of the hikes in this book.

Hiking Time is an estimate of the average time (in hours) it takes to walk the prescribed distance. In general, most people can walk about three miles in one hour on level terrain at a steady pace; the pace is about the same on a level forest hiking trail or smooth dirt road. But hiking time can increase when the terrain becomes uneven or hilly.

Moderate uphill walking slows you down to about two miles per hour, and steep hills to one mile per hour or less. Hiking time also will be increased if you stop frequently to enjoy the scenery or take photographs.

Nevertheless, the hiking time given is this book is a fair approximation of the time you will spend walking at a normal pace without taking time to rest or snack.

Vertical Rise refers to the total rise in elevation for the hike. This total is calculated by multiplying the number of ascents by their distance, measured in feet. If your hike is all uphill, then the vertical rise is the distance in feet from the lowest to the highest point. But virtually all hiking terrain is an up-and-down affair. The vertical rise, then, is the total distance when all your hill climbs are added together.

Any rise of less than 300 feet is an easy walk. A rise of 300 to 699 feet means moderate climbing. A rise of 700 to 999 feet means some demanding climbs, and any rise of over 1,000 feet usually means steep and perhaps even difficult climbs.

Map(s) may include one or more United States Geological Survey (USGS) topographic maps. All USGS maps used in this book are in the 7.5-minute quadrangle series. They usually have contour lines at 20-foot intervals, although some have lines at 10-foot intervals.

The New York Department of Transportation (DOT) also makes topographic maps available. These are based on the USGS 7.5-minute series but with several differences. The DOT maps have contour lines in only one color, brown, and there is no green to indicate forest areas. Otherwise, the DOT maps are virtually the same as the USGS maps. The DOT maps can be obtained from the Map Information Unit, New York State Department of Transportation, State Campus, Building 4, Room 105, Albany, New York 12232.

A Sense of Place

Geographers like to speak of "a sense of place" to justify gaining knowledge about geographical locations. It involves more than simply knowing where you live or the name of the forest through which you are hiking. It also involves knowing the similarities and differences between various large geographic areas, such as the Cattaraugus Hill Region and the Finger Lakes Region. It means knowing the relationship between the land's current physiographic features and its geological origins.

A sense of place is also enhanced by knowing the various life forms in an area's ecological systems. Such knowledge provides an understanding of the location of various plant species by the shape of hills, valleys, glens, and gorges. It is knowing the relationship between the flora and the fauna—between, say, the wetlands and the thousands of waterfowl that migrate to them to rest, feed, and nest. People, too, have a place in this natural environment and it takes a quiet hike to experience this complex and always interesting ecological scheme of coexistence.

The Land and Its Geology

Western New York, like the rest of the state, was formed gradually over 400 million years, dating back to the early Paleozoic Era. Its topography—or surface features—was shaped in part by the underlying bedrock.

The bedrock was laid down in the middle period of the Paleozoic Era, especially during the Silurian and Devonian periods, over 400 million years ago. During these periods, a shallow sea extended westward from the Adirondack and New England mountains. Great quantities of sediment washed into this sea from the mountains, resulting in thick accumulations of bed upon bed of sand, mud, lime, and salt. The sea sank under the weight of the sediment, and the sediment, in turn, hardened into sedimentary rock—shale, sandstone, limestone, and rock salt.

All through Western New York, the numerous fossil remains of marine life can be found in these rocks. These fossils are reminders of the brachiopods, trilobites, ostracods, crinoids, gastropods, and coral that lived in this sea. They also provide important information about the geology of the various layers.

The Paleozoic Era ended with the Appalachain orogeny, or mountain building, more than 220 million years ago, which permanently lifted the land above sea level, creating the Appalachian Plateau. The present landforms of Western New York are the results of erosion of this ancient surface.

Also during the Paleozoic period, gas and oil were formed in the land's bedrock, resources that today are brought to the surface by hundreds of wells scattered throughout Western New York from the Southern Tier west to Lake Erie. The oil comes from the permeable sandstone located in the late Devonian Conneaut and Canadaway group.

Many people are surprised to learn that New York is an oil and gas producing state. Oil was first discovered in New York in 1627 at a spot called Seneca Oil Spring, or "burning spring," located in the Seneca Indian Reservation (on the southern edge of Cuba Lake, in the west-central portion of Allegany County). This discovery occurred 230 years before the first successful oil well was drilled in Titusville, Pennsylvania. The first oil was drilled in New York in 1865 near the village of Limestone in the southeastern corner of Allegany State Park. Since then, wells have appeared throughout the state's Southwestern Region. Some have been pumped dry, but the many active wells add more than $65 million annually to the state's economy.

Western New York also contains conglomerate rock beds of the late Devonian Conewango group, the Mississippian Pocono group, and the Pennsylvania Pottsville groups, dating back to 320 million years ago. These massive beds manifest themselves as outcrops on hillslopes, in clusters of huge, two-story-high blocks, to form "rock cities." The large stones formed when the conglomerate beds broke into huge, joint-bounded blocks and were slowly carried downslope by erosion and soil creep. They separated into clusters to form caves, tunnels, and "streets"— passageways through which a person can walk. These rare geological phenomena are found in only a few places in Western New York: Olean Rock City south of Olean, Little Rock City north of

Salamanca, Panama Rocks west of the village of Panama, and Thunder Rocks and Bear Caves in Allegany State Park.

The topography of Western New York also was shaped by the Ice Age. Over a period of two million years, four glaciers advanced and retreated over most of New York, massively reshaping the region's terrain. The last continental glacier overrode Canada, parts of the United States, and northern Europe as well as most of New York State during the Pleistocene Period more than a million years ago.

Called the Wisconsin glacier, it was a mile high and advanced over New York like a huge bulldozer. The forward-moving glacier, by grinding and leveling, cut down hilltops, wore down ridges, deepened and widened valleys into U-shaped troughs and created new ones, called through-valleys. As it advanced southward, lobes of ice pushed into eastern Pennsylvania and across Long Island in the east and deep into Ohio in the west.

But the Wisconsin glacier never touched the area in and around what is today Allegany State Park. This is the northernmost unglaciated region in eastern North America. As a result, Allegany State Park retains a preglacial landscape and has a more rugged terrain than the rest of Western and Central New York. Its straight-sided hills have the appearance of peaked mountains. It has peaked and angular ridges and narrow valleys. The topography is deeply dissected by many little streams.

As the Wisconsin glacier receded northward, it melted and released a vast amount of meltwater. Sometimes these meltwaters followed preglacial streambeds and cut deeply into the valleys. Over aeons, the meltback produced spectacular gorges like the Genesee Gorge in Letchworth State Park, Chautauqua Gorge, Canadaway Creek Gorge, and the Cattaraugus Creek Gorge, near Gowanda. The glacial meltwaters also produced postglacial landforms such as outwash plains, recessional moraines, cross channels, kettle lakes, plunge-pools, eskers, and kames, most of which can be found in Western New York.

As a result of these forces, Western New York can be divided into four basic geological regions. The Cattaraugus Hill Region, which includes Allegany, Cattaraugus, and Chautauqua counties and the southern parts of Erie, Wyoming, and Livingston counties, is the largest. The Allegany Hill Region, which is completely encompassed by Allegany State Park, is the smallest. It is the part of Western New York that was not touched by the glacier. The Erie Lake Plain Region runs along the western edge of the Cattaraugus Hill Region, from Buffalo to Erie, Pennsylvania, in a long narrow strip. Finally, the northernmost region of Western New York is actually divided into two geological regions: the Southern Ontario Plain and the Ontario Lake Plain. These two lowland areas are separated by a scarp, in the form of an east-west slope, into two levels. In the Southern Ontario Plain are two of the state's wildlife management areas, Tonawanda and Oak Orchard, and the Iroquois National Wildlife Refuge.

Finally, tradition defines still a fifth region: the Niagara Frontier. This region is widely accepted and is conventionally thought to encompass the counties of Niagara, Erie, Orleans, Genesee, and Wyoming.

Hiking Regions and Locations

Although dividing Western New York into regions according to topographical landforms seems a helpful way to divide the state for the hiker, this is not the way the state arranges the area. Various state agencies—the Office of Parks, Recreation, and Historic Preservation, and the Departments of Environmental Conservation, Commerce, and Transportation—have somewhat different ways of organizing both the Niagara Frontier and other regions of Western New York into administrative units, each with its own appropriate rationale.

This book, however, defines Western New York with the hiker in mind and places the 50 hikes in three large geographical regions: the *Niagara Frontier Region, the Genesee Region,* and *the Southwestern Region.* The Niagara Frontier Region includes three counties: Niagara, Erie, and Orleans; six hikes in this book are in Erie County. The Genesee Region includes three counties: Genesee, Wyoming, and Livingston; five of the hikes fall in these counties. Finally, the Southwestern Region includes three counties: Chautauqua, Cattaraugus, and Allegany; comprising thirty-nine hiking sites here—10 in Chautauqua, 15 in Cattaraugus, and 14 in Allegany. Traveling by car, the prospective hiker can reach even the most distant sites from Buffalo in only about 1½ to 2 hours.

Rochester falls outside the half-circle and is usually considered to be in the Finger Lakes Region. But those who live in the Rochester metropolitan area who would like to hike in Western New York can reach 65 percent of the hikes in this book in about the same driving time.

State Land-Use Classifications

New York State classifies its lands in several different land-use categories, according to the general purpose for which a specific tract of state land is used. The three categories as administered by the Department of Environmental Conservation include state forests, wildlife management areas, and multiple use areas.

State forests, the dominant land-use category in Western New York, are managed for the purpose of developing tree stands for harvesting. Directed by state foresters, logging is done selectively by private individuals and companies which under contract, buy the trees from the state.

Wildlife management areas, by contrast, are developed and managed to improve the capacity of the land to sustain sizable populations of waterfowl and mammals.

Multiple use areas, in turn, are used for recreational activities, including hunting and trapping in season, cross-country skiing and snowshoeing, nature study, birdwatching, photography, and dog field trials.

To improve access to private lands for hunters, the state also has established *cooperative hunting areas* under the Fish and Wildlife Management Act. In this special arrangement, private land owners, with state assistance, allow their land to be used for recreational purposes. An example of such an arrangement is the Sulphur Spring Hill Cooperative Hunting Area, adjacent to the Carleton Hill Multiple Use Area in Wyoming County.

In addition to the public lands administered by the Department of Environmental Conservation are scores of state parks managed by the Office of Parks, Recreation, and Historic Preservation. Many of these parks are small and are found on the shores of Lake Erie and Lake Ontario; others are large, such as Letchworth State Park and Allegany State Park (the largest park in Western New York).

In addition to the state's categories of public lands, Western New York also contains county parks. Several of these are included in this book because they provide ideal hiking terrain and marked trails.

All the hiking areas in this book are located on public lands, to eliminate the possibility of crossing or camping on private property or other posted lands. The fifty hikes do not take you to all of the state and county lands in Western New York; they touch only about 70 percent of all the available public lands. Small state parks along the lakes, for example, are not included in this book because while these parks are extensively used for picnicking and swimming, they have limited acreage for serious hiking.

But other state parks offer plenty of room for hiking. Letchworth State Park is the site of the Genesee Gorge, dubbed the "Grand Canyon of the East"; its three great falls and impressively deep gorge should be seen from several different vantage points to be appreciated. Darien Lakes State Park allows the hiker to walk a section of the Conservation Trail. Finally, Allegany State Park is the state's largest park, with 62,000 acres of forested landscape, sharply peaked hills, narrow valleys, and scenic beauty. It contains more than 130 miles of groomed and marked hiking trails through some of the best hiking territory in Western New York. Through this large park, located in the southern portion of Cattaraugus County, runs an 18-mile section of the Finger Lakes Trail, which starts on the Pennsylvania border and runs eastward along the southern part of the state to terminate in the Catskill Mountains. Allegany, indeed, is a hiker's mecca.

Trail Systems

Several trails described in this book are part of larger trails and trail systems that pass through the region.

The Finger Lakes Trail (FLT). The Finger Lakes Trail system, white blazed, runs for 648 miles. It allows you to walk the entire southern region of upstate New York. Beginning at the Pennsylvania border in Allegany State Park, it takes a northerly course, passing through various state forests in the Cattaraugus Hill Region: Bucktooth State Forest, Rock City State Forest, McCarty Hill State Forest, Boyce Hill State Forest, Bear Creek State Forest, Farmersville State Forest, Allegany State Park, Bully Hill State Forest, Swift Hill State Forest, Slader Creek State Forest, and Klipnocky State Forest. Eventually it runs below the Finger Lakes, then into southern New York State, and has its eastern terminus in the Catskill Forest Preserve (see Hikes 23, 24, 28, 31, 34–39, and 50).

The Conservation Trail (CT). Coming out of the FLT system are several long spur trails, which run toward Buffalo, Rochester, and Syracuse. The Buffalo-directed spur is the Conservation Trail (CT). The CT begins in Allegany State Park as part of the FLT system. It switches off on its own about 5 miles northwest of Ellicottville and runs through Hunter Creek Park and Darien Lakes State Park (see Hikes 1 and 6). It ends in Akron Falls Park, northeast of Buffalo and east of Akron. The Conservation Trail was built and maintained by the Foothills Trail Club of Western New York. It is blazed in orange.

Letchworth Trail (LT). The other spur off the Finger Lakes Trail system in Western New York is the Letchworth Trail in Letchworth State Park (see Hikes 8, 9, and 10). This yellow-blazed spur runs the full length of the state park, from Portageville in the south to Mount Morris in the north.

Chautauqua County Trails. Chautauqua County's two long trails, the Westside Overland Trail (WOT) and the Eastside Overland Trail (EOT), are so named because they are located on the west and east side off Chautauqua Lake, respectively. Both are marked with light blue blazes, and both pass over state forest lands and private lands lined up along north-south axes. If you draw a line through all the state forests on both sides of Chautauqua Lake, you will approximate the routes of the two trail systems.

The two systems, extensively used in winter for cross-country skiing, make these areas of Chautauqua County a hiker's and skier's mecca. Well marked in blue blazes or blue discs and frequently groomed, these are the county's recreational pride and joy, as well as major attractions for serious hikers and casual strollers in the summer. In winter, Nordic ski races are held on these trails, including an annual long-distance race on the Westside Overland Trail.

The Westside Overland Trail (WOT) is a continuous trail of 25 miles that runs from Chautauqua Gorge in the north to Brokenstraw State Forest in the south. Along the way, it passes over county land, six tracts of state forest land, and private lands of a quarter-mile to 5 miles long. It was constructed in 1976 through the efforts of the Youth Conservation Corps, but it was developed and is currently maintained by Chautauqua County Park Commission and the Department of Public Works (Hikes 12–17).

The Eastside Overland Trail (EOT) has one terminus in the Canadaway Creek State Wildlife Management Area and the other just east of the hamlet of Gerry on NY 60. It runs over three large clusters of state land, including the Canadaway Creek State Wildlife Area, Boutwell Hill State Forest, and Harris Hill State Forest (Hikes 18–21).

Trails: Their Classification and Maintenance

Trailheads. A trailhead is the starting point of a route. If the hiking route is part of an officially marked and maintained trail system, such as the Finger Lakes Trail, the trailhead is usually marked with an identifying trail sign.

On unmarked routes, the trailheads are not marked with trail signs. Still, you should encounter no difficulty finding these trailheads. A careful reading of the "Access" directions for each hike should enable you to find both the marked and the unmarked trailheads with ease.

Trail Building and Maintenance. Twenty-three of the 50 hikes in this book are on trails that are groomed, marked, and maintained either by public agencies (state, county, federal) or by private organizations (such as the Finger Lakes Trail Conference).

In state parks, state officials do build and maintain a variety of foot trails. In state forests and wildlife management areas, however, the state generally does not mark or maintain trails, although it does assist private groups build and maintain trails through its Department of Environmental Conservation.

In one case, a county has built, marked, and maintained lengthy hiking trails, with assistance from state and federal agencies. Chautauqua County's Westside and Eastside Overland Trails were made possible by the unique cooperative efforts of local, state, and federal agencies, but Chautauqua County and its Department of Public Works and Park Commission was the prime mover in trail construction, and they continue to maintain the trails. The state helped locate the trails on state forest land, and the federal government provided funding for wages to various groups that actually constructed the trails. (Both trails pass through state forests and a state wildlife management area, which are all under the jurisdiction of the state's Department of Environmental Conservation.) Private landowners gave permission for the trails to cross their lands.

The private Finger Lakes Trail Conference (FLTC), which is generally made up of local hiking groups, has taken on the responsibility of developing, grooming, and maintaining the various sections of the Finger Lakes Trail (FLT).

The remaining 27 hikes in this book are located on public lands but are not groomed or maintained by either public or private agencies as hiking trails. These trails include dirt roads, truck trails, lanes, jeep trails, and paved roads.

A *truck trail* is a somewhat technical term used by state personnel to designate a dirt road through a state forest that has been built and is currently maintained by the state as an access route. These are excellent roads—well drained and rarely rutted. They usually are a lane and a half wide (sometimes two) to allow, among others, heavy-duty timber trucks to drive in and out of the state forest during logging operations.

A *dirt road* is usually a vehicular route found outside state forests. They are maintained by the county or, in some cases, by towns or villages; the conditions of these roads vary greatly. Please note that while all truck trails are dirt roads, not all dirt roads are truck trails.

A *lane* may or may not be maintained by a state or local agency or by a private individual (if the lane is located on private land). It is usually a single-lane route with low, if any, maintenance. On state land, lanes are frequently abandoned farm or logging roads and are generally off-limits to unauthorized vehicles, making them ideal routes for hiking.

A *jeep trail* is a route that is not main-tained either on state or private land but is still used by all-terrain vehicles (ATVs) and four-wheel-drive vehicles. Although frequently badly rugged, they can be used as impromptu hiking routes. They usually are shown on USGS topographical maps as dashed lines.

A *paved road* is occasionally used for hikes in this book, usually to get from one section of a state forest to another. A paved road is generally a two-lane hard-top highway, in this book, either a state or a county highway.

Lifeforms and Ecology

The animals, including reptiles and amphibians, found in Western New York are like those found in the rest of New York and in the Northeast generally. They include such mammals as opossum, porcupine, muskrat, beaver, several species of bat, several species of mole, shrew, and vole, red, gray, and flying squirrels, chipmunk, woodchuck, varying hare, Eastern cottontail rabbit, raccoon, skunk, ermine, weasel, mink, red and gray fox, coyote, black bear, and the white-tailed deer.

The birds here include more than 200 species. The largest is the wild turkey, which, through a state trap-and-transfer program, is now found across a broad range of the Southwestern Region. Other large birds include the turkey vulture, osprey, and the bald eagle. The latter were originally "hacked" (specially raised from eggs brought from Alaska) by the state in the Oak Orchard Wildlife Management Area and elsewhere. These eagles return to Oak Orchard and the nearby Iroquois National Wildlife Refuge to mate and raise their own eaglets, marking a successful restoration program.

Other predatory birds can be found, including several species of owl and a score of hawks—sharp-shinned, broadwinged, red-shouldered, red-tailed, marsh—and the American kestrel. Upland game birds include ruffed grouse and ring-necked pheasant, while waterfowl include the great blue heron, green heron, grebe, American bittern, common gallinule, American coot, snow goose, Canada goose, and about 25 species of duck. Local nesters include the Canada goose, mallard, wood duck, black duck, American widgeon, and green-winged teal. Dozens of shore birds also stop in Western New York during migration periods.

There are more than 300 kinds of wildflowers here, as well as most of the common trees and shrubs, including white, red, and scotch pine, spruce, hemlock, poplar, sycamore, walnut, hickory, oak, birch, American hornbeam, willow, Eastern cottonwood, aspen, cherry, locust, ash, and maple. Look for these and other trees in the state forests.

Black Bear and Rattlesnake: Caution! The black bear and the timber rattlesnake are both shy creatures and usually will take considerable pains to avoid contact with human beings. This doesn't mean, however, that you should not be cautious.

The habitat of both black bear and the timber rattler stretches across southwestern New York, and the rattler is found as far north as Letchworth State Park. There is even a place that publicly acknowledges the presence of the rattler—Rattlesnake State Wildlife Management Area.

There have been no reported cases of black bear attacks in New York in recent memory, but incidents have been reported in other states, particularly Maine and Michigan. In these incidents, an individual got between a sow and her cub, and the sow, feeling threatened or protecting her cub, was provoked into attacking. While such attacks are rarely fatal, they may result in serious injuries.

Such incidents, however, are rare. The likelihood of having a close encounter with a black bear while hiking in western New York is very low. But should such an eventuality occur, making a loud noise—such as shouting, clapping hands, or banging rocks—is usually enough to frighten a bear into a hasty retreat.

Nonetheless, treat the black bear with respect; you're dealing with a wild animal, not someone's stray but friendly pet. Remember, too, that there is a stable population of black bear in Chautauqua, Cattaraugus, and Allegany counties, with the largest population in the latter.

The cold-blooded timber rattlesnake likes to warm itself in the sun on cold days and cool itself on hot days. The rattler may select a trail or other open spot for sunlight, thus increasing your chances of seeing one. In summer, the rattler seeks out cool spots in holes, rock crevices, and narrow openings and under brush piles, so you are unlikely to spot a rattler during the heat of a summer day. Still, watch where you sit for a break or a snack.

Another species, the Massasouga rattlesnake, is found in swamp areas south of Rochester. But in Western New York, the timber rattler is the more common of the two.

Generally, a snake will move off when it hears or senses your approach, greatly decreasing the chances of an encounter. If you do see one, give the snake time to leave. In any event, don't crowd the snake. And don't kill it—it belongs in this habitat and is a natural member of the environment.

Neither black bear nor rattlesnake should keep you from enjoying your hike. Just be aware that these animals are indigenous to this area.

People and Ethnology

The history of New York Indians extends back thousands of years. It is generally believed that the Iroquoian group migrated to New York from the Midwest in the thirteenth or fourteenth century. Over time, this group divided into five nations: the Senecas, the Mohawks, the Cayugas, the Onondagas, and the Oneidas.

By 1570, these five Iroquois nations had formed a confederacy. In the early 1600s, the confederacy occupied the lands that run eastward from an imaginary line just west of Rochester to include all of the Adirondack region. The Senecas were the Keepers of the Western Door, and the Mohawks were the Keepers of the Eastern Door. In between were the Cayugas, the Onondagas, and the Oneidas. In 1714, a sixth tribe, the Tuscaroras, were added to the Iroquois Confederacy.

During the seventeenth century, other tribes that did not belong to the Iroquois Confederacy also occupied parts of Western New York. The Erie tribe settled the land along Lake Erie and the western part of Lake Ontario. The Susquehannas, pushing up from Pennsylvania, occupied the land that extends approximately from Rushford Lake, in northeastern Allegany County, to Binghamton, where the lands of the Delawares lay. But the rest of New York was occupied by the Iroquois Confederacy. These two basic groups spoke two dialects, classified as Algonkian and Iroquoian.

In time, the French and the British moved into Western New York. In 1679, French explorers reached the shores of Lake Erie. From there they searched and found a southward passage to the Ohio and Mississippi rivers via an overland route from Lake Erie to Chautauqua Lake and then by streams to the Allegheny River, which led to the Ohio River. The overland parts of this route became known as the Portage Trail. The importance of controlling this route gave rise to a dispute between the French and the English and led to the French and Indian War.

The members of the Iroquois Confederacy were scattered after the American Revolution, and today they are found throughout New York and the Canadian province of Ontario. "The Lands of the Senecas," however, still exist in Western New York and consist of three Indian reservations: the Allegany Reservation, the Cattaraugus Reservation, and the Oil Spring Reservation (which is unoccupied). These lands were set aside by the Treaty of Canadaigua in 1794; the Seneca Nation holds the title to them.

The 22-mile-long Chautauqua Lake, called "Jad-dah-gwah" by the Indians, ultimately gave its name to Chautauqua County. This county is one of the large grape-producing areas in the state, and more Concord grapes are grown here than anywhere else in the country. The narrow strip of land running along Lake Erie is known as the Chautauqua Wine Trail and boasts five large wineries.

Among the more recent arrivals to Western New York are the Amish, who first settled in Cattaraugus County in 1949, after moving there from Pennsylvania and Ohio. The heart of New York's Amish country is found in the Randolph area, located between Chautauqua Lake and Allegany State Park. The Amish people speak a frozen German called Pennsylvania Dutch. ("Dutch" is the Anglicized version of *Deutsch*.)

Amish homes are recognized as the ones that lack fancy window curtains and electric lines; no electric appliances are found in Amish homes. Their religious beliefs also forbid them to use modern appliances or farm implements. Instead, they use horses for farm work and transportation. The Amish are thrifty, hardworking, and successful farmers in spite of their old ways, and their homes and farm buildings are always neatly painted and are kept in excellent repair.

On highways, you can see horse-drawn buggies driven by Amish men in black hats and women in bonnets. Children are clad like their elders and walk to and from Amish schools, sometimes several miles.

Outdoor Pursuits

Camping and Backpacking. Most of the hiking areas in this book are suitable for both camping and weekend backpacking.

In state forests, the general rule regarding camping is that you may pitch a tent anywhere, unless signs indicate otherwise, for three days; beyond three days, you have to obtain a permit from the nearest regional office of the Department of Environmental Conservation.

State parks—such as Letchworth, Darien Lakes, and Allegany—have special areas designated for camping, but they prohibit camping outside these areas.

County parks usually do not allow camping, but when in doubt, check with the county department of parks and recreation.

For long-distance backpacking, you have a number of options. You can use long trails, such as the Finger Lakes Trail or several of its spur trails, or you can use the long trails in Chautauqua County.

On Chautauqua County's two overland trails, camping should be restricted to the lean-to areas in the several state forests through which the trails pass. Similarly, when hiking long distances on the FLT, plan to stay in or camp next to the existing lean-tos found on state land.

The Conservation Trail, on the other hand, passes over a large portion of private land; camping, if anywhere, should be on the few available public land sites.

Ski Touring and Snowshoeing. The hiking areas described in this book were selected with Nordic skiing and snowshoeing in mind. For those who have never engaged in these two modes of winter travel, now is the time to start. Every hiking trail in this book can be used for snowshoeing, and most can be used for Nordic skiing. Of course, you need a fair amount of snow to make snowshoeing or ski touring worthwhile and pleasurable—at least a half-foot.

A few of the hiking areas contain moderately steep ascents or descents into gullies and ravines. The novice may wish to avoid these, although an advanced skier can handle the terrain with ease. With snowshoes, no one will have difficulty in these hilly areas.

Several of the trails are suitable for backcountry skiing—that is, for overnight excursions where the skier carries a backpack and tenting gear. Try trails in Mount Pleasant State Forest and Boutwell Hill State Forest in Chautauqua County; Harry E. Dobbins Memorial State Forest, Rock City State Forest, McCarty Hill State Forest, and Golden Hill State Forest in Cattaraugus County; and Jersey Hill State Forest, Phillips Creek State Forest, Palmers Pond State Forest, and the adjoining areas made up of Rush Creek State Forest, Crab Hollow State Forest, and Hanging Bog State Wildlife Management Area in Allegany County.

A number of hiking areas are ideal for shorter cross-country skiing trips. Try various sections of Chautauqua County's two overland trails, trails in Letchworth State Park, and trails in the three wildlife areas—the state's Tonowanda and Oak Orchard areas and the Iroquois National Wildlife Refuge, where a special circular trail is marked for ski touring.

Other Outdoor Pursuits. The hiking areas can also be used for birdwatching, outdoor photography, hunting, fishing, canoeing, and other outdoor activities.

Photography mixes well with birding and hiking, especially using a telephoto lens to get closeup views. State lands also are open for hunting in season, whether for small game, upland game, or large game. Many of the hikes take you to streams, ponds, and lakes where you can fish and, in many cases, canoe. Game fish are plentiful in Western New York and include bass, walleye, bullhead, sunfish, crappie, pickerel, Northern pike, muskellunge, and the three species of trout—brook, brown, and rainbow.

Weather and Climate. Western New York's weather is about the same as that of Central New York. It has warm and generally sunny days in summer and cold, snowy ones in winter, inviting you to hike when it is warm and ski or snowshoe when it is snowy.

Summer temperatures are usually around the 70- or 80-degree mark; winter temperatures drop into the low 30s or high 20s. In January, the mean monthly temperature is 21 degrees Fahrenheit in the highlands of southwestern New York and around 25 degrees Fahrenheit along the plain areas bordering Lake Erie and Lake Ontario. In July, the mean monthly temperature is 65 in the highlands and 70 along the two lakes.

Summer temperatures, of course, can get high, sometimes into the 90s for short periods. This is the time when you should head for the woods; hiking shady forest trails on such days can prove pleasantly cool and comfortable.

As for precipitation, Western New York has cool, wet summers and cold, snowy winters. Much of this is the result of "lake effect": conditions produced by westerly winds blowing across Lake Erie. The mean monthly precipitation for much of Western New York is more than three inches, making the area a little wetter in summer and snowier in winter than the rest of New York State.

In winter, snow squalls coming off Lake Erie can dump several feet of snow in short periods of time, providing excellent conditions for Nordic skiing and snowshoeing. In summer more than four inches of rainfall per month, with rainfall occurring about 30 percent of the month; it is a kind of summer climate that suggests carrying rain gear in your backpack on every outing in case of a sudden summer shower.

Hiking Gear and Clothing. Weather affects what you wear and the kind of gear you will use on any given hike. In summer, your gear can be minimal and your clothes light; the reverse is true for winter hiking. In any season, however, you will always need a sturdy day pack to carry a number of items that you should always have even on a short trip. There is nothing sacrosanct about the following list; you can and should adjust the inventory to fit your needs as a hiker. A useful list would include (1) food (usually lunch) and some on-the-trail mix of, say, raisins, peanuts, and candy to keep your energy level constant; (2) extra clothing, including a rain parka or poncho, windbreaker, or wool shirt or sweater to keep you from getting wet or chilled; (3) a pocket knife (a Swiss army knife is a good choice); (4) a plastic bottle with water (for safety's sake, never drink water from a stream or lake); (5) a small first aid kit; (6) map(s) of the area in which you plan to hike, and (7) a compass.

You may also want to carry insect repellent and sunburn preventive lotion (in season), toilet paper, a whistle to use if lost, sun glasses, lightweight binoculars, a camera with extra film, and field guides on birds, flowers, ferns, mushrooms or your other interests. In winter you may wish to carry extra socks and gloves, a Thermos of hot liquid (coffee, tea, or soup), waxes for cross-country skis, and other gear for skiing.

Good hiking shoes are a necessity; buy the best. Today you'll find a wide assortment of styles and brands of lightweight boots. A hiking boot should be sturdy, about six inches high, with a good sole to give you grip on wet trails or slippery rocks. You'll need half-packs or insulated boots when you hike in snow, or use snowshoes.

In summer it is better to wear pants or slacks than shorts; walking a trail that suddenly becomes filled with briers is an experience you can do without. In winter, layer the garments you are wearing. Wear several lightweight wool shirts and a windbreaker rather than a single heavyweight jacket. When you dress in layers, you can remove one piece at a time to reduce unnecessary sweating. You do not want your inner clothing to become wet—this will make you cold and uncomfortable when you stop to rest.

Hiking Safety and Ethics. Safety and ethics go together. Ethics, the proper conduct imposed by morals and laws, means, among other things, that you behave responsibly when it comes to your safety and the safety of others with you on a hike. None of the hikes in this book will place you in a life-threatening situation, but there will be places where you must exercise caution and care: walking near the rim of gorge or making a steep descent, for example.

Compared with driving on the highway, hiking is a safe, low-risk activity. Even so, carelessness and thoughtlessness can lead to oversights, mistakes, and mishaps. These can range from getting blisters from poorly fitted boots to

getting lost for having failed to bring a map and a compass. The first step in safety is to be prepared. Always carry a first aid kit in your backpack.

Never walk alone in far-off or remote places. At the very least, hike with a partner; better still, hike in a group of three or more. If anything happens to one group member, one can seek help while another cares for the one who can't go on.

Know where you are going, and let others know as well. Use topographic maps, and know how to use a map and compass when you reach a trailhead. To hike an area for the first time without a map is to invite getting lost. While this is rarely a life-threatening situation in Western New York, it can be an unnecessarily harrowing experience for you and your family and friends; it may also involve many people and much time in a search. Let responsible people know where you are going, and when you reach the trailhead, leave a note under the windshield wiper outlining your hiking route.

Hiking ethics go beyond safety. They include the obligation to care for the land, forest, trail, and campsite. Do not litter; if you find some one else's litter, pick it up and carry it out. Leave the trail cleaner than it was before you passed through.

Don't chop trees for fuel. Don't deface lean-tos or cliff walls. Exercise care in the disposal of human feces; dig a hole and bury your feces at least 200 feet off the trail, well away from any water source. Don't bathe with soap in lakes or streams, and carry washwater or dishwater well away from the water's edge.

As more people become hiking and backpacking enthusiasts, problems of trail maintenance increase. Proper conduct minimally entails that you respect hikers who come to the hiking area after you, respect the area's plant life and wildlife, and respect the private landowners who have allowed a trail to cross their land. Please leave nothing behind but your footsteps.

For More Information

Books and Guides. It's easy to find out more about hiking, camping, cross-country skiing, and snowshoeing. Most outdoor stores carry books on these subjects. Moreover, there are now hiking guidebooks that cover virtually the entire state of New York. Backcountry Publications of Woodstock, Vermont, publishes a series of 11 "Discover the Adirondacks" hiking guides, as well as hiking and bicycling guides for the Hudson Valley and Central New York. The Adirondack Mountain Club has also published a series of hiking guides of the Adirondacks, as well as guides to canoeable streams in the Adirondacks.

Several of the more useful books and guides include:

Cayuga Trails Club. *Guide to Trails of the Finger Lakes Region.* 3rd ed., 1971. (Cayuga Trails Club, General Delivery, Ithaca, N.Y. 14850.)

Ehling, William P. *Canoeing Central New York.* Woodstock, Vt.: Backcountry Publications, 1982.

Ehling, William P. *Fifty Hikes in Central New York.* Woodstock, Vt.: Backcountry Publications, 1984.

Ehling, William P. *25 Ski Tours in Central New York.* Woodstock, Vt., Backcountry Publications, 1980.

Foothills Trail Club of Western New York. *Guidebook to the Conservation Trail.* 4th ed., 1984.

Niagara Frontier Chapter, Adirondack Mountain Club. *Wilderness Weekends in Western New York.* 3rd ed., 1983.

O'Connor, Lois. *A Finger Lakes Odyssey.* Lakemont, N.Y.: North Country Books, 1975.

VanDiver, Bradford B. *Field Guide to Upstate New York.* Dubuque: Kendall/Hunt Publishing Co., 1980.

Von Engeln, O. D. *The Finger Lakes Region: Its Origin and Nature.* Ithaca: Cornell University Press, 1961.

Organizations and Clubs. Several public and private groups provide maps, pamphlets, brochures, and guidebooks about hiking trails, state and county lands, and places to see in Western New York. The Adirondack Mountain Club publishes regional guides and other materials for hikers. It has many chapters throughout New York State, including the Niagara Frontier Chapter, which maintains trails in Western New York. These chapters conduct group outings and day hikes. They can be reached at:

Adirondack Mountain Club
172 Ridge Street
Glen Falls NY 12801

The Finger Lakes Trail Conference (FLTC) is made up of local hiking clubs that build, groom, and maintain sections of the 648-mile-long Finger Lake Trail, which runs from Allegany State Park to the Catskills. It provides a map series covering the FLT, as well as information about member hiking clubs and conferences. Write to them at:

Finger Lakes Trail Conference, Inc.
P.O. Box 18048
Rochester NY 14618

State and County Offices. These, too, provide information for the hiker. The state's Department of Environmental Conservation provides brochures of state lands and a variety of pamphlets on outdoor subjects. It also publishes a magazine, *The Conservationist.*

New York State Department of Environmental Conservation
50 Wolf Road
Albany NY 12233

The regional districts into which New York State is divided also provide information and pamphlets on state lands in their regions. Western New York's Region 9 is made up of Allegany, Cattaraugus, Chautauqua, Erie, Niagara, and Wyoming counties. Serving Region 9 is a staff made up of the regional director, regional supervisor for natural resources, regional forester, regional ranger, and regional operations supervisor; all can provide detailed information about state lands and facilities to a hiker.

Region 9
New York State Department of Environmental Conservation
600 Delaware Avenue
Buffalo NY 14204

The state's Division of Tourism issues a New York tourist highway map, brochures, and pamphlets on various regions of the state, and an annual state travel guide to places and events in each region.

New York State Division of Tourism
Department of Commerce
99 Washington Avenue
Albany NY 12245

The Office of Parks, Recreation, and Historic Preservation issues an annual *Guide to New York State Parks, Recreation, and Historic Preservation,* which contains information about each of the state parks and historic sites.

New York Office of Parks, Recreation and Historic Preservation
Empire State Plaza
Albany NY 12238

Map Legend

– – – – main trail

· · · · · · connecting trail

CT Conservation Trail

FLT Finger Lakes Trail

⇥ lookout

Ⓟ parking

⋔ shelter

Niagara Frontier Region:
Niagara, Erie, and Orleans Counties

1

Hunter Creek Park

Total distance: 4.9 miles
Hiking time: 2–3 hours
Vertical rise: 350 feet
Maps: USGS 7½' East Aurora; USGS 7½' West Almond

Hunter Creek Park is unusual for a host of reasons, not the least of which is its location—just a hop, skip, and jump from the greater Buffalo metropolitan area and only a couple of miles from the city of East Aurora. Yet this heavily wooded area gives you the feeling of a wilderness experience. The scenery is merely appealing until you reach the gorge edge—and then it becomes eye-popping.

The park sits astride the lower part of Hunter Creek, whose headwaters are in the rolling highlands about 10 miles southwest of Aurora. The valley through which Hunter Creek flows in its northerly course is deep and narrow, and it becomes more so as it reaches the park, where it suddenly changes into a magnificent gorge, located just north of Center Line Road.

The 185-foot gorge, cut aeons ago by what was then the young Hunter Creek, comes as a sudden surprise in a land that hitherto had given the appearance of being relatively flat. The gorge can be viewed easily from hiking trails found on both its sides, and its northwest edge can be reached by a road running south from NY 78.

Another unusual feature of the park is that it really isn't a park—at least, not yet. Erie County officials report that the hiking site and gorge area are actually on a tract of land that belongs to the county land bank under the jurisdiction of the county's Park, Recreation and Forest Department. But to locals, this tract always has been known as Hunter Creek Park (although some are given to calling it Hunter's Creek Park).

Local lore gives a host of interesting names to the areas surrounding the park. To the south are the town of Wales and the villages of South Wales and Holland. On the east side of Hunter Creek is Crow Hill, and on the west side, Vermont Hill, each rising to an elevation of 1,500 feet. To the north you find Big Tree Road, East Blood Road, and Two Rod, Three Rod, and Four Rod Roads.

Since it is not really a park, Hunter Creek Park receives no maintenance. In the late 1970s, a conservation group constructed a number of trails, shelters, and bridges throughout the park, but it provided no backup maintenance. As a result, virtually all evidence of this effort has vanished, and nature has reclaimed the land.

Only the section of the Conservation Trail (CT) that runs through Hunter Creek

Deer in Hunter Creek Park

Park is maintained. After it passes through Hunter Creek Park, the CT continued north for another 24 miles, passing through Darien Lakes State Park (see Hike 6), 17.8 miles north of Hunter Creek Park.

To the south, a portion of the CT, called the Mabel James Section, runs for 13 miles from Hunter Creek Park at Center Line Road south to Warner Hill Road, and south from there along the eastern edge of Vermont Hill for 7.9 miles to Holland County Road, which in a short distance leads west to the village of Holland. If time and energy permits, you may wish to try the Vermont Hill portion of the CT after completing your hike in Hunter Creek Park.

Access. From Buffalo, take the Aurora Expressway (NY 400) to East Aurora exit, which intersects the east-west highway with a double route number, NY 78 and US 20A. Turn east onto this highway (which also is named Big Tree Road), and drive 2.1 miles to a fork; turn right here and continue on NY 78 for 1.2 miles to the intersection with Hunter Creek Road. Turn right (south) on Hunter Creek Road for little over 0.2 mile, where you intersect a gravel road on the right (just past a house). Turn here, and follow the

gravel road a few hundred feet to where it ends and the trailhead begins. Park here.

Trail. For the first half of this hike, follow the orange-painted blazes of the Conservation Trail, which crosses Hunter Creek Road at the parking entrance. On a path beginning at the west end of the parking area, follow the orange markings west. Cross an usually dry, shallow streambed, then another, and at 0.15 mile from the parking area, cross a third and larger one in a ravine, ignoring markers that go to the right. This ravine is also dry for most of the summer. Turn sharply left, then follow the ravine bank uphill. The compass direction will be SSW.

After the trail becomes nearly level again, 0.3 mile from the parking area, you reach a Y junction. Take the orange-blazed trail to the right, west. A little past 0.4 mile, the trail turns to the left in a southeast direction. At nearly 0.5 mile, you reach a T junction. Turn right, following the orange blazes, but note the appearance of this intersection. On your return, you can use the unmarked trail here as a quicker way back to your car.

Proceed southwest on the marked route. The trail is now mostly level and easy. The direction changes to more

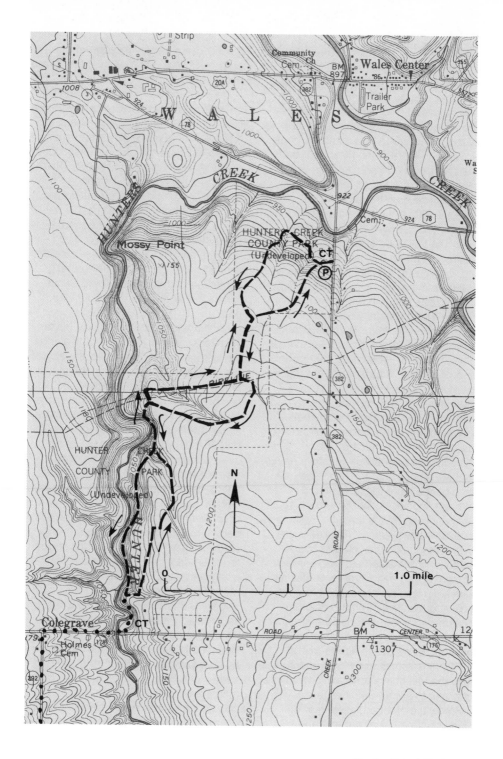

nearly south. At 0.9 mile, you reach a clearing along a gas pipeline running east-west, with a good path in the center. Look around this area. On your return, you will be following that path from the west, and you will have to be able to recognize where to turn into the woods.

Standing there in the clearing, you may not be able to see the next orange blaze. It is to the left on the other side. Turn left (east) on the pipeline trail and go about 90 yards to the corner of the woods. You can see the blaze ahead now. The trail goes southeast, then south, and about 0.1 mile from the clearing, it comes to a Y junction with another trail crossing a few steps beyond. Follow the blazes straight through the Y, then right in a southwesterly direction; 100 yards farther on, there is another trail junction. Go straight through here. In another 140 yards, you cross the upper end of another little dry watercourse. Be careful! A good wide trail continues straight on, but the marked one you want turns right here and is less obvious. It follows down along the bank of the little gully, which becomes a ravine.

You follow the ravine, generally going northwest, for about 0.3 mile. The trail then bends more to the west and through another Y junction. About 100 yards beyond that is a major crossroads. You have now walked 1.6 miles. Here the marked trail turns left and heads south. The unmarked old woods road straight ahead descends to Hunter Creek. (This is an interesting side trip, only about 0.1 mile to the creek. Upstream past a low waterfall the stream flows through a high-walled gorge, which provides a beautiful place to rest.)

From the "crossroads" you should also note the trail going north, which you will use later to get to the pipeline clearing.

Follow the orange blazes from the junction at the 1.6-mile mark, and you quickly come to the top edge of the gorge wall. You can look over and down, but make no attempt to climb down. The shale rock and earth are loose and will crumble underfoot. The lower wall is vertical. Stay on the level ground here. The trail follows the gorge south and shortly comes to where the gorge is less steep at the top and ravines cut into it. The first is at the 1.8-mile mark, the second only about 50 yards beyond. (The side trip mentioned above isn't included in our trail distances.) On the little ridge between these ravines, a path comes in from the east. If you follow the route described here, you will be using that unmarked path to return to the Conservation Trail at this point on your way back.

Continue to follow the orange blazes. The Conservation Trail now runs along the hillside, about midway on the slope, generally south but following the contour of the land. The path is marked, but little has been done to smooth it in this area. At 2.2 miles, you are near the top of the slope. There is an open field on the east. At 2.5 miles, you reach the top of another small ravine. There is a second ravine just beyond that is spectacular after a heavy rain, but before you reach it there is a trail junction.

To avoid returning by exactly the same path, turn left here and follow the loop north. To the south only 0.2 mile is Center Line Road. The Conservation Trail continues south, crossing that road east of the Hunter Creek Bridge.

Make the turn, and leave the Conservation Trail. Proceed southeast then east into the field for only about 50 yards. Here you find a good path, once used by farm vehicles, running from south to north in the field. Turn left onto the path. Ignore any trails in other directions, and stick to the slightly rutted old farm road, going north for 0.3 mile. You may pass a trail coming in at an angle from the southeast. Some paths have been mowed in these fields for the benefit of local horse riders, but we do not know whether this will continue. You will find that the field has become narrower as woods come closer on the left and a line of small trees and bushes on the right changes to solid woods. At this point, look for a path crossing the north-south one and going directly east into the woods. Do not go all the way to the north end of the field. Take the path to the right (east) about 70 yards to another trail junction in the woods. Turn left there. Your total distance is now 2.9 miles.

At 3.0 miles you have come down to a stream, which is nearly dry unless there has been a recent rain. You may have trouble seeing the trail ahead. Look around. There is a rotting wooden bridge just upstream, over which the trail crossed at one time. Ignore the bridge; instead, just walk across the stones and pick up the trail going north on the other side. This once was a forest road. Ahead you see more decaying bridges built by the group that worked on the hiking trail. The builders used poor-quality material that has not had a long useful life. Con-tinue through mixed hemlock and hard-wood forest, and soon you are back on the Conservation Trail at 3.2 miles. At 3.4 miles, you reach the point where the Conservation Trail turns right. Continue past the Conservation Trail and go straight; about 80 yards farther north, you are in the pipeline clearing.

Turn right (east) on the path in the clearing. It dips to a wet spot that you can usually step over, then rises and continues to the 3.8-mile mark, where you find the Conservation Trail; turn left into the woods, on the route you used earlier. At 4.2 miles, the Conservation Trail turns left, but a good wide path goes straight ahead. Take this unmarked path. It goes northeast, then more to the east, then east. At 4.4 miles, at the edge of an overgrown field, it turns north downhill into the woods with a small ra-vine on the left. At the fork, go left for the shortest way to the 5.2-mile point and your parked car.

Because there are multiple trails in the park, some unmarked and several marked with orange blazes, it is easy to become confused. If you are unsure which trail to take, check to be sure there are blazes on both sides of the trees.

Erie County Forest

Total distance: 4.75 miles
Hiking time: 2½ hours
Vertical rise: 470 feet
Map: USGS 7½' Sardinia

In the southeast corner of Erie County, just north of its boundary with Cattaraugus County, you will find a sizable preserve, the 3,100-acre Erie County Forest. It is tucked into rising highlands that pitch down steeply southward to the east-flowing Cattaraugus Creek. Deep gullies have been cut into the hill slope.

The deep ravines in the county forest are the work of two south-flowing streams, Hyler Creek in the forest's western section, and Dresser Creek in the eastern section. The gullies here range in depth from 150 to 200 feet, and the Hyler Creek gully where it narrows, takes on the appearange of a gorge.

This rugged and attractive chunk of public land is maintained by the Erie County Bureau of Forestry, of the Department of Parks and Recreation. The bureau makes available a booklet describing the forest's flora and fauna, as well as the several trails found here.

Two connected footpaths, called the Scarbuck Trail and the Silent Woods Trail, run in elongated loops almost the entire length of the county forest. They are also a part of the Conservation Trail (see introduction).

Both the Scarbuck and Silent Woods trails are well blazed in yellow and easy

to follow. Although readily accessible, these trails are only lightly used during the warm months; they are extensively used in winter by cross-country tourers. The Erie County Forest also contains two loops with blue blazes, Sugarbush and East Trail, which have been put in specifically for Nordic skiiers.

The recent history of this parcel of public land dates to the early 1900s, when it was acquired by Erie County as abandoned farmland. Reforestation was begun in 1927, and at present the area is a mature forest containing second-growth hardwoods and planted conifers.

Since much of the land is low, the forest is cool in summer and peaceful at any time. It lends itself to casual walking and nature study. It is well suited for bird-watching, especially during the spring and fall migration periods. This portion of Erie County lies within the state's wild turkey range; on a quiet morning you may be able to see a flock moving up the hillside in search of food. Here, too, you find the ruffed grouse, the migrating woodcock in spring and fall, and the white-tailed deer. Flora are well-enough represented to give you, guidebook in hand, a full day's enjoyment identifying various species.

Access. The Scarbuck and Silent Woods trails are accessible from Genesee Road, midway between NY 16 on the east and NY 240 on the west. Coming from Buffalo or points east, you can take the state's Thruway (I-90) to exit 54, where you pick up NY 400 running east and then south as the East Aurora Expressway. This expressway ends just south of East Aurora, where it changes into NY 16. Continue on NY 16 south for about 15 miles to the hamlet of Chaffee, and go to the intersection with Genesee Road.

Turn right (west) onto Genesee Road, and drive 4.7 miles. This brings you into the county forest and to the trailhead, which is well marked with Bureau of Forestry signs. At the trailhead you find adequate parking as well as restroom facilities.

An alternative route from Buffalo is to exit off the Thruway onto US 219, and drive south about 20 miles to the Genesee Road exit. Follow Genesee Road east for 5.8 miles, past NY 240, to the trailhead.

Trail. The start of Scarbuck Trail is on the south side of Genesee Road. It runs a narrow loop of 1.75 miles that, at the south end, ties into a smaller 1.25-mile extension loop; by combining both loops, you can hike 3 miles without retracing your steps.

Directly across from the Scarbuck Trail on the north side of Genesee Road is Silent Woods Trail, which is a single 1.75-mile loop. It takes you up and down a series of hills, some of which descend steeply into narrow gullies.

Both trails use yellow markers. Half of both the trails are also marked in orange to designate the route of the Conservation Trail, which uses part of the county forest trail system as it passes through the area.

The Scarbuck Trail, to the south, starts at a wooden gatehouse next to the trail-

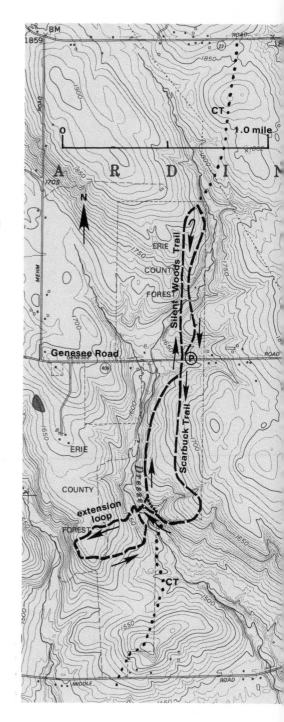

head parking lot. The trail initially follows a portion of the Conservation Trail (orange blazes). A short distance uphill, the trail reaches a fork.

Veer to the left, and follow the trail as it runs along the side of the hill in a southerly direction for 0.4 mile; then it swings left and heads uphill for a short distance, only to descend into a gully. Across the gully the trail continues uphill a short distance, then makes a turn to the right near the hill's crest. Just beyond is a bench where there was once an overlook, but it is now overgrown and the view is obscured.

The trail now makes a steep descent, dropping more than 100 feet in 0.3 mile, where it crosses a creek just after the Conservation Trail forks to the left to head south. The Scarbuck Trail, however, continues west now following a larger creek.

When you come to a wooden bridge, a sign that says "Extension" greets you. Here is the junction of the second loop, the so-called Extension Loop. To take this Extension Loop, cross the bridge and follow the yellow trail markers uphill, crossing a dirt road en route; this dirt road runs in a north-south direction, intersecting the Extension Loop first on the northern part of the loop and then again on the southern part. The dirt road runs from Genesee Road in the north to Middle Road, 1.5 miles to the south. It provides yet another route to enjoy in this forest.

Continue on the Extension Loop west 0.1 mile beyond the dirt road; the loop trail now turns south, following the rim of the Hyler Creek gorge, which drops precipitously on your right 100 feet to the stream below. In a short distance, the trail swings left and heads in a straight line over level ground, then starts downhill, where it crosses the dirt road

crossed earlier. The next 0.2 mile is all downhill, and the descent becomes steeper as you near bottom. There the trail turns sharply to the north; in 0.15 mile, the trail completes its loop, crosses the bridge, and then heads north along the east side of a narrow valley, through which Dresser Creek flows.

The yellow-blazed Scarbuck Trail continues north along the base of the hill, with the creek on your left. At 0.5 mile, the trail begins to swing a little to the right and head uphill for another 0.1 mile to intersect the eastern portion of the loop you walked earlier. Turn left here and head north; a short distance brings you to Genesee Road.

You are now ready for the Silent Woods Trail across the road. At the start you come to a fork. Take the left leg, and head uphill along an open area. The trail continues its uphill route, crossing several wider trails that are used by foresters when they tap the sugar maple trees in the spring.

As you reach the 0.75-mile mark, the trail begins to loop to the right; at this point you meet the orange-blazed Conservation Trail, which becomes part of your return route. As you continue turning on this short loop, you pass through an attractive stand of evergreen trees.

At first the trail—now heading south—passes over fairly level ground. But after 0.3 mile, the terrain begins pitching downward, gently at first and then more steeply, ending with an almost precipitous drop into a narrow gully. The trail climbs out of the gully and heads up a breath-gasping hill for 50 feet, then levels off at the top of a hill. The trail immediately starts down the other side. From the hilltop it is 1.5 mile to the trail's end at Genesee Road.

While the Silent Woods Trail is less muddy during wet seasons than Scarbuck Trail, its grades are far steeper. In winter this trail should be used only by intermediate or advanced Nordic skiiers. The Sugarbush Trail, on the north side of Genesee Road, and the East Trail, which borders Scarbuck on the south, are less demanding for the average recreational skiier.

Tonawanda State Wildlife Management Area

Hiking distance: 4.2 miles
Hiking time: 2½ hours
Vertical rise: 12 feet
Maps: USGS 7½' Akron; USGS 7½' Medina

The Tonawanda State Wildlife Management Area can be described as a land of dikes, drainage channels, and dammed ponds. In its vast waterfowl refuge, you will find a magnificent variety of ducks, geese, herons, hooded mergansers, hawks, and even the bald eagle.

The land here is open wetland, and from all directions you can see impounded cattail-choked marshes or duckweed-covered swamp ponds. Small woodlots and tree stands line the network of dikes and form backdrops for those watery areas that often take on the appearance of small lakes.

Tonawanda is one of three large public wetland areas located in Western New York; it is one of two state wildlife management areas in the Niagara Frontier Region, the other being Oak Orchard (see Hike 5). Situated between these two wildlife management areas is the 10,818-acre Iroquois National Wildlife Refuge (see Hike 4). Tonawanda is located on the west side of the national refuge, and Oak Orchard on the east. Only the highways separate one area from the other. Together, the three units provide over 20,000 acres of prime waterfowl habitat. This is also home to the newly reared bald eagles, as well as to ospreys and a variety of hawks native to New York State.

The three units are located between Buffalo and Rochester; they lie 7 miles north of the New York State Thruway (I-90) in the Southern Ontario Plain. The three wildlife areas are situated between the New York State Barge Canal, which passes through the village of Medina, 3 miles north, and US 20, located 13 miles to the south. The east-west US 20 marks the northern reaches of the Appalachian Plateau; the Southern Ontario Plain north of it is a low, featureless landscape with an elevation that barely rises over 600 feet. The result is that part of the plain is a flat wetland area containing swamps and marshes filled with cattails.

The state's Oak Orchard area and the federal government's Iroquois wildlife area both drain northward via Oak Orchard Creek to feed into Lake Ontario. The state's Tonawanda area drains westward to the Niagara River via Tonawanda Creek.

Throughout the summer, the three areas abound with waterfowl activity, as young are reared and then take to flight. Filled with resident ducks, geese, and herons calling sounds, the place is downright noisy. But the sights and

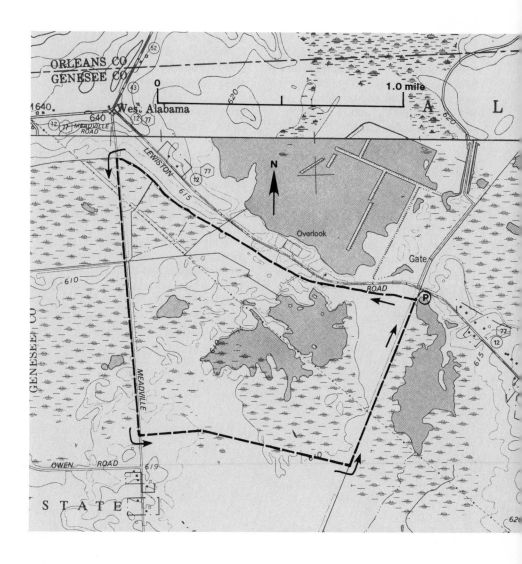

sounds reach their peak during the spring and fall migrations, when thousands of waterfowl descend on these wildlife areas for food and rest. This scene is especially striking in the Tonawanda area, with its many sloughs and large ponds.

Tonawanda allows waterfowl hunting in some parts and prohibits it in others. So there's no need to skip Tonawanda dur-

ing hunting season, since all you need to do is seek out the parts where it isn't allowed: these areas are especially inviting since waterfowl, undisturbed by hunters, are numerous and active. But the entire wildlife area is closed during spring waterfowl nesting periods until July 1 of each year.

Access. To get to the trailhead from the east or west, take the New York

State Thruway (I-90) and get off at Exit 48A. Turn north on NY 77, and drive 6.5 miles to the hamlet of Alabama, where it turns left and heads in a northwesterly direction. It is 2 miles from Alabama to where you enter the wildlife areas on what is now called Lewiston Road (NY 77).

On your right is the Iroquois National Wildlife Refuge, and on your left the Tonawanda State Wildlife Management Area. When you reach Casey Road on the right, a sign directs you to the headquarters of the Iroquois refuge (where information and maps can be obtained). A short distance farther, you reach the Tonawanda area on the west. From here it is 0.6 mile to the trailhead on the left. This is a dike road intersecting the main highway from the south. On the USGS topographical map, it is called Klossen Road; but there is no road sign here, just a sign telling you that this is a public hunting area. You are now on the east-

ern edge of the Tonawanda wildlife area, where you begin your hike. Park here.

Trail. Your hiking will take the form of a loop, which will be identified here informally as the Cinnamon Marsh Trail since it circles the marshland of that name. (The state has not labeled any of the dike routes with hiking trail names.) This 4.2-mile loop brings you back to your starting point after about 2½ hours of steady walking. If you stop to watch the endless activity of waterfowl and other birdlife, your hiking time will be longer.

To the right of Klossen Road, where you parked your vehicle, is a small pond. Stretching off on the left (east) side is a cattail-filled wetland area called the Feeder Marsh. A similar picture is found to the south, where Cinnamon Marsh is located; this is the area you will circle in a counterclockwise direction.

Intersecting Klossen Road at the point where you parked your vehicle is an-

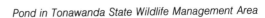

Pond in Tonawanda State Wildlife Management Area

other dike road. This is the road you take as you start your hike; it parallels the main highway, Lewiston Road (NY 77), on the right as you head in a northwesterly direction. Between the dike road and Lewiston Road is a wide drainage channel.

As you proceed on the dike road for 0.3 mile, you see on your left (south) first a large cattail-filled marsh and then an area of exposed water. Before you reach a small stand of trees next to the dike road, another dike road intersects from the south, and 0.2 mile past the treestand, another dike road intersects from the south.

The area on your immediate left (south) is called Finks Paddy; a narrow strip of this muckland is farmed. On the right, across the drainage channel, is a leased hayfield that is mowed during the summer, and just beyond on Lewiston Road are two white houses. An additional 0.6 mile brings you to the paved Meadville Road, which runs straight south from Lewiston Road.

Turn onto Meadville Road, and walk south on it over a narrow bridge and under power lines for 0.3 mile. There a dike road intersects Meadville Road from the east. The landscape here is made up of open fields, with a scattering of small woodlots that break the terrain's flatness.

An additional 0.2 mile brings you to the second bridge and to a set of two dike roads intersecting from the west. The two dike roads, running in an east-west direction, pass on either side of a drainage channel that extends 2 miles to the west; this whole area is a restricted refuge, where hunting is prohibited but hiking is allowed. This set of dike roads are a good route to use during hunting season. Where it is allowed, hunting occurs on Tuesdays, Thursdays, and Saturdays; the other days of the week are set aside to permit waterfowl to rest.

Turn off Meadville Road at this point, and climb to the top of the dike. Continue south on the dike road for 0.2 mile. You see the exposed water of an inundated swamp on your left (east) and a line of trees ahead. As you walk, you encounter several short spur trails (about 50 yards long) leading down to Meadville Road, which continues parallel to the dike road.

Within the next 0.4 mile, the open water on the left gives way to a large area of cattails. The dike road turns first a little to the left and then to the right away from the marsh as it enters an area of young growth. On your right you see a couple of tall maples that are part of a long line of maples along Meadville Road.

The dike road levels as it intersects a single-lane dirt road that runs east from Meadville Road. Turn left here, walking past a woodlot and a small wetland area on your left and a clearing on your right. The clearing soon gives way to a dense woodland area that ends at the eastern edge of a large wetland called Klossen Marsh. The marsh resembles a small lake.

The road bends gradually left and then right as it starts to run on a dike past the impoundment on your right and the cattail-filled Cinnamon Marsh on your left. In 0.9 mile, you intersect the dike road called Klossen Road, running in a northeast-southwest direction. Turn onto Klossen Road and head north.

On your right is a 10-foot-wide drainage channel that parallels the dike road, lining the channel on the far side is a thin string of trees. Follow Klossen Road north under the power lines and past Cinnamon Marsh on the right for 0.6 mile, where you complete the loop at the parking area and your original starting point.

Iroquois National Wildlife Refuge

Hiking distance: 2 miles
Hiking time: 45 minutes
Vertical rise: none
Maps: USGS 7½' Akron; USGS 7½' Medina;
  USGS 7½' Oakfield; USGS 7½' Knowlesville

The Iroquois National Wildlife Refuge is a diversified habitat—deep-water swamps, wooded marshes, and wet meadows surrounded or interspersed with forest-land, grassland, and cropland. It is primarily made up of a vast wetland called the Oak Orchard Swamp.

The 10,818-acre refuge shares the Oak Orchard Swamp with its neighbors, the Tonawanda State Wildlife Management Area (see Hike 3) to the west and the Oak Orchard State Wildlife Management Area (see Hike 5) to the east. These three areas are separated only by highways. NY 77 separates Tonawanda and Iroquois, and Knowlesville Road separates Oak Orchard and Iroquois. Iroquois is a federally owned and maintained refuge; the other two are owned by the state.

Together, these state and federal areas provide over 20,000 acres of prime waterfowl habitat, as well as good cover and food for many other wild species, from the white-tailed deer to the cotton-tailed rabbit. Combined, the three areas are 14½ miles in length and 5 miles in width.

When the Wisconsin glacier, which covered this section of New York state 12,000 years ago, melted, the water

filled a depression in the land between today's village of Medina and the city of Batavia and became what geologists call Lake Tonawanda. Over the centuries, this lake filled in with sediment, evidently shrinking to the present wetland area.

Early white settlers who came here around 1820 attempted to drain the wetland's swamps and marshes, but the effort to drain all of what is today called Oak Orchard Swamp proved too costly. Instead, the land around the wetland area was farmed, saving the wetland from complete destruction. In 1985, the U.S. Fish and Wildlife Service acquired the wetland to establish a wildlife refuge.

The water level and water flow of the refuge are controlled by dikes, impoundments, drainage channels and ditches, and sloughs. This assures that the refuge provides the kind of environment where waterfowl can rest, feed, and nest. Approximately 4,000 acres are flooded, covering about 40 percent of the refuge's land.

The federal refuge is named after the Iroquois Confederacy; the names of the original five nations have been bestowed on the refuge's marsh pools—Seneca Pool, Cayuga Pool, Onondaga Pool, Oneida Pool, and Mohawk Pool. While

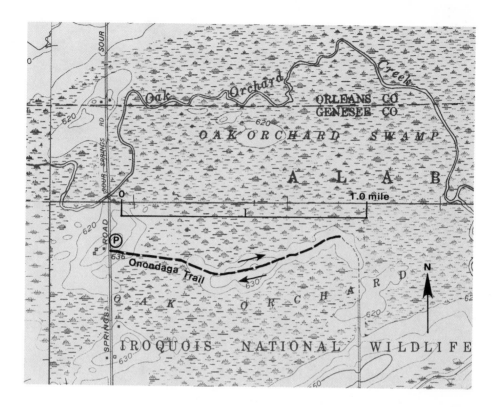

the Iroquois Confederacy existed, the Seneca Nation occupied the land that includes today's Iroquois, Tonawanda, and Oak Orchard wildlife areas.

Like its neighboring wildlife areas, the Iroquois refuge supports a large resident population of waterfowl during the summer months. But during the spring and fall migration periods, the waterfowl population explodes. Between 40,000 and 80,000 geese appear here in March and April, and between 7,000 and 8,000 geese in September and October; several thousand migrating ducks, representing dozens of species, appear with the geese in the spring and fall.

The marsh pools can be reached by various hiking routes, but the refuge is closed during nesting time, which lasts until July 1. The longest trail follows Feeder Road and runs for 3 miles from Lewiston Road (NY 77) in the south across the entire width of the refuge to West Shelby Road in the north. This trail takes you past four of the pools—Cayuga and Seneca to the west and Oneida and Mohawk to the east. Farther east, a mile-long foot-trail takes you past Onondaga Pool. This is the route for the hike described here. In addition, a mile-long trail that circles Swallow Hollow Marsh pond is found on the refuge's eastern boundary, just off Knowlesville Road.

There also is a short nature trail, called Kanyoo Trail, next to the southern end of Feeder Road on Lewiston Road (NY 77) and another short trail at Cayuga Over-

Onondaga Pool

look on Lewiston Road.

In winter, when ice covers the pools and snow makes for good Nordic skiing, you can ski a 4-mile loop through the four marshes, starting at the refuge headquarters site on Casey Road. A large outdoor map at the headquarter building shows you this ski route.

The hiker has many routes from which to choose, but the one recommended here is the Onondaga Trail, which covers a round-trip distance of 2 miles. It allows you to see a mixed habitat of wetland and forestland and scores of the water-fowl residing in the Onondaga Pool.

Access. The Onondaga Trail can be reached via NY 77 and NY 63. You can reach NY 77 from the west or east via the New York State Thruway (I-90). Leave the Thruway at Exit 48A and drive north on NY 77 for 5 miles to the inter-section with NY 63. Follow NY 77 north for the next 1.5 miles to the hamlet of Alabama; the road is a doubly marked one—NY 77 and NY 63.

In Alabama, NY 77 turns west, while NY 63 continues north. Stay on NY 63 for 0.8 mile, until Roberts Road intersects on the right (east). Turn here, and drive east for little over a mile to Sour Spring Road. Turn north here, and drive 0.9 mile to a sign that directs you to the Onondaga Trail parking area. Across the road is a white house and garage. Drive into the parking area on the right and leave your vehicle.

Trail. The Onondaga Trail begins next to the parking area at a wooden gate that keeps out unauthorized motor vehicles. A sign with a figure of a Nordic skier tells you that the trail is also open in winter for cross-country skiing. Surrounding the parking area is a large stand of trees; these trees mark the beginning of a forest that extends through the marsh area to Knowlesville Road in the east, where the refuge ends.

A hundred steps take you through the trees' canopy to the northwestern edge of the Onondaga Pool. As the trees give way to the swamp waters of the pool, you see two wood duck houses in the water and a small birdhouse on the left side of the trail.

On your left as you walk, the woods fill the lowland north of the mowed path. The Onondaga Pool gets bigger as you move on. The Onondaga Pool is a fairly large body of water, but much of its irregular shoreline lies out of sight of the walkpath. During the late summer you can expect to see numerous ducks leaping from the water to take flight as you approach; you may also see the big blue heron and the small green heron.

At the 0.3-mile mark, you reach the end of the Onondaga Pool and enter the forest. Trees arch over the trail. In summer, the trail is lined with ferns; some are typical wood ferns, but the overwhelming number are bracken fern.

Soon you come to a fork. The right leg of the fork is unmowed and little used; ignore it. Bear to the left, instead. After a short distance, you come to a narrow footpath that angles right off the main trail. A few steps take you to an opening, through which you can see a shallow, weed-cluttered pond; here are three more wood duck houses; the one made of metal is a double house.

This unmarked trail circles the small marsh pond. You can follow the path around the pond now or on your return trip. If you do it now, in a few minutes you will be back on the main trail. A swale of bracken fern extends downtrail on both sides of the path.

You now come to a bench with "YCC 86" cut into the top. It was built by members of the Youth Conservation Corps. Two other benches, built at the same time, are found on this trail. All were erected for the benefit of bird-watchers or anyone who wishes to pause to take in the sights and sounds of the forest environment.

The trail, still canopied by trees, brings you to where the forest brightens on your right. At this point, a small marsh area with low growth allows more light to penetrate the woods.

You come to the second bench, and just beyond you see a small clearing about 50 yards off to the left. A short distance from here you come to the third bench in the middle of the path. This tells you that you have reached the end of the trail. Your turn-around is provided by a small loop that circles the bench. It is a mile back, and a 20-minute trek brings you to your parked vehicle.

Oak Orchard State Wildlife Management Area

Hiking distance: 4.8 miles
Hiking time: 3 hours
Vertical rise: none
Maps: USGS 7½ Oakfield; USGS 7½' Knowlesville

Oak Orchard State Wildlife Management Area holds down the eastern flank of the tripartite wildlife refuge that also consists of the Iroquois National Wildlife Refuge (see Hike 4) in the middle and the Tonawanda State Wildlife Management Area (see Hike 3) in the west. All share a similar environment; the land is flat and is mostly wetlands, surrounded by or interspersed with wooded swamps, forested land, wet meadows, brushland, and cropland.

Running across the Oak Orchard wildlife area is Oak Orchard Creek, which drains into Lake Ontario, 16 miles to the north. About eighty percent of the area consists of marshes and swamps as well as two large ponds—Windmill Marsh Pond and Goose Pond.

Within the Oak Orchard area is a large "waterfowl refuge," which includes Windmill Marsh and some adjacent land. This is a no-hunting part of Oak Orchard, and the recommended hiking route is located within this refuge. Hunting, however, is permitted in the rest of the wildlife area.

The name Oak Orchard is somewhat unusual, considering that a stand of oak trees does not normally consitute an orchard. The explanation involves the history of this unusual area. During the

Iroquois Confederacy, the Seneca Indians occupied this area. When white settlers came to the region, they saw that the Indians had placed their garden patches around their villages amid the oak trees. This made the oak stands look like orchards. Hence the name Oak Orchard Swamp for the wetland and Oak Orchard Creek for the stream that flows through the swamp.

In the Oak Orchard Wildlife Management Area, as in the other two wildlife areas, the ecological balance depends on obtaining and retaining the right amount of water to maintain a waterfowl habitat. As a result, the state has constructed dikes, dams, channels, and drainage ditches and created sloughs, pools, and ponds so that water is retained the year around.

The result is that thousands of resident waterfowl make their home in Oak Orchard, as well as in the Iroquois and Tonawanda wildlife areas. The predominant nesters are Canada geese, mallard ducks, black ducks, gadwalls, blue-winged and green-winged teal, wood ducks, hooded mergansers, and herons. During the spring and fall migration periods, the skies darken with thousands upon thousands of geese and ducks

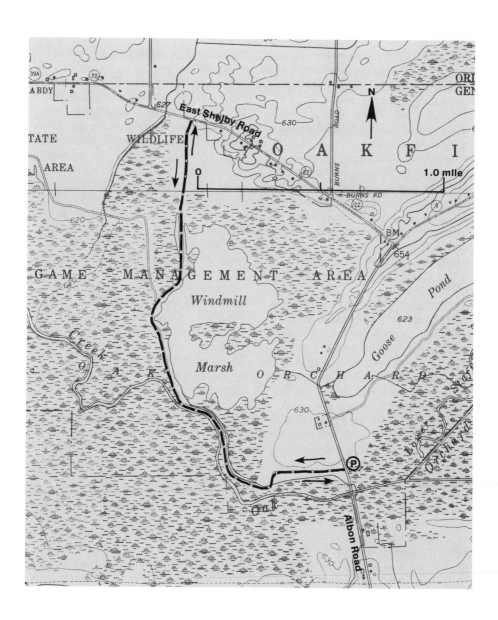

stopping to feed and rest in the marsh ponds and wooded swamps.

Oak Orchard, which is 3.2 miles long and 1.6 miles wide, provides homes for more than 30 mammal species as well. White-tailed deer, opossum, mink, red and gray fox, squirrel, and cotton-tailed rabbit make their home in the brushland and forests, and muskrat and beaver live in the wetland area. In addition, over 200 species of birds have been identified in Oak Orchard.

The network of restricted roads in this management area makes for excellent hiking routes. The roads, many of which run on top of dikes, are used only by vehicles driven by state personnel managing the area. Hence, summer hikers and winter Nordic skiers are not bothered by vehicles other than those used occasionally by state officials.

The road network takes you to all sections of Oak Orchard—the North and South marshes at the western end, Supply Pond and Windmill Marsh Pond in the central area, and Goose Pond and Oxbow Marsh in the eastern section. The best highway access to Oak Orchard is on Knowlesville Road on its western boundary and Albon Road on the eastern boundary.

A short distance off Knowlesville Road is the unmanned Oak Orchard Environmental Education Center. It is an open-sided building that serves as a lecture hall. Look for an outdoor sign next to the building showing six short hiking trails that radiate from the parking area. One of the trails takes you over a wooden footbridge, across a wide channel, then across the highway to the mile-long trail that circles Swallow Hollow Marsh Pond in the Iroquois National Wildlife Refuge (see Hike 4). You can walk more than 3 miles on this network of trails.

Access. The trailhead can be reached from the west or east via the New York State Thruway (I-90). Leave the Thruway at Exit 48A and drive north 6.5 miles on NY 77 to the hamlet of Alabama. Turn right onto Lewiston Road (which, after the hamlet of Wheatville, becomes Lockport Road). After 8.5 miles, you intersect Albon Road. Drive north on Albon Road for a mile. As soon as you pass over Oak Orchard Creek, a single-lane dirt road intersects the highway. This is the trailhead. Park here.

Trail. The trail, from the trailhead on Albon Road to East Shelby Road in the north, is 2.4 miles. You can arrange to have a vehicle waiting for you at East Shelby Road. But the recommended hike is a round-trip trek of 4.8 miles, which has you retracing your steps after you have reached East Shelby Road.

At the trailhead a sign on a tree tells you that you are entering a "wildlife refuge." This means that no hunting is allowed. Start by walking west on the dirt lane. This route takes you through a narrow hayfield that usually is mowed in summer. To the left of the field is a wooded area extending south over Oak Orchard Creek; to the right is a line of trees marking the field's old boundary line.

Continue on the dirt lane through the field for 0.3 mile. A stand of trees on the right forms a backdrop for a small pond. This pond is filled with clear water, contains no duckweed during the summer, and is stocked with bass.

The road turns first left and then right, then passes a clear-cut area on the left. On the right is the southern edge of Windmill Marsh, which is filled with waist-high and then head-high cattails. Looking north, you see a vast expanse of the cattail marsh containing a half-dozen dead trees. This marsh area seems to go on forever.

The land becomes lower on each side of the road, and you are now traveling on a dike that keeps the marsh waters from flowing into Oak Orchard Creek, which is visible on the left. The dike road turns gradually to the right, closely paralleling the creek—a 20-foot-side stream that hardly appears to move. Towering high over the stream edge are red maples, willows, and ash trees, which soar to heights of four and five stories.

At the 0.5-mile mark, you pass over a controlled water outlet. Through this flows water from Windmill Marsh and passes under the road to Oak Orchard Creek. Just ahead is an old metal tower, overgrown by climbing vines. An additional 0.2 mile takes you to the point where the creek turns away from the road and heads in a northwesterly direction through the dense wooded area on your left.

The dike road heads north, past the cattails that dominate the marsh on the right for the next 0.4 mile. Here, finally, you catch your first glimpse of open water, some distance east of the road. This is Windmill Marsh Pond, which is large but shallow. The dozens of small patches of vegetation on it look like tiny islands.

During the spring and fall migrations, the pond fills with thousands of geese seeking food and rest. As you continue northward, the pond becomes larger and approaches nearer to the road. At the same time, a line of trees appears between the road and the pond, partially obscuring the view. The road now follows higher ground rather than the dike.

On your left, you pass two potholes. These were constructed to provide water for land mammals like white-tailed deer. The first is now filled with cattails, and the second only partially so. The low, wet area on the right has given way to higher, drier ground with a scattering of trees amid grassland. Soon you reach a clearing and encounter a single-lane dirt road that angles south to form a fork with the road on which you are now walking.

This intersecting road runs north and then west and eventually reaches Knowlesville Road, the wildlife area's western boundary. You can follow this route if you wish to lengthen your hike.

Windmill Marsh

For now, however, stay on the main route by bearing right at the fork. Follow the road as it hugs the western edge of the marsh pond, which gives you a better view of the pond's open water. You pass several more potholes on your right.

From the fork it is 0.3 mile to a new swamp area that appears on the left. On maps it is identified as Supply Pond, and is a narrow, water-filled wetland about 0.2 mile long, running parallel to the road. Standing back from the road is a mix of live and dead trees. The road here again runs on a dike.

Soon you leave the water-exposed wetlands on both sides of the road and enter a low-lying wooded area. This, in turn, soon gives way to more open areas and brushland. A short distance more brings you to East Shelby Road.

If you have not arranged for a car-shuttle, this is your turnaround point. If you retrace your steps south, in 1½ hours you are back to Albon Road and your parked vehicle.

Darien Lakes State Park

Total distance: 4 miles
Hiking time: 2½ hours
Vertical rise: 130 feet
Maps: USGS 7½' Corfu

Darien Lakes State Park is best known for its camping, swimming, and picnic facilities, but these facilities occupy only a small portion of this small, attractive park's 3.5 square miles. The much larger and more secluded portion is ideal for hiking in summer, cross-country skiing and snowshoeing in winter, and nature study at any time of the year. The park's terrain is relatively flat, containing stands of hardwoods and evergreens, open areas, swamps and marshlands. There are four miles of hiking trails, and several loops come off the Conservation Trail, which passes on its northward course through the park, parallel to Elevenmile Creek. The park also has numerous gas wells and several miles of pipeline road. A fine day may be had by combining a short day hike in relative solitude with a picnic and swim in the more populated section.

Darien Lakes State Park is rectangular in shape and is bordered on the north by Sumner Road, on the south by Broadway (US 20), on the east by Allegany Road (NY 77), and on the west by Harlow Road. The state park should not be confused with the large, privately operated theme park called Darien Lakes Park located a short distance northeast

of the state park. The two have no connection other than the name.

The state park's benign appearance belies its important geological and ecological position. It lies almost at the center of one of the more interesting transitional areas in Western New York, on the line that separates the Cattaraugus Hills, rising to the south, from the Southern Ontario Plain (elevation 950 feet) or the midlands, immediately to the north. This plain pitches downward ever so gradually until it merges with the narrower but much lower Lake Ontario Plain, which borders Lake Ontario itself (elevation 250 feet). To the west and southwest, the terrain also slopes downward to the Niagara River in the Buffalo area and merges with the Erie Lake Plain. That narrow strip of land between Lake Erie and the Cattaraugus Hills rises only 100 feet or so above the lake.

Due to this topography, the region surrounding the park also serves as a divide for watersheds. Some of the rivers and streams, such as Elevenmile Creek and Tonawanda Creek, flow west toward Buffalo, and others, such as the Oatka Creek and the Genesee River, flow north toward Rochester.

Ecologically, this area also divides

open farmland, primarily to the north, from the higher southern region, where forest equals or exceeds farmland.

Occupying the southwestern corner of Genesee County, Darien Lakes State Park lies 20 miles east of Buffalo and 45 miles east of the greater Rochester metropolitan area—far enough away for a tranquil atmosphere in its rural setting,

welcoming the day hiker and overnight camper.

Access. From Buffalo, take US 20 east through Alden to the intersection of Harlow Road and US 20. Harlow Road is the first road after crossing County Line Road at the border of Erie and Genesee counties. Proceed past this intersection on US 20 for a half-mile to the trailhead

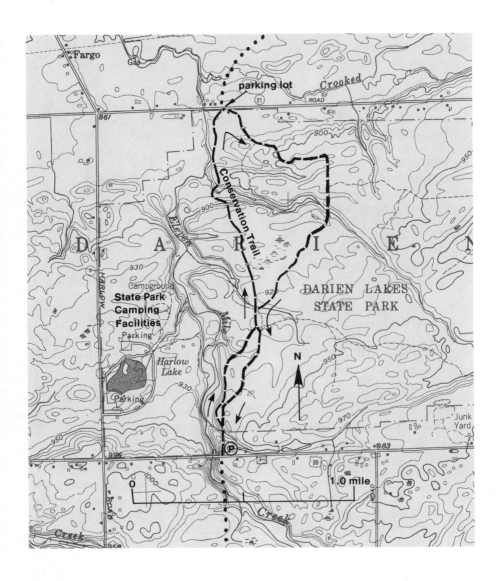

at a small parking lot located on the north side of US 20. From Rochester via Batavia (16 miles northeast), take NY 98 south out of Batavia to the intersection with US 20 at Alexander; then drive west on US 20 for 8.5 miles to the trailhead.

Trail. For the first half of this hike you will follow the orange-blazed Conservation Trail to Sumner Road. Take the gravel roadway north from the parking lot. At 0.1 mile, turn left off the gravel road onto a woods road. Note the dark, deep ravine to the left of the trail. About 150 feet from the gravel road, where the woods road goes downhill, the trail turns right (north) and continues along the edge of a steep dropoff.

As you follow the orange blazes, the trail enters a densely planted stand of evergreens. At 0.5 mile, the trail exits the evergreen stand and reaches the junction of a blue-marked trail. You turn right (east) and follow the orange and blue marks on the grass-covered roadway. In 100 yards, just before reaching a gravel roadway, the trail makes a left turn (north) and enters a short, thick section badly in need of brushing out. Shortly, the trail enters a large, overgrown meadow. Follow the trail northward for 0.25 mile to the forest on the northern edge of the meadow. Just before entering the forest you cross a gravel roadway and then make your way over a short swampy area on some decaying log bridges.

Inside the woods you reach a major trail junction at the 0.9-mile point. The blue-marked trail separates from the orange and goes right (northeast). You proceed on the orange trail, which goes left (northwest). A little later on in the day, you will return to this trail junction via the blue trail.

Your route continues northward beyond the trail junction through a mature hardwood forest. It makes its way past

some open wet areas to the right of the trail and over a few small stream crossings. At the 1.3-mile point, the trail crosses a woods road, where a sign hanging on a nearby tree indicates "foot trail only." From this point the trail winds

Foot trail beginning in Darien Lakes State Park

its way up a very short climb through the hardwoods to a ridge top, turns right (east), then follows the ridge line for 0.1 mile. At the 1.5 mile point, the trail turns left (north), descends off the ridge, enters an overgrown clearing, and shortly reaches a gas pipeline.

The trail turns right (east) and follows the gas line downhill to a small creek crossing and then up to the top of the small hill beyond. Turning left (north) off the gas line, the trail proceeds along the top of a steep embankment for a short distance and then descends over the edge into the brush below. Shortly, you reach a large meadow with Elevenmile Creek on the left.

From here the trail stays close to the creek, proceeding through the thick meadow. It enters an overgrown abandoned apple orchard at a point where an old fenceline reaches the creek bank. The trail passes dangerously close to the creek bank here, so be cautious.

The trail winds through the orchard, bordered by the creek on the left, until at the 2-mile point, the trail turns right and reaches the park's northern terminus of the Conservation Trail at a parking lot on Sumner Road. NY 77 is 1.5 miles to the east and Harlow Road is 0.5 mile to the west.

If lack of shade is presenting a problem, you may want to consider retracing your steps back to your vehicle now. If not, go through the parking lot, exit to the southeast, and follow the stone roadway.

For the next mile, the trail follows stone roadways through open fields until it reaches the blue-blazed trail. The trail follows a stone road up a gentle climb, then makes a sharp right turn to the south, then a sharp left turn to the east, then another sharp right turn back to the

south. About 0.7 mile from the Sumner Road parking lot, at a point where the stone road again makes a sharp left to the east, you find a dirt road that leads straight ahead to the south. Leave the stone road and follow this dirt road. It takes you down into a small ravine and up the other side, to a point where the dirt road turns right (west) at a junction with a grassy lane.

Proceed south on the grassy lane for 100 yards until you reach a lean-to situated 100 feet from the righthand side of the lane. The lean-to, with its picnic table, located at the 3-mile mark, makes a fine spot for a break.

When you are ready to continue, walk behind the lean-to and locate the blue-blazed trail that proceeds to the west. This trail is the other end of the blue-blazed trail that turned off the Conservation Trail back at the 0.9-mile-mark trail junction. From the lean-to, it is 0.5 mile to the orange-blazed trail.

Along the way, you pass many wet swampy areas and cross log bridges over the wettest sections. Avoid the blue-blazed trail that splits off to the east toward NY 77 shortly before you reach the orange-blazed trail. Stay on the blue trail going straight ahead (south). When you reach the junction with the orange-blazed trail at the 3.5-mile point, turn south onto it. Follow the orange trail south for 100 yards to the gravel roadway that you crossed earlier.

From here, you have a choice. You can follow the orange trail 0.8 mile back to your vehicle along the same route you traversed earlier, or for a little diversity, you can follow the gravel roadway 0.5 mile back to your vehicle. If you decide to follow the gravel roadway, turn left onto the roadway and take the right fork at the next two intersections.

Genesee Region:
Genesee, Wyoming, and Livingston Counties

7

Carlton Hill and Sulphur Spring Hill Areas

Hiking distance: 5.2 miles
Hiking time: 2½ hours
Vertical rise: 379 feet
Maps: USGS 7½' Dale; USGS 7½' Wyoming;
 USGS 7½' Batavia South

The public-use section of this large hilly area in the Genesee Region covers almost an entire highland area that rises above two valleys. Officially, it is called the Carlton Hill Multiple Use Area and the Sulphur Spring Hill Cooperative Hunting Area—a mouthful to say without drawing a second breath. Besides its name, this area of the Genesee Region has some other unique features as well.

One is its topography. The whole area looks like the round portion of a whale's back as it breaks water before sounding. From the high spot at the area's midpoint, the land tapers downhill in all directions, ending in the mile-wide Wyoming Valley in the east and in the narrower Dale Valley in the west.

Another unique feature of the area is its cooperative arrangement. To improve hunting access to private lands, the state's Division of Fish and Wildlife has worked out a cooperative arrangement with private landowners in the area. The 2,000-acre Sulphur Spring Hill Cooperative Hunting Area is the result, established in 1981 through the Fish and Wildlife Management Act.

The state-owned 2,700-acre Carlton Hill Multiple Use Area is adjacent to the cooperative hunting area. The state acquired this large tract under the Park and Recreation Act of 1962, and it manages the land so as to make it available for a host of recreational activities, including hiking, cross-country skiing, bird-watching, and nature studies, as well as hunting, fishing, and trapping in season.

The section that makes up the largest chunk of cooperative land is found in the northwest, abutting the state land both in the east and in the south. Another piece of private cooperative land is found in the area's east side; it, too, abuts the state land.

The Carlton Hill and Sulphur Spring Hill landholdings are located in the north central region of Wyoming County on the border with Genesee County, 6 miles east of Attica and 3 miles north of Warsaw.

Together, the two tracts of land are situated on the lower slopes of the Portage escarpment, one of several such scarps found in central and western New York. The Portage scarp marks the northern edge of the Allegheny Plateau, which covers most of Western New York except for the Erie Lake Plain. Generally, the plateau is made up of weak upper Devonian shale rock and interlayered resistant sandstone rock.

Much of the region's terrain—the elevation and hummocky relief—is the result of glacial sediment from the so-called Alden moraine, produced during the last Ice Age more than 10,000 years ago. It covers a section running from the village of Alden to the village of Avon in a west-to-east direction along US 20. Actually, the Portage scarp begins in the more resistant upper Devonian beds a few miles south and parallel to US 20. All this gives the region, including the Carlton Hill–Sulphur Spring Hill area, a gentle rolling, undulating landscape.

Several high spots line up in a north-south direction along the highland ridge where the Carlton Hill and Sulphur Spring Hill areas are located. The high areas include Skates Hill (elevation 1,358 feet), just north of the state land; Dutton Hill (elevation 1,365 feet); and Page Hill (elevation 1,620 feet). These lie within the state land. Sulphur Spring Hill (elevation 1,642 feet) is in the central section, and Fox Hill (elevation 1,676) and Jenkins Hill (elevation 1,647), outside of the state land, are in the south. As you travel south from Skates Hill, the land rises steadily and reaches its highest elevation at Fox Hill; from there, the land pitches downward toward Jenkins Hill and then into Wyoming Valley.

Unlike the densely forested state lands farther south in Allegany County, the Carlton Hill–Sulphur Spring Hill area is open country, made up of fallow fields and small stands of woods. Specifically, the Carlton Hill area comprises primarily abandoned farmland interspersed with a number of small woodlots. This diversified habitat provides good food and cover for a great variety of wildlife. The Sulphur Spring Hill area also consists of diversified upland habitat that includes a sizable section of mature forest, tapering off into brushland and fallow fields, and

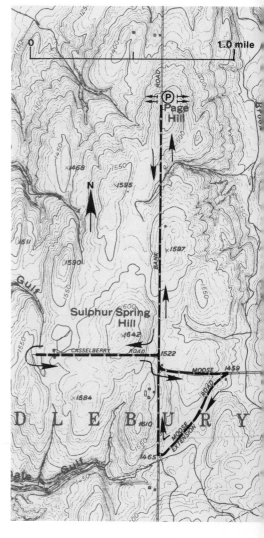

finally farmlands.

In both these areas are found such small game animals as squirrel, rabbit, raccoon, grouse, and especially white-tailed deer, the area's largest game species.

As you hike over the ridge's backbone, you can see a number of vistas in all directions, and there is little to obstruct your view. The land's openness literally invites you to walk the high ground and drink in the spectacular scenery.

This recommended hike takes you along the north-south Bank Road, which runs the full length of the Carlton Hill–Sulphur Spring Hill area. It provides a large number of fine views from its high vantage point. From Bank Road, there are several side trips to complete your day's trek of a little over five miles.

Access. The Carlton Hill–Sulphur Spring Hill area lies 8.5 miles south of Batavia and 11 miles southwest of LeRoy; it can be reached from the east or west via the New York State Thruway (I-90). From the west, drive to Batavia, leaving the Thruway at Exit 48. Drive south to the middle of the city of Batavia to intersect with NY 63. Drive southeast on NY 63 for 4 miles to the intersection

with Bethany Center Road; turn south on Bethany Center Road and drive through the hamlet of Bethany Center to the intersection with West Middlebury Road. You are now next to Dutton Hill (elevation 1,365 feet), with fine views to the north, east, and west.

Turn right (west) on West Middlebury Road, and drive 0.8 mile to where Bank Road intersects from the south. Turn onto Bank Road, and drive south 0.8 mile to a small parking area next to the road. Park here.

Trail. The parking area is located on top of Page Hill (elevation 1,620 feet), one of the high spots in the Carlton Hill–Sulphur Spring Hill area. Bank Road runs straight south, cutting the area in half. You begin your hike by enjoying the vistas over open fields. Looking downhill in a westerly direction, you see a fair-size forest covering the hill's lower

Carlton Hill Multiple Use Area

slopes; looking eastward, you see wood-lots. The views to the east, west, and south take in not only the nearby valleys but also the hills beyond.

As you start south on Bank Road, you head gradually downhill for 0.4 mile. There the road crosses a gully, through which flows the headwaters of a stream-let that feeds into Middlebury Brook. The brook is a half-mile to the east in a nar-row valley where the land pitches steeply downhill.

From here you start gradually uphill and then down; 0.8 mile brings you to Casselberry Road, intersecting from the west. The elevation at the intersection is 1,522 feet, but immediately northeast of the intersection is Sulphur Spring Hill. The views, especially those to the east, west, and south, are spectacular.

Turn onto Casselberry Road. Walk first uphill and then downhill past open areas on both sides of the road. Two man-made ponds lie where the road ends. The second and smaller pond is the headwaters of a streamlet that flows west through Dersam Gulf. The term *gulf*

is used extensively hereabouts: virtually all the deep cuts made into the hillsides by streams are called gulfs: Dale Gulf, Kennedy Gulf, Pflaum Gulf, and the like.

Return to Bank Road and continue south. A few more steps take you to the unused Moose Road, intersecting from the east. Turn left here, and follow Moose Road gradually downhill past several small woodlots for a little over 0.3 mile, to where Moose Extension Road intersects from the south. Turn here, and follow this extension in a southwesterly direction for 0.5 mile, to where it intersects Bank Road.

You are surrounded by fallow fields. At the corner of the intersection, you find a feeder streamlet that has its origin in the hill area 0.8 mile southeast. This stream-let flows west through Dale Gulf to feed into Little Tonawanda Creek, which flows north through Dale Valley.

This intersection is your turnaround point. You now can head north and uphill, and in 1.7 miles you reach the top of Page Hill and your parked vehicle.

Letchworth State Park (Gorge Trail)

Hiking distance: 6.4 miles
Hiking time: 4 hours
Vertical rise: 420 feet
Maps: USGS 7½' Portageville; USGS 7½' Nunda;
 USGS 7½' Castile; USGS 7½' Mount Morris

Letchworth State Park is a hiker's mecca, whether the hiker is a serious foot traveler or just a casual walker making a first visit to the park. The park comprises not only 14,350 acres of scenic beauty and awesome magnificence, but twenty-six individually designated, marked, and maintained trails, totaling 67.25 miles—enough to keep anyone hiking for a dozen weekends.

The trails range in length from a short trek of a quarter-mile to a demanding 21.5 miles. They take you through lush woodland area, to trout ponds, to small cascading falls, along gorge rims, down to the river bottom and the gorge floor, and over a stone bridge spanning a flume and the only spot where you can cross the river.

The longest of the hiking trails—21.5 miles—is the yellow-blazed Letchworth Trail, a spur off the Finger Lakes Trail that runs the full length of the state park in a north-south direction along the gorge's east side ending at Mount Morris in the north (see Hike 9).

The state park offers more than hiking paths; it is attractively forested and contains "the Grand Canyon of the East"—the deeply cut Genesee Gorge, through which flows the Genesee River, an In-

dian name meaning "Great and Beautiful River." Indeed, the river is all that.

The river is almost the width of a city block as it enters the park at its south end, and has a mild-mannered disposition there. But it changes its character as it passes 16 miles through the park and becomes a wondrous performer, hastening its pace until it is eager to plunge and roar over three awesome waterfalls, one of which is 107 feet high.

Over 10,000 years in the making, the Genesee Gorge runs the length of the park, but its most dramatic dimensions are found in the park's southern half. There, the twisting river cut a gorge with perpendicular walls almost 600 feet high.

The park's many trails have all been designed to take you to the scores of overlooks and vantage points. All these spots show you the towering falls on the Genesee River or bring you to the rims of the gorge itself, allowing you to enjoy the vast panorama of the gorge as it winds its way north.

The Gorge Trail is the one route specifically constructed to allow you to walk 7 miles along the western gorge rim. It brings you head-on to the Lower Falls, on top of the Middle Falls, and next to the Upper Falls. It is located in the "pay"

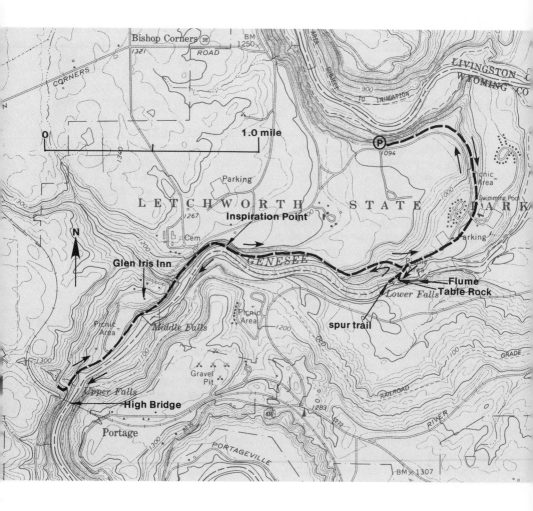

section of the state park; an entrance fee is charged to enter this side of the park either at the north or south end.

In this section of the park are also tent and trailer sites, rental cabins, swimming pools, fishing areas, winter sports facilities, restaurants, picnic areas, picnic shelters, snack bars, and restrooms. There is also the Glen Iris Inn, famous for its cuisine; the restored Seneca Indian Counsel House; the grave of Mary Jemison, the famous "White Woman of the Genesee"; and the William Pryor Letchworth Museum.

Letchworth, a wealthy hardware merchant from Buffalo, came to this area in the late 1800s in search of land on which to build a summer home. Upon seeing Genesee Gorge and its three falls, he was immediately taken by the spectacular beauty, but he was displeased that areas had been clear-cut for timber to build the railroad trestle. He quickly purchased 1,000 acres, which included the three falls, to save them from further exploitation. He bought an old tavern overlooking the Middle Falls and converted it into his home. He called his home Glen Iris, after the ancient goddess of the rainbow—a name inspired by the perpetual rainbow that rises in the mist from the Middle Fall. The home has been preserved as the Glen Iris Inn, where lodging and fine food are offered.

In 1907, Letchworth gave his land to the state on the condition that it be always preserved for public enjoyment. The state has added to the original holding with land purchases that have brought the park to its present size of 14,350 acres, running from Mount Morris in the north to the hamlet of Portageville in the south.

The entire Gorge Trail runs between the St. Helena picnic area in the north to the Upper Falls in the south. The full distance of 7 miles is a fair stretch and would take you about 4 hours to hike one way; but a round trip of 14 miles and 8 hours of hiking can be pretty demanding even for a seasoned hiker.

The recommended hike here cuts this down to 3.8 miles going one way, or 7.6 miles round trip. A friend with an automobile can provide a car-shuttle by leaving the car at the destination end to keep your hike to a short 3.8 miles. Otherwise, plan on about a 4-hour hike to cover your round trip—a good afternoon trek.

The recommended hike starts at the Lower Falls and proceeds upstream to the Middle Falls, ending at the Upper Falls, which are spanned by a high railroad trestle. The hike takes you to a number of other scenic spots as well, including Table Rock, Cathedral Rock, the Flume, and the man-made arch footbridge over the Flume—the river's narrowest spot.

Access. Letchworth State Park is only 35 miles south of Rochester. The park's northern entrance can be reached by the interstate expressway, I-390, which connects with the New York State Thruway (I-90) a few miles south of Rochester.

Drive south on I-390 to Exit 7; on leaving the expressway, turn onto NY 408, and 0.2 mile brings you into the center of the village of Mount Morris. Turn north onto NY 36, and drive a mile to the park's northern entrance.

Once inside the park, follow the paved Park Road for 16.5 miles to where a sign directs you to the Lower Falls Area. Turn left here, and drive downhill 0.3 mile to the first turnoff overlook parking site. Park here.

Trail. Running alongside the stone wall by the parking area is a footpath, which is the midportion of the Gorge Trail. The Gorge Trail is marked by a white double-diamond set on a red square; the numeral "1" sits in the center of the double-diamond, telling you that the Gorge Trail is also designated Trail 1. This is the trail marker that you follow south on your trek.

At the start, the Gorge Trail parallels the road on the left side. As you begin your descent to the Lower Falls picnic and parking area, it cuts left into a wooded area. This area contains picnic tables, shelter, a swimming pool, a restaurant, a snack bar, a store, restrooms, and public telephones.

At the bottom of the hill, as you enter the parking area, the Gorge Trail crosses the road and enters the wooded area. It proceeds along the west side of the river to a second parking and picnic area a short distance away. Just beyond this second picnic area, you come to a fork. The main Gorge Trail follows the right leg (the left leg follows a short, 0.2-mile spur trail). A large sign directs you to

Lower Falls

take the left trail to the Lower Falls. The spur trail begins with a long flight of stone stairs leading downward.

At the bottom of the stairs the trail splits. The short left leg goes to Table Rock, and the longer one goes to the Lower Falls. Follow the latter for about 0.1 mile, to where a sign reads "Trail Ends." To your immediate left is an overlook to the Lower Falls.

Two sets of falls, rising 70 feet in height, are found here; the first falls is the high one. A short distance downstream from the falls is the river's narrowest point—the 10-foot-wide Flume. Upstream, the river is about 60 feet wide and 10 feet deep; in the Flume, the river is channeled into a narrow passage—about 8 feet wide and 60 feet deep.

To reach the Flume, leave the falls overlook and head back on the trail a short distance. Another short trail on the right takes you in a few steps to the Table Rock, a large flat area of resistant sandstone that was swept clean when the river was higher and before the Flume was cut. From Table Rock looking upstream you have a fine view of the Lower Falls in front of you.

From Table Rock, a path leads down a set of stairs to the stone arch footbridge crossing the Flume—the only spot in the park where a hiker can cross the Genesee River. At the Flume the river must plunge through a narrow gatelike outlet, so the water literally turns on its side to pass through the Flume. At the outlet is a high pinnacle called Cathedral Rock, which towers over the footbridge a short distance downstream. Cathedral Rock is a relatively recent phenomenon; in 1835, the falls were located at Cathedral Rock, but as the falls eroded upstream, the river cut first in one direction and then in another, finally leaving behind the pinna-cle called Cathedral Rock.

From the bridge, retrace your steps back to Table Rock and then up the long flight of stairs to the main Gorge Trail at the top. Turn left at the top of the stairs and follow the trail a short distance to another set of stairs. These lead uphill to a dirt path; this path, too, continues uphill for almost a mile to follow the gorge rim. A chain-link fence and a stone wall separate you from the rim it-self.

In a stand of red pine, the dirt path changes to a paved walk. You have now arrived at Inspiration Point. The name is well chosen, since the point gives you a long-distance view upstream to the Middle Falls and still farther to the Upper Falls. If you look across the gorge, you can see what remains of the old Genesee Valley Canal that was cut into the

Middle Falls

side of the gorge wall. When the canal was sold, the canal towpath was converted to railroad line (for more details, see Hike 9).

As you continue along the paved walkway, you pass a small pond, whose outlet water spills down the gorge wall. After a short distance the paved footpath changes to a dirt trail, passing a rock with an inscription. The trail parallels the Park Road on the immediate right and then comes to a fork. Bear left and cross the one-way road that makes up the left leg and heads down a pair of stone stairs to a paved walk.

In front of you is the 107-foot-high Middle Falls. A short distance farther on are several overlooks that allow you more good views, including one that looks over the top of the falls. Far below, at the base of the falls, you see a rainbow arcing through the mist on a sunny day.

The trail now takes you along the river's edge, through a parking-picnic area, past Glen Iris Inn, and into a wooded area beyond. At 0.5 mile, you reach the brink of the 71-foot-high Upper Falls. The trail is just slightly above the river's edge, but park regulations prohibit visitors from leaving the trail to venture down to the edge.

Towering above the falls is a steel railroad trestle called High Bridge, which is still in use. This is the second bridge that was built over the river at this spot. The first one, an all-timber construction, was built in 1852 but went down in flames in 1879, set off by a spark from a passing locomotive engine. That wooden trestle, Portage Bridge, was over 300 feet high and was considered at the time to be the world's highest trestle. After the fire, work crews labored day and night, and the present steel bridge was erected in three months.

From the Upper Falls, the Gorge Trail turns right. It heads up a long flight of stairs that takes you through a wooded area covering the hillside. Once it reaches the top, the trail runs a short distance parallel to Park Road, then crosses the road to end at the parking area on the other side.

If you have not planned for a car-shuttle, this is your turnaround point. You now can head back, descending the stairs to Upper Falls, and then take the Gorge Trail back to your starting point at the overlook parking site.

Letchworth State Park (Letchworth Trail)

Hiking distance 3.8 miles
Hiking time: 2 hours
Vertical rise: 230 feet
Map: USGS 7½' Portageville

Of all the hiking trails in Letchworth State Park, one stands out by virtue of its distance—21.5 miles. It runs the entire length of the state park, from Portageville at the south end to Mount Morris in the north.

This trail is called by several names. Officially, its name is the Letchworth Trail and is one of several spur trails running off the 648-mile long Finger Lakes Trail (FLT). The Letchworth Trail is blazed yellow, whereas the FLT is blazed white. But entrances to the Letchworth Trail are marked by "FLT" signs, and the park map also uses the designation "FLT" to identify the trail route. The section of the Letchworth Trail that runs on the old Genesee Valley Canal route is also called Trail 7.

The FLT runs from the Pennsylvania border in New York's Allegany State Park to the Catskill Mountains. When the Finger Lakes Trail enters the southeastern section of Wyoming County, it heads toward Portageville but turns southeast when it crosses the Genesee River south of Portageville. It is at this point that the Letchworth Trail begins its northward route into Portageville. There it follows Main Street across the Genesee River to intersect NY 436. As soon as the trail crosses the Genesee River bridge, it turns sharply left and enters the park's wooded area.

The Letchworth Trail is known not only for its long distance but for the historical significance of the trail's southern end. A short distance into the park, the Letchworth Trail intersects the roadbed of an old abandoned railroad line. The railroad bed, in turn, was constructed on top of a section of the old Genesee Valley Canal.

The Genesee Valley Canal was commissioned to run south from Lake Ontario and the east-west Erie Canal at Rochester, past Mount Morris, to the Allegheny River in southern New York State. The purpose of this "lateral" canal was to tap the resources of the state's southwestern region and to capture the commercial trade that up to that time had been flowing down the Allegheny River to Pennsylvania. Construction was authorized in 1836.

The canal's first section—from Rochester to Mount Morris—was opened in 1840, and a branch to Dansville was finished in 1841. But the most difficult stretch was still to be dug—the part that passes through what is today the state park's south end. An overland route was needed to and across the Genesee River at Portageville and then south to Caneadea.

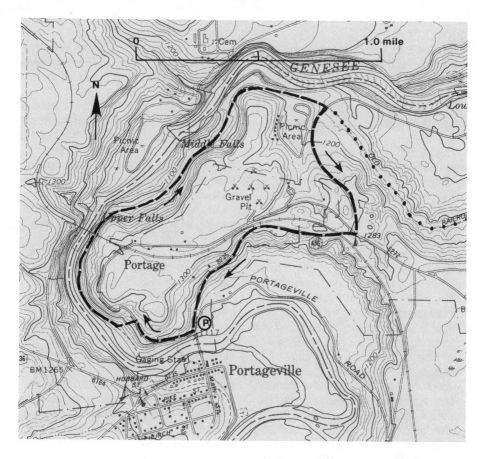

The building of this most difficult stretch was an engineering marvel in its day. Hundreds of workmen literally cut the canal into the gorge wall. They notched the canal into the side of the gorge as an open cut and traversed the gorge from what is today the Park Road near the Parade Ground on the park's east side to NY 436. Here an aqueduct for the canal was built across the river. Several locks also had to be built along this route. In fact, in this stretch there were 120 locks—almost one for every mile of canal.

This portion of the canal was not finished until 1850, and in 1862 the canal finally reached the Allegheny River near Olean. The canal was 124 miles long and linked Lake Ontario at Rochester with the Allegheny River at Pennsylvania.

But the canal was unable to compete with the railroads, which had already penetrated this section of New York. To make up for the loss of money in the endless repairs that had to be made, especially in the gorge area, the state sold the canal in 1880 to the Genesee Valley Canal Railroad Company, which immediately began to lay rails along the canal's former towpath.

The railroad bed was built in the narrow ledge that had been cut into the side of the east gorge wall for the canal. Only several feet separate the roadbed from the edge of the Genesee Gorge, popularly referred to as "the Grand Canyon of the East." From the roadbed there is a perpendicular drop of several hundred feet to the gorge bottom. In the days when trains ran this route, passengers looking out the window and into the gorge must have held their breath the whole way.

This railbed is today part of Letchworth trail. The route here is wide, level, and attractively canopied by arching trees—white and yellow birch, oak, and maple—making the trail a sheer delight to walk. Patches of black cinders still poke through the low-cut grass on the trail, reminding you that you are walking on an old railroad bed. Most of the rails and ties were removed in the mid-1960s, but from time to time, old railroad ties are still found alongside the trail.

After 2.2 miles on the old roadbed, the Letchworth Trail turns north on River road for a short stretch, then follows its own route north along the high ground overlooking the gorge to Mount Morris.

The recommended hike is confined to the trail's southern portion, which traverses the old canal route. You start at NY 436, near the Genesee River bridge, and eventually come back to your starting point in a loop 3.8 miles long. En route, you have countless opportunities to peer over the rim edge and take in the many breathtaking vistas of the gorge.

Access. The trailhead is in a small parking area off NY 436 on the north side of the Genesee River bridge. It can be reached from the north via the I-390 expressway, which connects with the New York State Thruway (I-90) a few miles south of Rochester. Leave the I-390 expressway at Exit 7 and take NY 408 southwest 2 miles to the center of Mount Morris. Continue on NY 408, first southwest and then south for 9 miles to the village of Nunda.

In Nunda, turn onto NY 436 and drive west for 5 miles to the northern end of the Genesee River bridge. En route you pass the remains of the old canal locks at the hamlet of Oakland, a short distance west of Nunda; the locks can be easily seen on the right side of the road. You will also pass the east entrance to the state park. Unlike the park's west side, no entrance fee is charged on the east side. After your return loop, you will be leaving the park by this entrance.

Just before the bridge, there is a small parking area on the right side of the road. Park here.

Trail. Your hike begins by climbing a small weed-covered bank that displays a sign that says "Road Closed." But you also are greeted by an FLT sign and yellow blazes painted on trees, assuring you that you are on the Letchworth Trail, an FLT spur trail. After a short walk through a wooded area, you come to a small open spot. Here rain and ground seepage caused a mud-slide that carried this portion of the trail with it. But with care, this short section can be negotiated and you cross to the other side, where a road ends and another sign also says "Road Closed."

Continue a short distance on this road to a fork. Here a double yellow blaze tells you to turn left. After walking a short distance on a little-used lane, you head downhill for about 100 yards. At the bottom, you intersect a wide, flat trail that looks like an abandoned road.

This is the remains of the old railroad bed, attractively canopied by the trees that line both sides of the yellow-blazed walkway. It once was the route of a railroad that replaced the Genesee Valley Canal. Years later the railroad also ceased to operate, but it was not until the mid-1960s that the rails and ties were removed to open the route for hiking.

As you walk, notice the limestone cliffs

on the right side of the roadbed. This is where the workmen cut back into gorge cliff to make room for the canal. Further uptrail on the right, you see several wide, long ditches next to the roadbed; some are filled with water. These ditches are all that remain of the Genesee Valley Canal.

Through the thin screen of trees on your left, you can see the Genesee River making its way north far below. Soon the sound of the river increases—the first hint that you are approaching the Upper Falls. Then high above you you see a railroad trestle over the falls.

Angling downhill on your left a narrow footpath takes you the short distance to the trestle's concrete base. If you carefully make your way to the far edge of the base, you enjoy a fine view of the top of the falls as the water cascades down in a roar. The Upper Falls are 71 feet high.

Return to the main trail, and continue your hike in a northeasterly direction on the level roadbed. As the sounds of the Upper Falls die away, another sound begins to replace them ahead. You are now approaching the 107-foot-high Middle Falls, which is located 0.5 mile downstream from the Upper Falls.

Both these falls can be seen even more closely from the opposite (west) side of the park, especially if you take the Gorge Trail (see Hike 8). The denseness of the woods covering the steeply sloped gorge on the left prevents you from seeing the Middle Falls except at times of year when the trees have shed their leaves.

As the sound of the Middle Falls recedes, the roadbed comes to an end. Young growth and trees block your progress. The Letchworth Trail, however, turns right and heads uphill for a short stretch. Then it turns left, to bring you to an open area filled with low shrubs and a few small trees. The area is open enough to allow you to glimpse the Middle Falls again a short distance upstream.

The trail again turns uphill into the forested section of the hillside. Then it turns left and straightens its route along the hill for a short distance before starting a gradual descent. Soon you come into a small clearing. On your left, a large sign reads "Keep Out Slide Area Dangerous." Now you know why the roadbed ended a ways back; a slide took a sizable chunk of the roadbed down the gorge wall to the river below.

You are once again on the roadbed, and the yellow blazes tell you to continue. An additional 0.5 mile brings you to a metal fence across the roadbed; the fence is there to prevent unauthorized motor vehicles from using the trail. Immediately beyond the fence, you intersect a paved park road.

Once on the park road, turn right; after a little over 0.1 mile, you come to a turnoff on your right that leads to an attractive open area on the right called the Parade Ground (which serves as a picnic site) and the "D" Camping Area on the left. You, however, continue on the Park Road for 0.6 mile to the park entrance. Here you intersect NY 436.

Turn right (west) onto NY 436 and follow it for a mile as it curves southward. You pass under a railroad bridge en route to finally reach the parking area. Although you are walking along a state highway, this portion of the highway runs inside the state park until you reach the Genesee River and your starting point.

10

Letchworth State Park (Big Bend Trail)

Hiking distance: 4.5 miles
Hiking time: 2½ hours
Vertical rise: 420 feet
Map: USGS 7½' Portageville

After more than 10,000 years of hard work, the Genesee River has cut a breathtaking gorge through sandstone and shale rock to give New York its "Grand Canyon of the East"—a 16-mile geological wonder with perpendicular rock walls, which are almost 600 feet high at some places.

Within the gorge, the Genesee River cascades in a series of noisy plunges over three high cataracts, identified simply as the Upper Falls, the Middle Falls, and the Lower Falls. The highest and the most spectacular are the Middle Falls, at a height of 107 feet. At their base in the mist on sunny days you can see the "perpetual" rainbow.

Striking views can be had from special overlooks on both sides of the canyon. On the park's west side, the Gorge Trail takes you to some of the best spots to see the gorge and the three falls (see Hike 8). On the east side, the Letchworth Trail's south end takes you to another set of overlooks of the gorge and falls (see Hike 9).

Still another trail in the south end of the state park is the Big Bend Trail. Like the Letchworth Trail, it is located on the park's east side, but it is much shorter—only 3 miles long—than the 21-mile

Letchworth Trail. It takes you into an area called the Big Bend and along the gorge's rim and gives you some of the best views of the gorge itself.

The Big Bend overlooks—all of them undeveloped—are the highest in the park, and the canyon walls rise to 550 feet. In the south end of the park, the river's route through the canyon is so tortuous that it almost doubles back on itself. One canyon looks like a huge *S*. In the upper part of the *S* is the Big Bend area and the Big Bend Trail. Here, as the name indicates, the river makes one of its more spectacular turns on its way north.

It is unusual for a river to wind and twist when it is confined by high rock walls. The reason the Genesee River does this is because it started out on a plateau during the postglacial period more than 10,000 years ago. On this plateau, the river would move sideways, first one way and then another, as it flowed north. Once its early course was set, the river cut downward along that winding route.

Before the Wisconsin glacier overran New York, drainage to the north was by way of a trunk river called the Dansville River. This river took its headwaters from

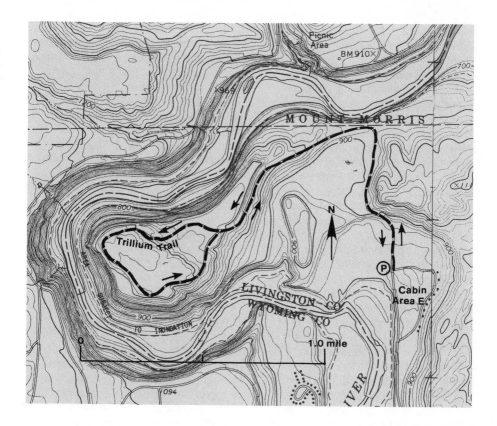

feeder streams in the Canandaigua Lake valley and directed the water flow into what is today Irondequoit Bay. After the ice sheet melted back, the modern Genesee River could have returned quickly to its old route from Pennsylvania to Portageville. But in the Portageville-Nunda area a high moraine blocked the river from using its old channel on its course through what is today the hamlet of Sonyea. Instead, the river found a passage over the Letchworth plateau, farther west, and began to cut its way through, creating the present Genesee Gorge.

When you come into the park's east side, you follow the main paved park road for 3.2 miles to what is called Cabin Area E. A cluster of wooden cabins are available to rent from the state. The grounds around the cabins are well groomed and provide a huge, attractive lawn, lined with sugar maples along the road.

This is also where signs of civilization end and the wilder part of the park begins. The paved road ends, and the beginning of a dirt lane is the start of the Big Bend Trail and its surrounding undeveloped area. Here you find no picnic areas, playfields, restrooms, or snack bars. As a result, vehicular and foot travel is almost nonexistent—adding to the area's remoteness.

You also may expect to meet some of the park's wildlife here. Over 150 different species of birds have been observed, including the huge, gracefully soaring turkey vulture and the wily wild turkey.

Other animals include the white-tailed deer, raccoon, woodchuck, opossum, striped skunk, porcupine, cottontail rabbit, and, on occasion, the red fox. The park also contains the shy timber rattlesnake. This species of snake is sighted each year, but the number of sightings are few. The rattler usually goes where people do not—into rock crevices and other hiding places. Nevertheless, the rattler is part of park's wildlife, so be alert.

Access. Letchworth State Park is only 35 miles south of Rochester and can be reached easily via interstate expressway I-390. The expressway connects with the New York State Thruway (I-90) just 5 miles south of Rochester.

Drive south on I-390 for 32 miles to Exit 7. Here you turn west onto NY 408; 2 miles brings you into the center of the hamlet of Mount Morris. Continue on NY 408, first in a southwesterly direction, then in a southerly direction, for 9 miles to the village of Nunda. In the village of Nunda, turn west onto NY 436 and drive 5 miles to the state park's east entrance.

Drive north on the paved park road for 3.2 miles, where the paved road ends and the dirt lane begins. Park here.

Trail. An open area where the trees are set back from the road is the start of the Big Bend Trail, which follows a single-lane dirt road north. Follow the road for 0.2 mile. There, as the road turns left and heads uphill, you enter a forested area. The upward climb is fairly steep for 0.2 mile, but then it levels off. The road turns right and continues straight north for 0.3 mile; the land on the left is flat, but on the right it rises to form a forested ridge 100 feet high.

At the 0.6-mile mark, the road turns sharply to the right. Running off the road

at this spot is another trail. A sign by the road tells you it is Trail 10A, also called the Trillium Trail. It runs northeast for little over 0.6 mile to join Trail 9 (the Dishmill Trail) at Dishmill Creek.

The Trillium Trail is an easy trail to walk and adds only a half-hour to your trek. It takes you down the lower side of a hill along a level path until you reach Dishmill Creek, which flows north and eventually spills over the gorge rim to the river below. The descent to Dishmill Creek is about 100 feet.

At the junction of the Big Bend Trail and the Trillium Trail is your first opportunity to walk a short distance north through the forest to the gorge rim for a view of the gorge and river below.

Back on the road, continue walking in a southwesterly direction. The road now begins to climb, gradually at first, then more steeply, for the next 0.3 mile. Here the road flattens and remains level for the next 0.6 mile. After a short ascent, you come to a fork. You have reached the top of the Big Bend Knob. A sign indicates that the road is one-way to the right. This begins a loop that eventually will bring you back to this spot.

Turn right and head in a westerly direction for about 0.1 mile. Here the road again comes close to the gorge edge; a few dozen feet to your right through the woods is another view, north and downstream, of the high-walled gorge.

Continue on the road for another 0.3 mile until you come to a turnoff that provides another overlook. The road now turns in a southwesterly direction, then more sharply to the south, as it completes the first half of the loop. Again, there is an opportunity to leave the road and walk through the woods to the rim. Now you are looking upstream in a southwesterly direction.

An additional 0.3 mile brings you to where the road turns even more sharply

View of Canyon from Big Bend Trail

to the left. About 20 feet off the road to your right is another overlook to the south; here the river flows west.

An additional 0.6 mile brings you past a large clearing with scotch pine set back from the road and finally to the fork where the loop began.

The next 0.8 mile takes you gradually downhill as you start your return trip, and an additional 0.6 mile brings you back to your parked vehicle.

11

Rattlesnake Hill State Wildlife Management Area

Total distance: 5 miles
Hiking time: 3 hours
Vertical rise: 409
Maps: USGS 7½' Ossian; USGS 7½' Nunda;
  USGS 7½' Canaseraga

To locals, it is known simply as the Hill. To officials of the state's Department of Environmental Conservation, it is known as the Rattlesnake Hill State Wildlife Management Area. To hikers new to this area, it's a place with an ominous name.

Don't let the word rattlesnake put you off, though, because this area is much too attractive to miss owing to unwarranted fears of snakes under every log and bush. The main difference between Rattlesnake Hill and other hiking spots in Western New York and upstate New York is that this area is up front about the existence there of one of its denizens, the timber rattlesnake. The other places have this snake too; they just don't advertise it.

In fact, this rattler is found in virtually every New York county that borders Pennsylvania (which has a sizable rattlesnake population). The timber rattlesnake's range extends through southwestern New York, across the southern tier, northward into the Lake George area, and to the eastern Adirondacks, where quite a few rattlers are found. Another species, the Massasauga rattlesnake, which is about as small as the pygmy rattler (2 to 3½ feet long), can be found not too far from Rochester in the Bergen swamp area.

Rattlesnake Hill lives up to its name. A few rattlers can be found in the more remote spots of the Hill. But you can do all your walking on open roads, where snakes are rarely seen. In early spring and late fall, when the temperature drops enough during the night to bring snakes—the timber rattlesnake as well as nonpoisonous varieties—come out into open areas to warm themselves in the sun. Still, it is rare to see any kind of snake in an open road.

Rattlesnake Hill covers 5,100 acres and contains nearly two dozen natural and man-made ponds. It occupies the top of the relatively flat highlands, which rise over 2,000 feet and spill over into two counties, Livingston and Allegany. About two-thirds of Rattlesnake Hill is in southern Livingston County, and the rest is in northern Allegany County. This wildlife management area lies on the imaginary boundary marking the eastern edge of Western New York. It is very accessible. It can be reached easily from Canaserage, 5 miles to the southeast, from Dansville, 8 miles to the east, and from Nunda, 5 miles to the northwest.

The wildlife management area sits on relatively level highland, and several

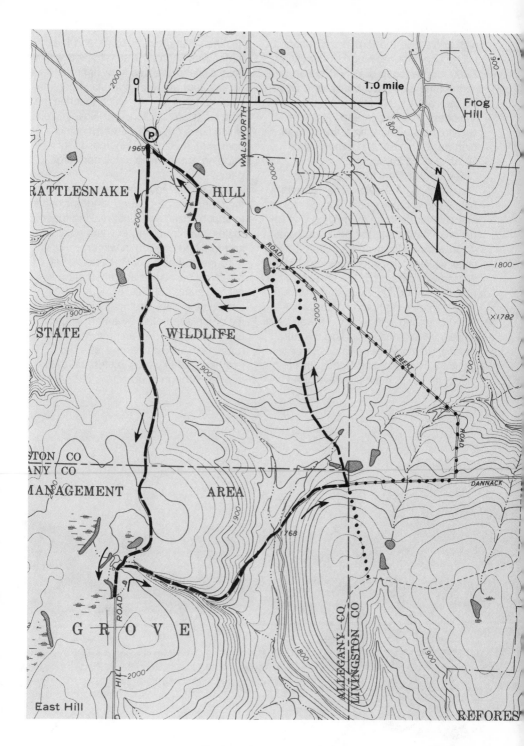

high spots give the terrain a pleasant, rolling appearance. Frog Hill (elevation 2,000 feet) is located a short distance north of the area's boundary, and Scott Hill (elevation 1,942 feet) looms to the southeast. In between and within the wildlife management area are several high points without hill names, all of which exceed 2,000 feet.

The area is ideal for hiking, cross-country skiing, bird-watching, studying nature, horseback riding, and picnicking. The hiker will find an interesting combination of habitats in the area, including woodlands of hardwood, conifer stands, small wetland areas, old apple orchards, overgrown fields, and open meadow—a nice mix to add variety to one's travels. Here, too, are the homes of the white-tailed deer and wild turkey, as well as smaller inhabitants, including the ruffed grouse, gray squirrel, and cottontail rabbit. Mink, raccoon, and beaver live in the marsh areas. In ponds in developed marshes, waterfowl abound, and the larger impoundments are stocked with trout. Several streams in or near the wildlife area are known trout waters, including Sugar Creek, which touches the area's eastern section, and Hovey Brook, which flows out of the area's southern portion. It is also used in season for trapping and hunting small and large game.

Still another advantage is that many of the roads are barricaded, hence closed to unauthorized vehicles, making these routes ideal for hiking in warm weather and for Nordic skiing in winter.

To the southeast of Rattlesnake Hill lie two large parcels of unnamed state forest, covering 2,600 acres. One parcel touches the Hill's southeastern corner; the other, separated by a narrow gap, extends eastward in a somewhat elongated fashion. The parcels can be reached and explored by the dirt roads that run through them.

Pond with ducks

Access. The main route from which Rattlesnake Hill may be reached is NY 436, which runs between Nunda and Dansville. These two towns in the southeastern part of Livingston County are located south of Rochester, about 10 miles from the southern tip of Letchworth State Park.

If you are coming from Dansville, drive west on NY 426 for about 6 miles to the Shute Road, which intersects at an angle from the southwest. Turn left here, and drive on Shute Road for 2.3 miles to Ebert Road, which intersects at an angle from the left. Turn left on Ebert Road, which is a dirt road, and drive uphill for 1.3 miles to the point where you see a barricaded road intersecting on the right (south). Park here.

From Nunda, take NY 436 east for 3.5 miles to the intersection of Carney Road. Turn right here and drive south on Carney Road for 1.1 miles to the intersection with Shute Road. Turn right (west) on Shute Road and drive 0.2 mile to the intersection with Ebert Road; turn left and drive uphill for 1.3 miles to the barricaded road intersecting on the right. Park here.

Trail. The recommended route is a loop that begins at the barricaded road, heads south, loops eastward, and returns to Ebert Road by way of a marked hiking trail. The state maintains two interconnected hiking trails in the wildlife area. One is a small loop, running a little less than a half-mile from and back to Ebert Road. The other, making use of the lower part of the smaller loop, goes from Ebert Road for 2 miles in a southeasterly direction and eventually intersects a one-lane dirt road that runs east and then north and comes out on Dannack Hill Road. It is this longer hiking trail that you intersect and use for your return route.

Sometimes weeds grow fairly tall on the hiking trail before they are cut back. On a wet day, this can make for pretty soggy feet, and even on a dry day, it is not all that pleasant to hike in the weeds. If the weeds are too high, you can complete the loop by hiking the dirt roads that take you to Ebert Road and back to your parked vehicle.

Walk around the barricade and head south on an unmarked dirt road—what the state calls a truck trail, a little over one vehicle width. The road is treelined, and woodlands run along the road on both sides. Although unmarked, this is the extension of England Mill Road that comes from the southern portion of the wildlife area.

The unmarked road runs south for 2 miles over level terrain with hardly any change in elevation for the whole distance. With the exception of a couple of bends, the road is also relatively straight, making this portion a leisurely one.

About 0.3 mile from your start, the road curves a little to the left, then again straightens out. After a short distance you cross a hardly noticeable streamlet that feeds water from a small pond some distance in the woods on your left to another pond about equally distant on the right. The road makes a bend to the right and then turns south again and continues over level land for the next mile.

At the mile mark on your right near the road is a fair-sized pond that has been dammed on the near side. This is the first of four such ponds that lie close together in this area. They are connected by streamlets that feed water from one to the next and are part of the headwaters of Hovey Brook, which flows south. Since the ponds are close together, they can be visited easily with a short walk.

By the time you spot the second pond on your right, you have reached a junction with England Hill Road coming from the south and Dannack Hill Road coming from the east. A short distance down what is now England Hill Road brings you to the third pond on your right; it literally touches the road. Hidden from sight in summer is a very small pond in the woods on your left; it feeds into the large pond on your right.

Return to the junction and turn onto Dannack Hill Road. It starts going downhill and into a gully, which widens and deepens as you continue your descent. A short distance from the junction, a small creek, taking its water from the cluster of ponds you just passed, moves from the left side of the road to the right side and continues there until after a descent of a little less than a half-mile, the road turns northeasterly out of the gully. The creek continues its descent, but now more gradually, for another 0.3 mile. There it crosses a brook that also feeds water to Hovey Brook.

Once across the streamlet, the road starts climbing and continues for the next 0.35 mile, then flattens out. Here the hiking trail crosses the road. If the weeds are down and the footpath is clear, turn left here and head north on the hiking trail. If the weeds are high (or if you prefer the road to the footpath), continue on Dannack Hill Road for a distance just short of a half-mile. When it intersects Ebert Road on the left, turn left and continue north, then northwest on Ebert Road for almost 2 miles to your parked vehicle.

If you select the hiking trail, 0.1 mile brings you to a cluster of three fair-sized ponds that sit on a divide. The two joined ponds on the west feed their water west into the headwaters of Hovey Brook, while the pond to the east feeds its water in the opposite direction, east down the hill to Sugar Creek.

The trail goes between the two western ponds, and then climbs uphill as it runs through the surrounding woodland. After a short walk to the north, you pass a small pond on your right. From here it is a half-mile to the intersection of the main foot-trail on which you are walking with the smaller loop running south from and then back to Ebert Road.

Turn left and follow the bottom of the loop until it heads north for 0.1 mile where a foot trail—part of the main hiking trail—intersects on the left. From this intersection, it is only 0.1 mile to Ebert Road, which lies due north. But continue on the main hiking trail by turning left (west).

The hiking trail now runs west for about 0.1 mile, then loops southwest, to make a semicircle around a fairly large impoundment that lies north of the trail. The trail now turns to the right and heads north. Along the next 0.4 mile, the trail first passes a small pond on your left, then a large one on your right adjacent to the large impoundment, and finally another on your left. From the last pond it is a little over 0.1 mile to Ebert Road. Turn left and follow Ebert Road for 0.3 mile past a pond well off the road on your right. This road leads to your parked vehicle.

Southwestern Region: Chautauqua County

12

Chautauqua Gorge State Forest

Hiking distance: 2.6 miles
Hiking time: 2 hours
Vertical rise: 270 feet
Map: USGS 7½' Sherman

The Chautauqua Gorge State Forest lies at the northern end of the large upland area known as the Cattaraugus Hill Region. Amid this region's vast expanse of relatively level land are rolling farmlands and a sparse population thinly scattered. The upland region was only lightly exposed to the Wisconsin glacier, which advanced over New York State more than 15,000 years ago, and so the terrain is different here from that of the Genesee and Niagara Frontier regions, where the hilltops were bulldozed, the ridges worn smooth, and large U-shaped valleys deepened and widened.

The spine of the upland area runs in a north-south direction, more or less paralleling the long and narrow Chautauqua Lake. Hence, streams and creeks on the northeastern side flow down to the lake, on the southwestern side into French Creek, and on the northwestern escarpment of the Allegheny Plateau into Lake Erie.

This northwestern route is the one Chautauqua Creek takes. Its headwaters are in the upland region, immediately north of the village of Sherman and Titus Road, which runs east-west on a divide. The feeder streams come together at Nettle Hill Road to form Chautauqua Creek; a half-mile north, the creek enters the south end of the gorge at Putnam Road.

Chautauqua Creek drops more than 800 feet on its way to its outlet in Lake Erie, a short distance north of the village of Westfield. During the postglacial period, the steep downhill pitch of the northwestern escarpment allowed the creek to cut the impressively deep Chautauqua Gorge.

Whether viewed from the top or from the bottom, the gorge is a breathtaking development in this otherwise benign landscape. The steep sides of the gorge already rise 150 feet at Putnam Road, but by the time it reaches the southeastern boundary of Chautauqua Gorge State Forest, the gorge has deepened to 230 feet. When it reaches the end of the state forest a mile north, the creek bottom lies almost 300 feet below the top of the narrowing but straight-sided gorge.

The Chautauqua Gorge State Forest is a terminus of the Westside Overland Trail (WOT). Blue-blazed, the WOT is a continuous trail of 25 miles that runs from Chautauqua Gorge in the north to Brokenstraw State Forest (see Hike 17) in the south.

Access. You can reach Chautauqua

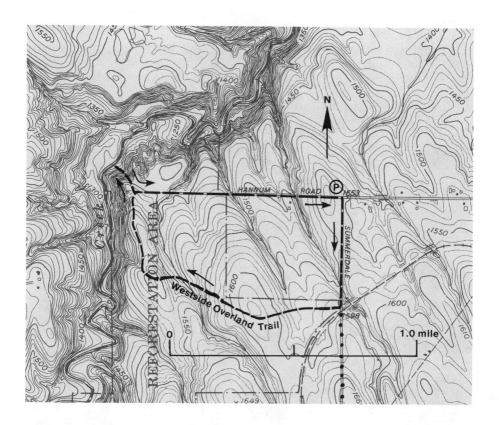

Gorge State Forest by taking the New York Thruway (I-90), coming from Erie, Pennsylvania, in the southwest or from Buffalo in the northeast.

Use Thruway Exit 60 at Westfield. Turn onto NY 394, and drive in a south-easterly direction for 6 miles to the village of Mayville; turn right on NY 430 and drive 1.6 miles, where the paved Hannum Road intersects on the right. Turn here, and drive first north and then west on Hannum Road for 2.4 miles where the dirt Summerdale Road inter-sects from the south. Park here.

Trail. Start your hike by walking south on Summerdale Road. The road goes gradually uphill, and in a short distance you see a gas well in the field on your

left. The area on your left is wooded; on the right, however, are fields. After 0.4 mile, as you descend to cross a feeder stream, the fields give way to woods. As you climb up the other side, you see the beginning of Chautauqua Gorge State Forest on your left and a sign informing you that you have reached the northern portion of the Westside Overland Trail.

Turn onto the WOT by climbing the road bank into the forest. From here, the WOT climbs gradually for the next 0.3 mile to reach one of the area's high spots (elevation 1,620 feet). Look north at this point to get a view of the fields and woods that lie beyond. A steady downhill walk from the high point for the next 0.3 mile brings you to a north-

flowing stream that eventually feeds into Chautauqua Creek.

A short but steep climb brings you past an open area on your right and to a one-lane dirt road. The WOT crosses the road, then turns north, staying in the forest as it goes. Soon you pass two picnic tables on your left; also on your left, looking through the trees, you have a view across the gorge to the hillsides beyond. An additional 0.3 mile brings you to a small parking area where Hannum Road ends.

The WOT now makes a sharp left turn and starts a steep descent into the gorge itself. At a little over 0.2 mile, you reach the gorge bottom, where the narrow and fairly shallow Chautauqua Creek is flowing north over hard bedrock. The WOT ends here for now, although future plans call for it to continue upstream along the east side of the gorge, presumably to Lyons Road.

The gorge's bottom and the creek's edge are a fine place to linger and enjoy the scenery up and downstream. It is also a good place to enjoy a bite to eat.

When you are ready, retrace your steps uphill to the parking area. From here, turn east on the dirt road, Hannum Road, and follow it past a bivouac area for 0.1 mile, where it crosses a feeder stream—the same one you crossed earlier on the WOT.

The road now rises, only to make another descent to cross a second feeder stream; it repeats this same performance once again to cross a third stream. All these streams flow north into Chautauqua Creek. From here, it is a 0.2-mile climb to reach the intersection with Summerdale Road and your parked vehicle.

13

Mount Pleasant State Forest (Northern Section)

Hiking distance: 5.6 miles
Hiking time: 2½ hours
Vertical rise: 440 feet
Map: USGS 7½' Sherman

Mount Pleasant State Forest is long and narrow, indeed one of the longer state forests in western Chautauqua County. It extends 5.6 miles from its northern tip at Nettle Hill Road to its southern end at Titus Road. The 1,522-acre state forest lives up to its name. The terrain is rolling, but never too steep: ascents and descents average 60 to 80 feet. There is just enough variation to make your hiking here both interesting and pleasant.

Both the northern and the southern sections of this elongated forest are located on the high ground of the region's upland. The forest area's drainage flows east to Chautauqua Lake by means of Wing Creek and north by way of Chautauqua Creek.

Chautauqua Lake, which lies a couple of miles east of the state forest, was a favorite route for the early French explorers as they traveled from Lake Erie to the Ohio River via both the lake and the Allegheny River.

The blue-blazed Westside Overland Trail (WOT) passes along the entire length of the state forest. You can walk this portion of the WOT round trip (11.2 miles) in a single day, but it might be somewhat on the demanding side. The better strategy is to divide the state for-

est in half: walk to the northern end of the WOT one day, and the southern half another day. That way, you can make your day hike easy and enjoyable.

This hike, in the state forest's northern section, follows the WOT from the trailhead at Nettle Hill Road to Brumagin Road in the forest's midsection. As you hike, keep an eye open for white-tailed deer. Back in the 1920s, deer herds were largely confined to the Adirondack Mountain region; a few deer were found along the New York–Pennsylvania border, but the rest of the state was devoid of deer. Today, however, every county in the state has sizable deer herds, especially the counties in Western New York. In Chautauqua County, the annual deer take by hunters now usually averages over 3,500, a figure exceeded only by the takes in Chattaraugus and Allegany counties in Western New York.

The color of both the buck and doe is similar with two seasonal variations. In summer, the coat is reddish-brown; in the winter, the color turns grayish-tan. The hair of the winter coat is hollow, giving the deer an air-cushion when it lies down on the snow. The buck sheds his antlers each year in December, and they are usually eaten by porcupines and voles. New antlers begin to grow in May; they are in "velvet" until September, when the buck rubs small trees to get rid of the covering.

If you spot a doe in the summer, you may be able to get quite close to her before she bounds off. But the white-tail is a shy animal, given to hiding in thickets and swamps to avoid detection by possible enemies, including man. Although the buck is often bold during the rutting or mating season, he is actually even warier than the doe.

When startled, the buck "blows"— emits a loud snort—before taking off in a spurt of speed. If you are not expecting such noise, the blowing sound can give you quite a start. All deer, does and bucks, are loners, although they come together during the brief rut and when they "yard-up" on the leeward side of hills during the winter. At other times, however, each deer goes its own way.

You have a good chance of spotting a deer in Mount Pleasant State Forest, but a deer will probably sneak away quietly and circle behind you before you see it. So from time to time look behind you; you may be surprised to see a deer in the trail watching you depart.

Access. The northern section of Mount Pleasant State Forest can be easily reached from either the west or the north on the New York Thruway (I-90).

Leave the Thruway at Exit 60 in Westfield and turn onto NY 394 going southeast; 6 miles brings you to the center of Mayville. In this village, turn right onto NY 430 and drive 3 miles to where the WOT crosses the road. On the north side of the road is private land, and on the south side is a narrow strip of public land and the northern tip of Mount Pleasant State Forest. Park here.

Trail. Follow the WOT south into the state forest. After a short distance, the trail turns sharply to the left; in little less

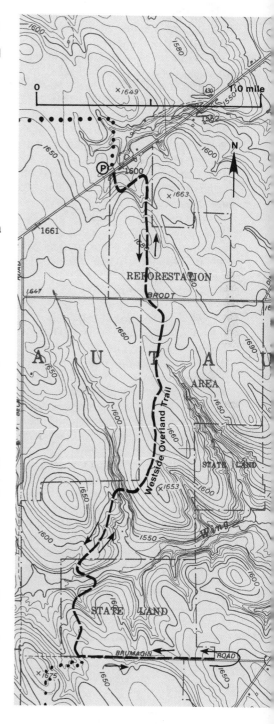

than 0.2 mile, the trail makes another sharp turn, this one to the right.

It now heads straight south, climbing gradually uphill; 0.3 mile brings you to the top of a small hill. Ahead of you the terrain is flat; an additional 0.2 mile brings you to a dirt road, Brot Road. The WOT crosses the road and reenters the state forest to make a quick turn to the left. Just as quickly, the trail turns right and again heads straight south. The land here is level, and walking for the next 0.6 mile is easy.

Now, however, the trail turns gradually uphill, only to reverse direction after 0.1 mile. The descent at first is gradual, but after 0.1 mile, the trail heads down steeply to cross a small stream that feeds into Wing Creek about 0.5 mile south.

Once over the stream, you have a short but steep climb as the trail heads southwest, first gradually uphill, then down a steep hillside to cross the main branch of Wing Creek. From here, the WOT climbs the stream's bank to continue on an uphill and winding journey for the next 0.4 mile. Then the trail intersects a narrow dirt road, the continuation of the east-west Brumagin Road.

Turn left here and follow this road east for 0.7 mile, where the state forest ends on the right side. An additional 0.1 mile brings you to the end of the state forest on the left side. This is your turnaround point. However, just ahead—0.2 mile— Brumagin Road intersects the paved Mt. Pleasant Road. When you are ready, retrace your steps northward and back to your vehicle.

Hiking path

14

Mount Pleasant State Forest (Southern Section)

Hiking distance: 4.5 miles
Hiking time: 2½ hours
Vertical rise: 390 feet
Map: USGS 7½' Sherman

The southern section of Mount Pleasant State Forest, which extends from Titus Road in the south to Brumagin Road in the north, displays a few high spots, but it is not as hilly or craggy as the northern section (see Hike 13).

Nonetheless, it does contain scenic landscapes, specifically several tall forested hills, a couple of attractive man-made ponds, a canopied hiking trail, and a comfortable lean-to. Anyone interested in a weekend backpacking trip may wish to spend the night in the lean-to; it saves bringing along a tent.

You will find the ponds at the southern end of the state forest and the lean-to a little over a mile north of the trailhead on Titus Road. If you plan a weekend outing, you can use the lean-to as your base camp; this will allow you to hike the Westside Overland Trail (WOT) through both the southern and northern sections of the state forest.

The southern section of the Mount Pleasant State Forest sits on a divide. Drainage north of the divide is to the east by way of Wing Creek and north by way of Chautauqua Creek; south of the divide, drainage is to the west and then to the south by way of French Creek. The high spot (elevation 1,775 feet) is at the lower end of the state forest's southern section.

There are a cluster of four hills in the southern section; all are higher than 1,740 feet, which is high for this area. None have names, but Mount Pleasant Road runs past these hills, and from it the state forest takes its name. Together, these hills are high enough to warrant being collectively called a "mount" and unofficially as the site of "Mount Pleasant."

Between several of these hills lie two ponds with man-made earthen dams that hold back the water. The ponds have an unusual location—right on the high ground that acts as a divide; however, there is enough drainage from the surrounding hills to keep the ponds full.

The outlet stream of the first pond flows under Mount Pleasant Road to the adjacent pond about 0.1 mile northwest. The second pond also drains westward into a wetland area a little over a mile away; from here the drainage is southward for over a mile past the village of Sherman and empties into French Creek, which eventually drains into Pennsylvania, 15 miles southwest of the state forest.

The state forest welcomes you any

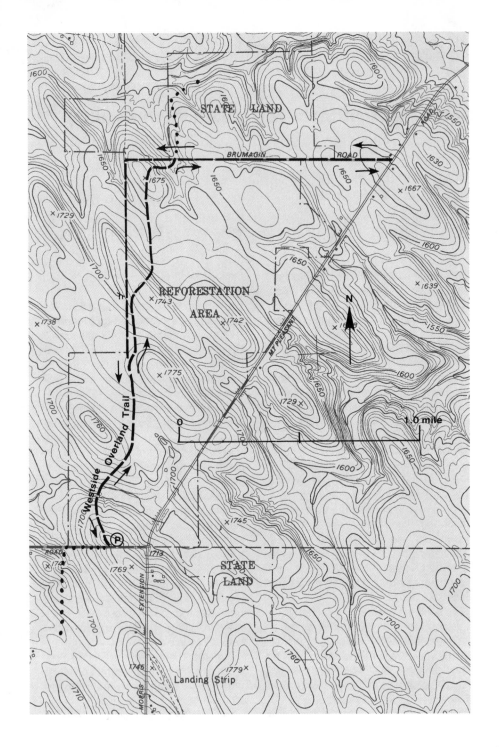

time of the year. In summer, the forest's canopy provides a cool walk even on a hot day. In fall, the colors of the autumn foliage always make hiking enjoyable. Spring is the time to see the woods take on new life. In winter, as the snow deepens, foot-travel changes to snowshoeing or cross-country skiing.

The state forest's southern section is ideal for such winter travel. Getting onto the WOT is easy since the plowed Mount Pleasant Road takes you close to the trailhead, and the blue-blazed trail is easy to follow with either skis or snowshoes.

Life continues in the woods even when the ground is covered with a thick mantle of snow. Sometimes wildlife activity is even more noticeable in winter than in summer—animals have to forage more openly for food. There are always a good variety of winter birds, including the slate-colored junco, the pileated woodpecker, the white-winged crossbill, the black-capped chickadee, the red crossbill, the white-breasted nuthatch, and the purple finch, as well as such predators as owls and hawks.

Other animals make their rounds in search of food: the red and gray fox, the short-tailed weasel (whose coat turns white in winter), mink, white-tailed deer, varying hare, opossum, porcupine, wild turkey, and ruffed grouse. The fox and mink search for mice and shrews that travel under the snow in tunnels. The fox listens for movement or squealing under the snow and then rises up and pounces with both front feet to pin down its quarry.

In winter, the ruffed grouse grows feathers on its toes—home-grown snowshoes—to allow easy travel over the snow. It has a habit of plunging into soft, powdery snow in the evening to spend the night in an enclosed, insulated chamber. The noise of someone approaching will cause the grouse to flush in an explosion of flying snow and whirling wings. It is an unexpected spectacle, so surprising that a skier or snowshoer can be quite startled.

If you come to this section of the state forest in winter, travel slowly and look about for movements of birds and other animals. In winter the woods are filled with tracks, visible signs of much activity here.

Access. The state forest can be reached by taking the New York State Thruway (I-90), from Buffalo or Erie to Exit 60 at Westfield, and take NY 394 south; 6 miles brings you to the center of Mayville. At the south end of this village turn onto County Route 301 (listed on some maps as 25). Follow this route southwest for 3.2 miles to a fork. County Route 301 takes the left leg and heads south; the other leg is the beginning of Mount Pleasant Road.

Turn onto Mount Pleasant Road and drive 3.4 miles. There you enter Mount Pleasant State Forest. An additional 0.3 mile brings you to a bridge over an outlet stream. Another 0.1 mile takes you to the intersection with the dirt Titus Road. Turn left on Titus Road, and drive 0.2 mile west to where the WOT crosses the road. This is your trailhead. Park here.

Trail. The trailhead is high, at 1,769 feet; you walk downhill on the WOT as you head north. The downward pitch of the trail is gradual at first, but it becomes steeper when you come to the bank of the outlet stream, flowing west from the pond on your immediate right.

Once across the stream, the trail starts uphill. For the next 0.2 mile, you climb steadily until you reach a level area. After only a short distance, you again head downhill; the downward pitch remains gradual for the next 0.4 mile. At that point you find a lean-to—a nice spot to take a short break, or even to stop for a while for snack or a refreshing drink.

But after this point, the trail steeply ascends a small hill (elevation 1,743). The downside of the hill, in turn, is steep also; when you reach bottom, the ground stays level for about 0.3 mile of flat walking. Then you reach another hill (elevation 1,675)—smaller than the previous one but just as steep.

When you reach the hilltop, the trail turns right and heads downhill. After less than 0.1 mile, you turn north again and intersect a dirt lane, an extension of Brumagin Road. Turn right on this road and walk east over relatively level ground for just over 0.5 mile, where the state forest ends on the right side of the road. Another 0.1 mile brings you to the spot where the state forest ends on the left side as well. Continue for another 0.2 mile, which brings you to the intersection with the paved Mount Pleasant Road.

Retrace your steps west to where the WOT crosses the road. If you continue on Brumagin Road in a westerly direction, 0.2 mile brings you to the western edge of the state forest. This is your turn-around point. The one-lane dirt road, however, turns right and heads north for 0.7 mile, where it joins the north-south Beck Road.

Return to the WOT and turn south; 1.05 miles brings you past the lean-to, over the outlet stream, and to Titus Road and your parked vehicle.

15

Edward J. Whalen Memorial State Forest

Hiking distance: 3.6 miles
Hiking time: 2 hours
Vertical rise: 572 feet
Map: USGS 7½' Sherman; USGS 7½' Chautauqua;
* USGS 7½' North Clymer; USGS 7½' Panama*

As soon as you enter the Edward J. Whalen Memorial State Forest, you notice that it is quite different from other nearby state forests—not only in its name but also in the lay of the land.

Some years ago, it was a state practice to name a forest after a forester who had made a significant contribution to the productive development of state land, including recreation and raising and harvesting trees for financial income.

Edward J. Whalen was such a person. He was the second district forester to oversee the expansion and improvement of the state forests in this area; in 1955, he succeeded the late Harry E. Dobbin. One state forest in Cattaraugus County is also named after Dobbins (see Hike 27). These are the only two memorial state forests in Western New York. The practice of memorializing forests has now been discontinued.

The terrain of this forest is more rugged than that of Chautauqua Gorge State Forest (see Hike 12), despite its impressively deep gorge, and than Mount Pleasant State Forest (see Hikes 13 and 14); these other state forests, while hilly, are fairly uniform in appearance.

The same conditions prevail farther south in North Harmony State Forest (see Hike 16) and in Panama and Brokenstraw state forests (see Hike 17).

The Whalen Memorial State Forest, by contrast, has a set of closely clustered steep-sided hills that peak at elevations exceeding 1,800 feet. These hills taper sharply downward on the east to form a 2-mile front that pitches precipitously into a narrow valley.

Through this valley Prendergast Creek flows in a northerly direction. Feeding the creek are several streams that originate high in the craggy hill country and that have cut deep gullies and gorges; all this gives the landscape a rugged, untamed look.

To get to this area, all you have to do is follow the 3-mile portion of the Westside Overland Trail (WOT) that takes you over the hilltops, through two gorges, and alongside Prendergast Creek. The WOT is a well-groomed 25-mile trail that passes over private land and through six state forests, beginning with Chautauqua Gorge State Forest in the north and ending with Brokenstraw State Forest in the south.

Wildlife in this region include white-tailed deer, black bear, wild turkey, ruffed grouse, a variety of hawks, the red and gray fox, cottontail rabbit, red and gray squirrel, striped skunk, opossum, raccoon, muskrat, bear, mink, and chipmunk. It also is home to more than 100 species of birds and more than 200 species of flowering plants and ferns, as well as a variety of broad-leafed and evergreen trees.

Access. To reach Whalen Memorial State Forest, take the New York State Thruway (I-90) to Exit 60, at Westfield, and drive south on NY 394 for 6 miles to the village of Mayville. At the south end of the village, turn onto County Route 301 (on some maps, it is listed as County Route 25).

Drive south on County Route 301 for 3.6 miles to a fork; the right leg becomes Mount Pleasant Road, while the left leg continues as County Route 301. Turn left and continue on County Route 301 for 2.8 miles, at which point you encounter the hamlet of Stebbins Corners. The paved county route now becomes the dirt Stebbins Road. Continue south on Stebbins Road for 2 miles, where the WOT crosses the road. This is your trailhead. Park here.

From the south, the trailhead can be reached from the village of Panama, which can be reached from the east or west via NY 474; from Jamestown in the east, it is 11 miles to Panama. In Panama, turn north on North Street, which takes you out of the village to become County Route 33 (on some maps it is County Route 76).

Drive north on County Route 33 for 5.5 miles, to where Eiden Road intersects on the left. Turn left, and drive 3 miles west to the intersection with Stebbins Road. Turn here, and drive south on Stebbins Road for 0.7 mile where the WOT crosses the road. Park here.

Trail. The blue blazes along Stebbins Road tell you that the WOT follows the

road from the south a short distance before turning east into Whalen forest. This portion of the WOT is actually a continuation of the trail passing through Mount Pleasant State Forest 5.2 miles away. (See Hikes 13 and 14)

About half of the recommended hike through Whalen Memorial State Forest follows the WOT, then switches to several dirt roads to allow you to walk a loop.

As you leave Stebbins Road at the trailhead, the WOT starts uphill immediately. In only 0.2 mile you reach the crest of the hill. For the next 0.1 mile, the terrain is level, but then it pitches downhill, gradually at first, then more steeply as the trail enters the top end of a deepening ravine through which tumbles a streamlet.

For the next 0.5 mile, the WOT follows the ravine and the stream in a southeasterly direction. The ravine gets deeper, until eventually it takes on the dimension of a gorge, over 200 feet deep. Soon the trail reaches the floor of the narrow valley. The stream that the trail has been following through the ravine and gorge now turns north to become part of Prendergast Creek. The WOT, on the other hand, turns south.

As it does so, it intersects an old dirt road. It follows the road straight south for 0.7 mile. On the left side of the road is a stream that channels the headwaters of Prendergast Creek northward.

The road on which the WOT is now traveling follows the feeder streamlet upstream. (This streamlet has its origin in a wetland area high in the hills.) The WOT, paralleling the creek, turns west, then north, as it starts to climb. An additional 0.3 mile finds the trail leaving the road and turning downhill in a southwesterly direction to cross another feeder stream. From here, the climb is steep, but in a short distance the ascent becomes less

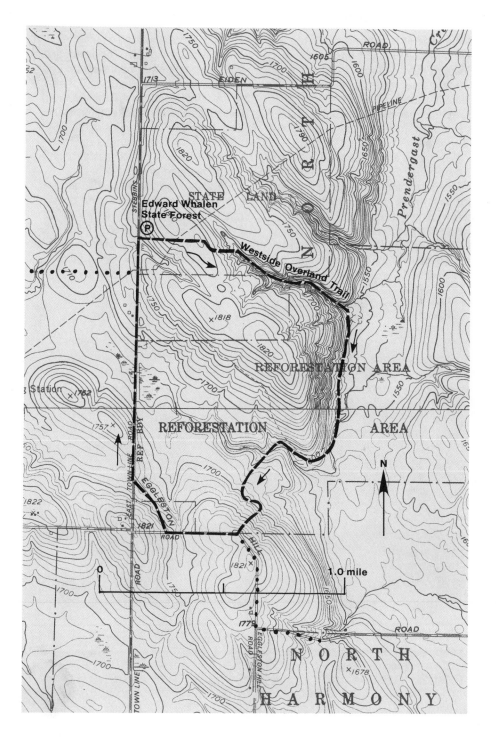

demanding. It resumes a steep climb until it reaches the dirt Eggleston Hill Road. At this point this road turns south. The hills are nameless, yet the road appears to be named after a nearby hill. Such an unnamed hill (elevation 1,820) is found 0.1 mile south on Eggleston Hill Road itself.

At the point where the WOT intersects Eggleston Hill Road, turn right and follow the road west for 0.3 mile in a gradual descent. At the fork, the right leg is the continuation of Eggleston Hill Road, while the left leg is Bailey Hill Road.

Bailey Hill Road reaches its highest spot (elevation 1,821 feet) just over 0.1 mile west of Eggleston Hill Road; this high spot may have been homesteaded by someone named Bailey, perhaps explaining in part the road's name.

You take the right leg, however, and your route takes you northwest on Eggleston Hill Road for just over 0.2 mile, where it intersects East Townline Road (which later turns into Stebbins Road). East Townline Road runs straight north, making a gradual ascent for 0.2 mile, then turning downhill to pass through a sizable wetland area.

Once through this area, the road changes to Stebbins Road and goes gradually uphill and past a farm for just over 0.2 mile. Here the WOT intersects on the left and turns to continue north on Stebbins Road for another 0.1 mile, where you find your trailhead and parked vehicle.

16

North Harmony State Forest

Hiking distance: 6 miles
Hiking time: 4 hours
Vertical rise: 703 feet
Map: USGS 7½' North Clymer; USGS 7½' Panama

North Harmony State Forest occupies a highland area defined by seven hills, all of which are more than 1,800 feet high. These heights are about average for this region, which itself is the highest land in Chautauqua County. From here, the land tapers gradually downward in all directions—in the north to Chautauqua Creek, in the east to Chautauqua Lake, in the south to Little Brokenstraw Creek, and in the west to French Creek.

The hills are not giants, but they are peaked and rugged, indicating that this part of New York was only lightly glaciated during the Ice Age that overrode the state more than 15,000 years ago.

The highest hilltop in North Harmony State Forest has an elevation of 1,863 feet and is almost in the center of the state forest. Next to it is another hilltop with an elevation of 1,822 feet. Between these two hills is a sizable wetland area, located at the surprisingly high elevation of 1,802 feet.

The 1,651-acre state forest takes its name from the Town of North Harmony (a *town* in New York State is the same as a *township* in other states). Passing through the entire length of the state forest is a 4-mile stretch of the 25-mile Westside Overland Trail (WOT), running

in a north-south direction.

North Harmony State Forest is situated between Edward J. Whalen Memorial State Forest (see Hike 15), only 0.4 mile north by way of the WOT, and Panama State Forest (see Hike 17), a mile south by way of the hiking trail.

As it runs through North Harmony State Forest, the WOT also passes through a small parcel of county land, situated in the east-central section of the state forest. There is a lean-to here that can be used by hikers who are planning a weekend hiking tour and would like to have a base camp; from here you can hike a good piece of the WOT to the north or to the south.

One small and two large man-made ponds are found in North Harmony State Forest some distance from the WOT. To reach these ponds requires bushwacking, using map and compass. The northern pond is part of the headwaters of French Creek, and the southern pond is part of the headwaters of Little Brokenstraw Creek.

Wildlife here is like that in other parts of southwestern Chautauqua: white-tailed deer, beaver, raccoon, opossum, porcupine, red and gray fox, woodchuck, cotton-tailed rabbits, short- and long-tailed

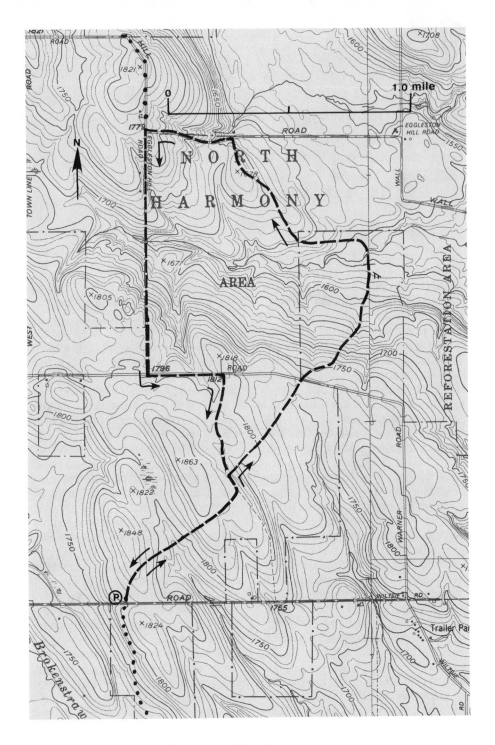

weasel, red, gray and flying squirrels, and striped skunk. Among the game birds are the wild turkey and the ruffed grouse, while predator birds include the red-tailed hawk, red-shouldered hawk, marsh hawk, sharp-shinned hawk, and coopers hawk, as well as the kestrel, the great horned owl, the barred owl, the saw-wet owl, and the screech owl.

With some quiet walking and just plain good luck, you may see some of these animals. Also remember that you are walking through prime deer country. Walk softly, and keep an eye open. Stop for a while—say for 15 to 20 minutes—and remain quiet; you'll be surprised how many birds and animals you will see.

Access: The best route to North Harmony State Forest is by way of NY 474, which passes through the village of Panama, a short distance from the state forest.

From the east, NY 474 can be picked up on the western edge of Jamestown in the community of Lakewood. Once you have reached Panama via NY 474, continue west for 4.1 miles past the southern boundary of the state forest, to where the WOT crosses the highway to intersect Wickwire Road. Turn here, and drive north a little more than 0.7 mile to where Wiltsie Road intersects from the east. Take Wiltsie Road east for 2 miles to where the WOT crosses the road. This is your trailhead.

The trailhead also can be reached from the north via the New York State Thruway (I-90). Leave the thruway at Exit 60 in Westfield and drive south 6 miles on NY 394 to the village of Mayville. In Mayville, turn right on NY 430 and drive southwest for 10 miles to the center of the village of Sherman, where you find NY 76. Turn south on NY 76 and drive 5 miles, to where NY 474 intersects on the left (east) in the hamlet of North Clymer.

From here drive 0.9 mile east on NY 474 to the intersection with Wickwire Road. Turn onto Wickwire Road and drive north 0.7 mile to the intersection with Wiltsie Road. The latter road takes you east for 2 miles to where the WOT crosses the road. Park here.

Trail. In this forest, the WOT runs 3 miles from Wiltsie Road in the south to Eggleston Hill Road in the north. By combining this foot-trail with several roads, the hiker is able to walk almost a complete loop; only the last mile of your return trip is on the foot-trail.

The WOT takes you north and immediately uphill. In 0.2 mile, you reach the hill's crest as the trail turns slowly to the northeast. It continues this route, gradually descending for 0.3 mile. The trail then climbs to the top of the second ridge, where the ground levels for 0.2 mile. Here you intersect a state-maintained truck trail. The WOT crosses the truck trail and continues north on fairly level ground for 0.4 mile to the intersection with Warner Road.

From Warner Road, the trail descends steeply for 0.7 mile, where the footpath crosses a stream. This stream feeds into Goose Creek, 0.5 mile to the east. Your vertical drop to this point from Warner Road is 270 feet—a fair descent. Before crossing the stream, however, you pass a lean-to just off the trail. If you are on a weekend backpacking trip, this shelter may be used as a base camp. The lean-to also eliminates the need to haul a tent, rope, and pegs on your weekend hike.

From here, the WOT curves slowly northward and then more sharply westward before resuming its northwesterly direction. The climb from the feeder stream to Eggleston Hill Road is gradual, over a distance of 0.8 mile. The vertical rise is 158 feet.

Once on Eggleston Hill Road, the

WOT follows the road west for a little over 0.3 mile, where it turns north on the continuation of Eggleston Hill Road. Topographic maps show that Eggleston Hill Road runs not only west and then north but south as well. Nonetheless, this is the point where you change direction by leaving the WOT and turning south on the state-maintained truck trail.

For the first 0.4 mile, the truck trail makes a descent—gradually at first, and then more steeply as it crosses a feeder stream you crossed farther to the east earlier in your hike. Once across the stream, the climb becomes demanding as the slope of the hill steepens; 0.5 mile brings you back to Warner Road with a vertical rise of 196 feet.

Turn left (east) on Warner Road and walk 0.3 mile to where a truck trail intersects from the south. Turn here and follow the truck trail over fairly level terrain for 0.4 mile, to where it intersects the WOT. Turn right onto the hiking trail and walk southwest for a mile to Wiltsie Road and your parked vehicle.

Hiker in North Harmony State Forest

17

Panama State Forest and Brokenstraw State Forest

Hiking distance: 6.7 miles
Hiking time: 3½ hours
Vertical rise: 510 feet
Map: USGS 7½' Panama; USGS 7½' Clymer

To most people, "going to Panama" usually means taking a trip to a Central American country. But to knowledgeable hikers in Western New York, it means a visit to the village of Panama in western Chautauqua County and a walk through Panama State Forest, which is situated just south of the village.

This 1,224-acre state forest contains several features to attract hikers. In the eastern half is a well-shaded, 1.6-mile truck trail that can double as a hiking trail. In the western half is a 1.2-mile portion of the Westside Overland Trail (WOT). This wide, well-groomed trail begins in neighboring Brokenstraw State Forest, which takes its name from Brokenstraw Creek, which passes through its western section.

If you wish to enjoy a short one-way hike on the southern part of WOT with, say a friend who drove his/her own vehicle, you can use a car shuttle; this allows you to hike from the trailhead in Brokenstraw State forest through Panama State Forest to Rock Hill Road, a short distance southwest of the village of Panama. This one-way distance is 3.8 miles.

However, if you desire a longer hike to see more of these two state forests, you can combine a portion of WOT with

some local roads to form a loop for a total of 6.7 miles. On a cool summer or fall day, this is the route recommended.

The forest is located in the area of rolling terrain called the Chattaraugus Hill Region. This region includes Chautauqua, Cattaragus, and Allegany counties. Except for Allegany County, it was glaciated, so it consists of a relatively flat-topped upland. In the eastern part, the hills are moderately sloped, usually over 10 percent. But in Chautauqua County, especially the section containing the Westside Overland Trail, the land is much flatter and the hills are marked by gentle slopes ranging between 2 and 8 percent. Elevations range from 1,550 to 1,800 feet.

This portion of the Chattaraugus Hills sits on top of a vast reserve of natural gas; all around, you encounter the blue-painted wellheads—two in Brokenstraw State Forest and 11 in Panama State Forest. Access roads lead to all these wellheads to give you an additional network of roads to explore if you have the time and interest.

Access. From Buffalo and the Niagara Frontier area, follow the New York Thruway (I-90) south to Exit 59, Fredonia–Dunkirk, and then go south on NY 60 to

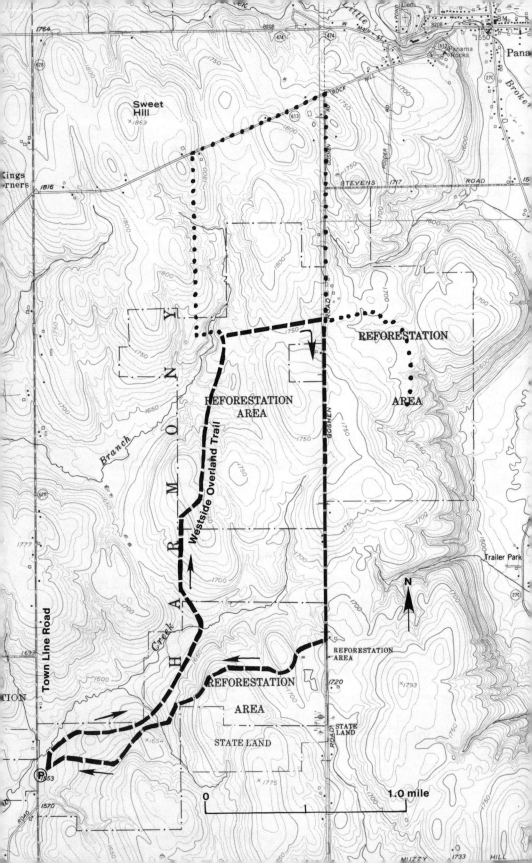

the Southern Tier Expressway (NY 17) just north of Jamestown. Get onto the expressway, and drive west to where it crosses Chautauqua Lake at Hadley Bay, on the west side. From Hadley Bay, go 3½ miles to Exit 7 and the intersection with County Route 33. Exit here, and drive south on County Route 33 for 6 miles to the center of Panama village. Here you intersect NY 474. Turn west on NY 474, and drive 2.4 miles to Townline Road (County Route 23 on some maps and County Route 628 on others). Drive south on Townline Road for 2.4 miles to Brownell Road intersecting on the right; here Brokenstraw State Forest begins on your right. An additional 0.5 mile brings you to a bridge that crosses Brokenstraw Creek. Just 0.1 mile more is a dirt road

intersecting on the left (east). Turn onto this truck trail and go 0.1 mile, to the southern trailhead of the WOT. Park here.

Trail. The WOT begins in a large stand of spruce trees; it runs north as if through a tunnel of evergreens. After 0.1 mile, the wide, well-groomed trail turns slowly to the right and heads gradually uphill in an easterly direction.

An additional 0.5 mile brings you to a large stand of hardwood trees, where you will see the truck trail (the same one on which the trailhead was located a half-mile back). From here the foot-trail veers to the left and then passes over two footbridges. The first one crosses a small feeder stream that flows north to Brokenstraw Creek, and the second, 0.5

Man-made pond

mile farther on, crosses Brokenstraw Creek itself. Once over the creek, the trail turns gradually to the left (west) and heads uphill, and in 0.15 mile leaves the state forest to begin a steady ascent in a straight line north over private land for the next 0.4 mile.

At the 1.8-mile mark, the trail enters the southwestern corner of Panama State Forest, and in 0.1 mile it reaches one of the state forest's smaller hills (with an elevation of 1,750 feet, only 197 feet higher than your starting point). The trail continues north over the hill, then down past a low marshy area on the right.

After 0.6 mile, you come to an east-west dirt road (a state-maintained truck trail); this road terminates at a natural gas wellhead, 0.5 mile to the west.

The WOT turns left (west) on this truck trail, crosses a stream called Brownell Branch, and turns north to leave Panama State Forest en route to Rock Hill Road. Your route, however, goes in a different direction. At the intersection with the dirt road, turn right (east); follow it for 0.7 mile to the intersection with a north-south black-top road, Goshen Road.

Directly across Goshen Road is another truck trail; it takes you to three nat-ural gas wellheads in the eastern portion of Panama State Forest. You may wish to explore this route; if you do, it will lengthen your hike by over a mile round-trip.

Back on Goshen Road, turn south; at the 0.5-mile mark you pass a short access road on the left to another well-head. An additional 0.4 mile brings you to still another wellhead access road on your left.

A short distance further south on Goshen Road, you come to another truck trail, intersecting on the right; it, too, takes you to a wellhead.

Continue south on Goshen Road for 0.6 mile until you reach a truck trail intersecting on the right (west). Turn here, and follow the dirt road in Brokenstraw State Forest. About 0.2 mile west on the truck trail, you see on your left a sizable pond containing upright dead trees.

The trail swings about the base of a hill on the right and proceeds southwest through a thick forest where the trees form a canopy over the road. The road wiggles back and forth for 1.8 miles, then brings you to your starting point at the trailhead of the Westside Overland Trail and your parked vehicle.

18

Canadaway Creek State Wildlife Management Area

Hiking distance: 4.6 miles
Hiking time: 2½ hours
Vertical rise: 520 feet
Map: USGS 7½' Forestville; USGS 7½' Hamlet;
  Chautauqua County's "The Eastside Overland Trail"

The Canadaway Creek State Wildlife Management Area sits on rolling terrain. Yet a cluster of three closely spaced hilltops of up to 1,900 feet collectively make up what is called Dibble Hill, the highest area on the state land. They overlook the Lake Erie Plain, which lies to the west, and they are the western beginnings of the Cattaraugus Hills.

Canadaway Creek begins 4 miles south of the wildlife area. The creek and its tributaries cut deeply into the eastern section, which is marked by steep slopes and sharply defined hilltops. The Canadaway Creek Gorge is located in the south-central portion of the area. It can be seen from Park Road (also called Ball Road), which follows the gorge's northern rim. In the western section is a 150-to-200-foot-deep gorge through which Canadaway Creek flows.

This wildlife area is a good place to get acquainted with the 19-mile Eastside Overland Trail (EOT)—the EOT's northernmost trailhead is here. The Eastside Overland Trail system is so called because it is located east of Chautauqua Lake, actually, 14 miles northeast of the midpoint of Chautauqua Lake, where the Expressway crosses. It is a sister trail to the Westside Overland Trail, which lies 7

miles west of Chautauqua Lake. Both trails pass through clusters of state forests that fortuitously line up along a north-south axis.

The two trail systems, extensively used in winter for cross-country skiing, make these areas of Chautauqua County a hiker's and skier's mecca. In winter, Nordic ski races are held on these trails.

The EOT is especially convenient for hikers coming from Fredonia, Buffalo, Niagara Falls, and other parts of New York, via the Thruway (I-90). Hikers coming from the south—from Jamestown, Olean, Hornell, or more eastern spots—via the Southern Tier Expressway can get to the EOT at this southern trailhead, which is 2.25 miles east of the hamlet of Gerry on NY 60. The wildlife area is located 46 miles south of Buffalo, 6 miles southeast of Fredonia, and 5 miles east of Cassadaga.

Access. Coming from Buffalo or points farther east, you can take the state Thruway (I-90) to Silver Creek (Exit 58). Leave the Thruway, turn onto US 20, and drive 8.5 miles to the village of Sheridan. At the intersection in Sheridan, turn left (south) onto Center Road; follow this road 7.6 miles south, where it crosses Markum Brook (which flows west and

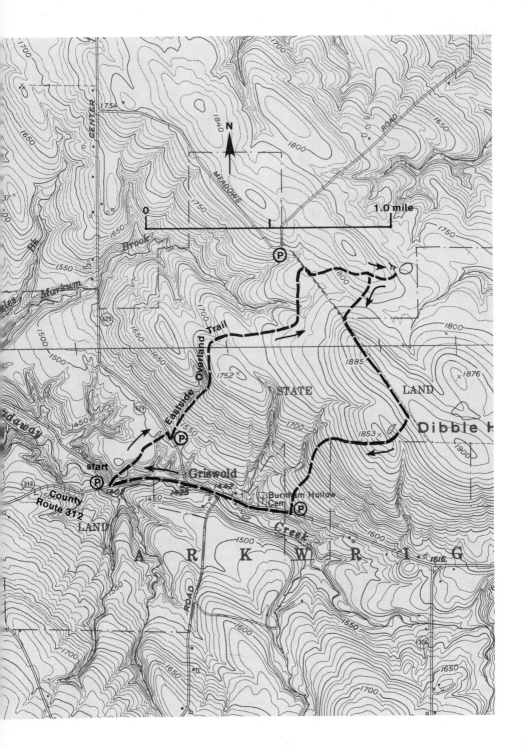

then south into Canadaway Creek, a short distance away). On the right is the boundary line indicating the beginning of the Canadaway Creek State Wildlife Management Area.

Continue south for another mile as the road veers slightly left to head southeast. It ends at an intersection with a paved road, County Route 312, at a point called Griswold on various topographical maps. Turn right (west) onto County Route 312 and drive 0.3 mile to a small parking area. Park here. There is a sign reading "Trail" at an unpaved forestry road with a gate that may be closed. The dirt road that angles to the northwest is Park Road (on some maps called Ball Road); this is the road that runs along the northern rim of the Canadaway Creek Gorge.

You can drive on Meadows Road, called Tygert on some maps, from Center Road for 1 mile to a parking place at the west end of Dibble Hill Road; from here it is only about 120 yards past the gate to reach the trail. If you are packing camping gear to the lean-tos, this is the recommended way to do it.

Trail. The EOT trailhead, at the intersection, runs uphill in a northeasterly direction into the thick forest. The trail is marked with blue-painted blazes. As soon as you enter the woods, you encounter a trail register. Sign in and continue uphill, moving through a mixed stand of hardwood and hemlocks. You ascend for the first 0.1 mile, but the second 0.1 mile is level as the trail bends slowly to the north; it then moves uphill again as it follows the edge of a small ravine containing a brook.

At 0.36 mile you reach Center Road. Walk about 100 yards to the right on the road, and cross it to a parking area. Follow the sign and trail markers north uphill, climbing steeply at times on a good jeep road. In the streambed, you

see level layers of sedimentary shale bedrock, and on the surface a few entirely different erratic boulders that were carried here by the Wisconsin glacier, which covered New York more than 12,000 years ago.

At 0.8 mile, the route becomes nearly level. Watch for another trail joining from the right, and another branching to the left. Your route turns to the right, and at 0.9 mile enters a clearing. Follow the left side and watch for the trail markers to show where to cross. If the weather is not too dry, you pass a tiny pond at 1.1 mile. Continue past the pond on the left side of the clearing, and turn onto a jeep trail at the northeast corner. The trail dips to cross a tiny stream at 1.3 miles, then continues as a wide grassy roadway going north and then northeast to bring you to a dirt truck road at about 1.5 mile.

The road you see is Dibble Hill Road, which is not open to the public; its gate is just out of sight to your left. The trail turns right (southeast) onto Dibble Hill Road, goes along the road about 90 yards, and turns left up a less-traveled forest road. At this point you are leaving the state land and entering Chautauqua County land. The road goes up a gentle slope through planted spruce and white pine trees. At 1.7 mile the marked trail turns right into the woods, leaving the roadway.

To get to the lean-to, do not follow the marked route at this point. Instead, take the little unmarked path turning to the left off the road. Follow it for about 0.2 mile over the hill through the trees, where you find the two shelters and a pond. (The road you were on also goes to the pond; the path, however, is shorter.) There are tables and a well with a pump by the pond. These lean-tos are the only place where camping is permitted. In contrast to county land, the state wildlife management area does not allow camping.

You return to the marked trail at the same point where you left it. You have now traveled about 2.2 miles. You follow the blue blazes down a wide path and across a footbridge over a small stream. You leave the deep shade of evergreens for hardwood growth again. The trail climbs a small slope to rejoin Dibble Hill Road at 2.4 miles. You are now back on state land.

Turn left on the road. You are now climbing to the area's second-highest hilltop, with an elevation of 1,885 feet.

Hiker in Canadaway Creek Wildlife Management Area

Toward the top of the hill, you pass an area where loggers have worked. At 2.85 miles, the trail turns right and leaves the road. (If you come to a bend in the road, you have gone too far.) Just southeast of this turnoff is the area's highest hilltop, at 1,900 feet.

The trail passes another shallow pond on the right, with nesting boxes for wood ducks. You curve west along another grassy roadway through young hardwood growth. You have reached the top of the area's third highest hilltop (elevation 1,876 feet); from here it's all downhill. At about 3.1 miles, the trail descends to the south.

Dropping steadily from this point, you follow the edge of a ravine for a while. The trail brings you to the highway (County Route 312 again) at 3.8 miles. There is another parking area here. (If you have two cars, you could have left one here before starting the hike.) Turn right on the paved road and walk downhill past the cemetery to return to your starting point.

As you drive back on Center Road to Sheridan, you have an excellent view of Lake Erie to the west.

Boutwell Hill State Forest (Northern Section)

Hiking distance: 8 miles
Hiking time: 4½ hours
Vertical rise: 366 feet
Map: USGS 7½' Hamlet; Chautauqua County's "The Eastside
*   Overland Trail"*

The Boutwell Hill State Forest occupies 1,484 acres of the highlands that overlook Farrington Hollow, a narrow valley a mile to the east, and the flat, mile-wide Cassadaga Creek valley, about 7 miles to the west. The northern boundary of the Boutwell Hill State Forest is only 1.25 mile south of Canadaway Creek State Wildlife Management Area (see Hike 18). The state forest is an elongated 5.5-mile-long parcel of high and rolling terrain; the steep slopes in its eastern section are cut by deep gullies and ravines. The highlands hereabouts are mostly forest covered, although the lower regions contain farmlands.

Most of the hilltops in and around Boutwell forest exceed 2,000 feet in elevation. Boutwell Hill, from which the state forest takes its name, is among the highest spots in the forest's northern half. With an elevation of 2,072 feet, it is located just 0.1 mile from the state forest's eastern boundary on Boutwell Hill Road. Boutwell Hill Road runs through the midsection of the state forest, equally dividing the forest into a southern section and a northern section.

Through the state forest runs 6.9 miles of the Eastside Overland Trail (EOT). This is as fine a walking trail as you can

find in Western New York, matched only by its companion to the west, the Westside Overland Trail (WOT). The EOT runs over three large clusters of state land, of which Boutwell Hill State Forest is the middle. The others are the Canadaway Creek Wildlife Area to the north and Harris Hill State Forest to the south (see Hike 21). The EOT also passes through several miles of private lands to connect these three.

The state forest also contains a network of state-maintained dirt roads, called variously forestry roads or truck trails. These and the adjoining county roads provide easy access to the state forest and the trail system, making it an attractive place for hikers and birdwatchers during the spring, summer, and fall, and for cross-country skiers and snowshoers in the winter.

It is convenient to start your hike at the northern end of the state forest, but you can also start just as well at the southern end at Thornton Corners and the Cockaigne Ski Area or at Arab Hill at the forest's midsection.

The state forest's portion of the Eastside Overland Trail continues south from Arab Hill for another 3.75 miles. Just over half passes through state land,

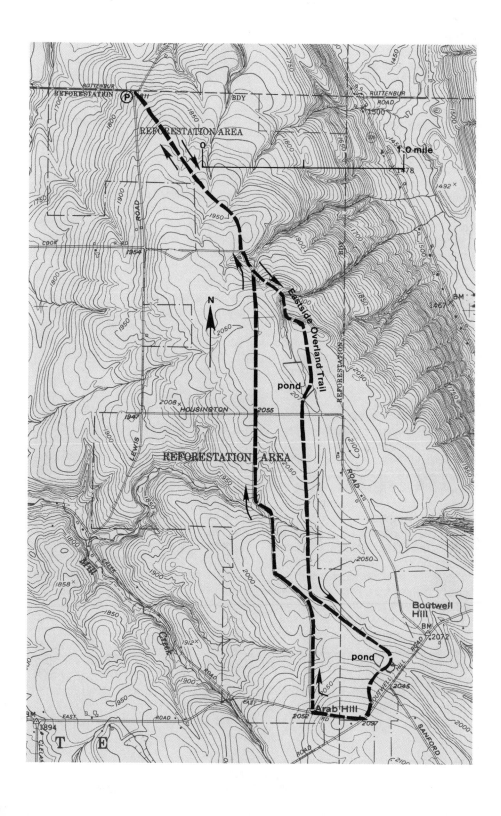

while the rest passes over open roads outside the state forest.

Access. Boutwell Hill State Forest can be reached easily from just about any direction. Coming from the north, east, or west, take the state Thruway (I-90) to Dunkirk–Fredonia at Exit 59. From here, take NY 60 south for 9 miles toward Cassadaga. Just after you pass a trailer park and before you enter the village proper, you encounter a paved county road intersecting on the left. This is County Route 312 (also County Route 72 on the state's road atlas). Turn northeast on this road.

It takes you in 6.4 miles past Center Road in the southwestern part of the Canadaway Creek area to Rood Road (County Route 326). Turn south on Rood Road, and drive a mile to Ruttenbur Road and turn left (east). Continue 0.5 mile on Ruttenbur Road to a parking area at its intersection with Lewis Road. Park here. The trailhead is in the southeast corner.

Coming by the Southern Tier Expressway, exit at Jamestown (Exit 12) and take NY 60 north for 18 miles through Sinclairville to Cassadaga. From there, go northeast via County Route 312 for 6.4 miles to Rood Road, then south, then east to the trailhead as described in the previous paragraph.

Trail. The state forest's trail is part of the EOT. The Ruttenbur Road trailhead is your starting point. The trail runs fairly straight south and uphill to the northern section's highest spot, Arab Hill, with an elevation of 2,097 feet. In contrast, the elevation at the Ruttenbur Road trailhead is 1,811 feet, making this a steady uphill route with a vertical rise of 366 feet—not all that demanding when spread over a 4-mile distance. En route you will encounter two sizable and lovely ponds—fine places for relaxing and having a bite to eat.

The trail markers are blue, either blazes or discs, and they are well placed for sighting. Enjoy this well-maintained trail: even the grass is frequently mowed in the trail area!

The total distance one-way from Ruttenbur Road to your turnaround at Arab Hill is 4.2 miles. Using a car-shuttle and leaving one vehicle at Arab Hill as a pickup point makes this a relatively short hike. For a full day of walking, you can take the recommended return route via the truck trails that parallel the overland trail most of the way back. This brings the round-trip hiking distance to 8 miles.

The trail, cut wide and clearly marked, leaves the parking area heading south into planted pine trees. In season, you may find an apple to eat from the abandoned orchard near the beginning of the hike. For the first half-mile or so, the path may be a little wet from seepage, especially after a rain.

The path climbs a slight grade for 0.2 mile, then levels out where it veers south and then southeast again. You pass the beginnings of a little stream, without much water, and after this the trail dries out. There is another gentle rise, and at 1.0 mile from the start, you reach a knoll with attractive hardwood trees.

After another 0.1 mile, you come to a truck trail, which the hiking trail now follows south for a short distance. On the truck trail you cross the beginning of a ravine and pass a parking spot. At 0.1 mile, the hiking trail turns left, leaving the truck trail.

From here the hiking trail is generally good walking, with a few wet spots that are not bridged. As you climb a low hill, you see a mixed stand of maple and beech of all sizes, and also some black cherry. The trail passes the edge of an old logging area on your right; brush and small trees are now growing back. At 0.2 mile from the truck trail, you cross

Pond in Boutwell Hill State Forest

a snowmobile trail and then descend by a switchback route into a ravine containing a small stream.

After crossing the ravine, the trail continues southeast on level ground, climbs a little, traversing the slope, and then turns south and uphill. At 0.7 mile from the truck trail, you reach a pond that contains enough fish to attract a few people with poles and worms on a nice day. As you pass along the east side of the pond you may find blackberries in late July or early in August. The trail now passes through a little group of hemlocks and then along the earthen dam of a smaller pond. This brings you to Housington Road. The total distance to this point from Ruttenbur Road is 2.1 miles.

The trail continues south, crossing Housington Road, and enters a thick stand of spruce trees, where the cool shade is pleasant on a hot day. Shortly, you leave this shady area for more open woods, where selective cutting has left only a few large hardwoods. Seedlings are growing between them; blackberries also prosper here where the sun reaches them. Fortunately, the trail is not only marked but mowed to keep the passage open.

At the 2.6-mile mark, the trail crosses the beginning of a stream and leaves the partly logged area to pass through a mixed hardwood forest. After another mile, another trail, visible on the right, comes in from the west, leading in 40 yards to another truck trail. Stay on the main trail, which bends at this junction to the southeast.

At the 3.3-mile point, there are some hemlocks and a little farther on some planted pines, then larches. Another 0.5 mile brings you to a pond and marshy area, where an old beaver lodge appears to be deserted. Crossing the dam, the trail enters another spruce plantation, and a short distance beyond, you come to a trail register, then to Boutwell Hill Road. Your hiking distance to this point is 4.2 miles.

You have now arrived at the state forest's highest point, Arab Hill. This landmark is also your turnaround point. Of course, you can return to your starting point via the trail that led you here, or as recommended, you can return by hiking the state forest's truck trail, which parallels the hiking trail on the west side a short distance.

Arab Hill is located at the intersection of Boutwell Hill Road and East Road. To reach the truck trail, take East Road and hike west 0.2 mile, to where the state's dirt road intersects on the right (north).

Turn here, and head north and downhill; a little over 0.2 mile brings you to a gully and the beginning of a streamlet. Out of the gully, the trail, which is well shaded by arching trees, levels for the next 0.5 mile, turning first slightly to the right, then straightening out as it enters a much deeper gully through which a brook flows west.

Once out of the gully, the truck trail heads north, but now uphill, for 0.4 mile to a level stretch. Then it intersects Housington Road. Crossing this road, the trail continues its northerly route over level terrain for 0.7 mile, where it intersects and becomes a part of the hiking trail over which you walked earlier.

At this point you can either follow the truck trail west to intersect Lewis Road, which you then follow north to your starting point on Ruttenbur Road. Or you can follow the hiking trail to Ruttenbur. The latter route is recommended since on a hot, sunny day the forest cover provides cool shade. A mile on the hiking trail brings you back to Ruttenbur Road and your waiting vehicle.

Boutwell Hill State Forest (Southern Section)

Hiking distance: 6.6 miles
Hiking time: 3 hours
Vertical rise: 597 feet
Map: USGS 7½' Hamlet; Chautauqua County's "The Eastside Overland Trail"

Boutwell Hill State Forest's highest spot is Arab Hill, at 2,097 feet, where Boutwell Hill Road and East Road intersect. This hill can conveniently divide the state forest into two sections: the longer northern section (see Hike 19), and the shorter southern section.

The southern section commands the more rugged part of the high terrain on which the state forest is located. Shaped like a huge wedge with the point facing south, the land drops steeply into narrow valleys on the northeast, southeast, and southwest. On the state forest's southern flank, the hill pitches sharply downward into a valley that acts as a divide; at the valley's midpoint, the drainage splits: the beginnings of one streamlet carry water north, while another streamlet, farther to the west, carries water to the south.

Similar terrain is found on the hill's southwestern side, which pitches into another narrow valley. Through this valley Clear Creek flows. The hill's southern slope is deeply cut by numerous gullies and ravines; some resemble gorges. Across the valley at the tip of the hill's wedge is the Cockaigne Ski Area, a popular winter resort and local landmark.

The southern section is only 2.2 miles long. The trail, which runs through most of the state forest, is slightly longer, covering a distance of 2.8 miles, in a general north-south direction. For those who like to do their climbing at the beginning of a hike so they can enjoy a leisurely downhill stroll on the return, the southern trailhead at County Route 62 is the best starting point. This will be the starting point of this hike. From County Route 62, the path goes north and uphill, ending at Arab Hill.

The trail in this section of the state forest is part of the Eastside Overland Trail (EOT). Most of the trail passes over state land, with the exception of a small 0.8-mile section that traverses a part of a county road and some private land as it leaves and then reenters the state forest.

Access. From the north, the state Thruway (I-90) brings you to Dunkirk–Fredonia (Exit 59), where you pick up NY 60 heading south. Follow NY 60 for 15 miles to the southwestern edge of Sinclairville. Drive north into the village; just north of the village center is Reed Street, on the right. Turn here, and drive east out of the village for 0.5 mile to an intersection with another road from the village. This becomes County Route 617 (or Route 64 on the state's road atlas). Follow this road for 1.5 miles (past the

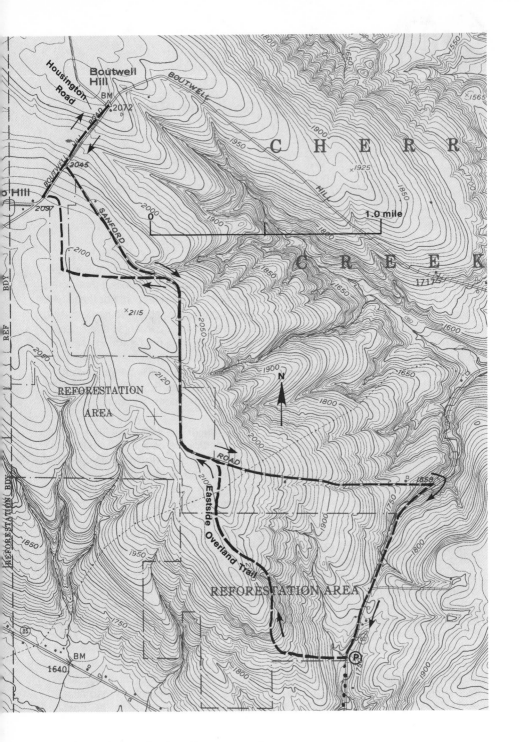

intersection of the curiously named C Johnson Road) to a fork with Engdahl Road running straight east and County Route 617 bearing southeast into a valley; 2.8 miles farther on County Route 617 brings you to the intersection with County Route 33. Turn and follow County Route 33 north. In 0.9 mile just before you reach Cockaigne Ski Area on the left, is the intersection with County Route 62 on the right. Turn onto this road, and follow it through the narrow valley northeast for a mile where a stream crosses the road. This is the southeast corner of the state forest and the site of the trailhead. Park here.

If you come by the Southern Tier Expressway (NY 71), get off at Jamestown (Exit 12) and head north on NY 60 for 10 miles to Sinclairville. From here, follow the directions given above.

Trail. The blue-marked trail begins at the base of a hill. There is a gully here, through which a small stream flows in a southerly direction. The climb from the trailhead is quite demanding, as the trail first heads west and then turns south as the steep climb continues. Only at the 0.7-mile mark does the trail begin to level out, at which point you have made a vertical ascent of more than 300 feet.

As the upward trek flattens somewhat, the trail turns right from its northwest course and moves straight north, crossing under a power line en route. In 0.3 mile, the trail intersects Sanford Road and turns northwest onto the road. In another 0.1 mile, the road on which the trail is now located turns north on level terrain. At this point the state land on the right side of the road ends, but it continues for another 0.1 mile on the left. Before you reach this boundary, you encounter a snowmobile trail on the left, angling in from a southwesterly direction over a nob (elevation 2,120) that is the highest spot in the southern section.

The trail and road continue north with private land on both sides. The terrain here is relatively flat on the left but drops steeply off to the right. From the last state forest boundary, the road and trail proceed together for 0.3 mile where they turn west for an additional 0.35 mile. Here the trail and road separate, with the road turning to the northwest. Stay on the trail, which continues straight ahead and enters a woodlot on private land. Another 0.45 mile on a westerly course brings you into a narrow strip of state land that runs north-south.

Here the footpath, joining a snowmobile trail, turns north. In another 0.25 mile, the trail, which is still level here, reaches a left turn; a short distance beyond, you arrive at the Boutwell Hill Road–East Road intersection. To the left is a knoll that marks the top of Arab Hill.

For a scenic view of the eastern and southern hills, walk east and down Boutwell Hill Road for 0.5 mile to the intersection with Housington Road. This is the top of Boutwell Hill, after which the state forest was named. From here the land drops into a narrow valley a mile to the east; the valley acts as a divide (the second in the area), and the beginnings of a nearby feeder stream flow north into the West Branch of the Conewange Creek. The beginnings of Cherry Creek, farther east, flow to the south.

You are now ready for your return trip. Retrace your steps along Boutwell Hill Road toward Arab Hill for 0.3 mile to the intersection with Sanford Road, coming from the south. Turn here and follow the road for 0.5 mile; when the road turns left, it meets the footpath you walked earlier coming from the west.

Continue to retrace your steps on Sanford Road for the next mile. This takes you beyond the road's left turn to a point where the trail, heading south, leaves the road. Stay on Sanford Road as it runs

Trail in Boutwell Hill State Forest

114 *Southwestern Region: Chautauqua County*

east. The road, crossing under the power line, heads steeply downhill; over the next mile, the vertical drop is an impressive 442 feet. At this point you reach County Route 62.

Turn right (south) and follow County Route 62 uphill along the beginnings of a north-flowing streamlet to a dead-end road that intersects on the left. You are now at still another divide; off the hill on your right is the beginning of a second streamlet. This one, however, flows south. Now the road slopes gradually downward, and after a 0.3-mile walk, you are back at your parked vehicle.

21

Harris Hill State Forest

Hiking distance: 6.9 miles
Hiking time: 4 hours
Vertical rise: 350 feet
Map: USGS 7½' Gerry; Chautauqua County's "The Eastside
Overland Trail"

Harris Hill State Forest is an elongated 3.8-mile parcel of state land in the central Chautauqua County highlands. Harris Hill (elevation 1,850 feet) is not itself in the state forest; it is located 1.7 miles south of the state forest's southern boundary. Nor is it even the highest spot in this area. The highest elevation is at an unnamed spot a short distance west of the state forest and south of Chautauqua Road. It is from here that the terrain slopes off in all directions. One tends to think of the entire highland, not just one spot on it, as Harris Hill, of which the state forest holds the highest ground.

Sitting astride the high terrain, the state forest area acts as a local divide. Drainage to the immediate north is into an east-flowing feeder stream and to the east into nearby Clear Creek. At the state forest's southern boundary, the land slopes south and eventually reaches the confluence of Cassadaga Creek and the Chadakoin River.

Harris Hill State Forest contains the southern trailhead of the Eastside Overland Trail (EOT). This trail, along with the Westside Overland Trail, is among the finest walking trails in Western New York. It passes from Harris Hill State Forest through Boutwell Hill State Forest (see Hikes 19 and 20) to the Canadaway Creek State Wildlife Management Area (see Hike 18), which contains the trail's northern terminus.

In Harris Hill State Forest, the EOT trail is 3.45 miles long and runs between Chautauqua Road in the north and 28th Creek Road in the south. The 28th Creek Road trailhead marks the southern terminus of the EOT. The recommended direction for this hike is from north to south and then back, for a round-trip distance of just under 7 miles.

You can hike the trail in Harris Hill State Forest in either direction comfortably. The elevation of the state forest's northern end, at the Chautauqua Road trailhead, is 2,012 feet; at the southern end, the elevation is 1,750 feet. The vertical rise, 262 feet, is not all that steep. You do notice the hill's upward grade as you walk, but it is a gradual one, hardly even noticeable when walking downhill.

Harris Hill Road passes over the entire hill in a north-south direction and runs lengthwise through virtually the entire state forest.

Access. Harris Hill State Forest can be reached without difficulty from the north or south. Take the New York State Thruway (I-90) to Dunkirk–Fredonia, Exit

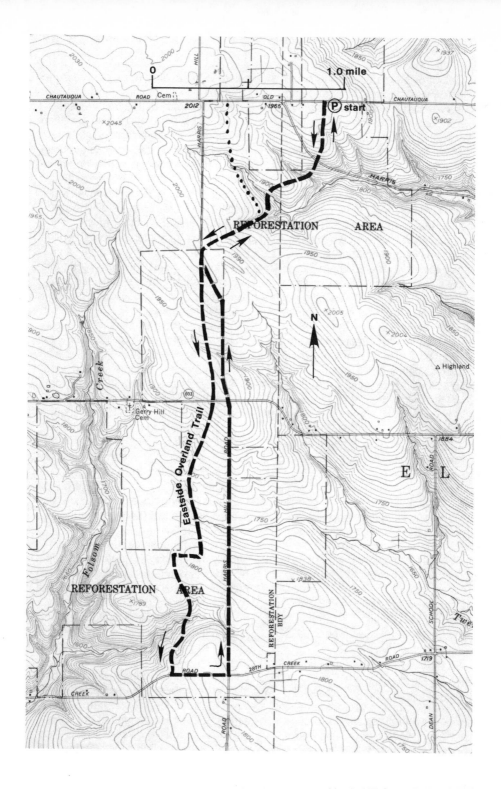

59. Get off onto NY 60, heading south. Drive 16 miles through Cassadaga and Sinclairville to the hamlet of Gerry, where County Route 603 intersects on the left.

Follow this county road for 3.1 miles, where it meets Herrick Road; turn left (north), and drive 1.9 mile uphill to the intersection with Chautauqua Road on the eastern edge of Hatch Creek State Forest. Turn right, and drive east on Chautauqua Road for 1.65 miles past the first trailhead to the parking area and the second trailhead on your right.

If you are using the Southern Tier Expressway (NY 17), get off at the Johnstown (Exit 12) onto NY 60 heading north. Follow NY 60 for 5 miles to the hamlet of Gerry. Turn onto County Route 603 on the right, and follow directions above.

Trail. This trailhead is one of two trailheads on Chautauqua Road; the second is 0.5 mile east of the first, just past the intersection with Harris Hollow Road. The second trailhead is actually the exit point (or entrance point) of the EOT, which runs from here via county roads to the Boutwell Hill State Forest, several miles to the north.

Of course, you can walk the Harris Hill State Forest trail one way for 3.45 miles, providing you have arranged with a friend for a car-shuttle, and leave a second vehicle at the endpoint on 28th Creek Road. A more interesting and longer hike is a round trip that makes use of the state forest's well-maintained truck trail, which closely parallels the hiking trail on the east side. This route, called East Road, allows a change of scenery on your return hike.

The starting point is 0.2 mile east of Harris Hollow Road. A small sign reading "Trail" directs you to the trailhead. Follow the blue trail markers south; the trail initially runs south along the edge of a plantation of spruce trees, and then veers to the southwest to cross a cleared strip of land (containing a buried pipeline) after a .25-mile walk.

Descending a hill, the trail crosses Harris Hollow Road at 0.3 mile and then descends even more sharply into a ravine and across an east-flowing streamlet. From here, the climb is somewhat more demanding: the slope becomes steeper the higher you go. Soon, however, you reach a level area. It gives way to another descent into another ravine through which another, larger streamlet flows eastward. Uphill you come to another trail intersecting on your right; this one comes from the first trailhead you passed on Chautauqua Road en route to your starting point.

Once past the trail intersection, the hiking path continues uphill, but now the grade is more gradual and continues like this for 0.3 mile to the intersection with East Road. You are now 1.2 miles from your starting point. The trail turns left here onto East Road and heads south a short distance, then turns right, off the road, to continue its route through the forest in a straight line to the south. The trees in this section are a mix of hardwood and pine.

The trail now gradually descends, noticeably for the first 0.4 mile, but then it levels out for the next 0.4 mile. You reach a paved county road, which, unhappily, has been assigned several different route numbers (County Routes 603 and 50) and several different names (West Hill Road and Gerry-Ellington Road). But the road's designation is not all that important, since you only need to cross it to continue on the trail south.

After crossing the road, the trail passes through an area in which a host of pine trees have been harvested, leaving it for brush, briers, and hardwood saplings. But this changes at the 2.95-mile mark to a mixed stand of older tree growth. Here you turn slightly to the right

Pine Hill State Forest

onto an old tote road running east-west. In season, about mid-August, you will probably find blackberries.

The old road runs west for 0.2 mile on fairly level ground. It turns sharply to the left and heads southeast for 0.3 mile, then makes a short but steep descent into a ravine. Here are the beginnings of another east-flowing streamlet. The trail now takes you across a bridge and up a 70-foot hillside in a southwesterly direction. The trail finally levels off, and in a short distance you emerge from the forest onto 28th Creek Road and your turn-around spot.

For your hike back, turn left on 28th Creek Road and walk east 0.3 mile to the intersection with East Road. Turn left here, and follow the road straight north. Initially, the road makes a gradual descent to the start of a ravine, then heads uphill to a level area. This extends for 0.2 mile before dipping more steeply into another ravine, through which flows another streamlet.

From here for the next 0.6 mile, the road continues its uphill route. It becomes steeper until you reach the county highway you crossed earlier. Once across the county highway, the truck trail runs along fairly level terrain for 0.2 mile, then crosses a small gully. For the next 0.4 mile, the grade is steadily uphill until the road turns slightly to the northwest on fairly level land. In just over 0.2 mile, the road intersects the hiking trail you walked previously. From here, retrace your steps back along the blue-marked hiking trail to Chautauqua Road and your waiting vehicle.

Southwestern Region:
Cattaraugus County

22

Pine Hill State Forest

Hiking distance: 6 miles
Hiking time: 3½ hours
Vertical rise: 420 feet
Map: USGS 7½' Steamburg

Pine Hill State Forest sits on top of the rugged hill country that overlooks Allegany State Park, 5 miles to the east, and the Allegheny River, which curves around the northern edge of the park on its way south to Pennsylvania. Spelling differences between "Allegheny" and "Allegany" notwithstanding, this region, with its wide, looping river is a grand place to do some hiking.

The shape of the hills on the river's west side are very different from the shape of those in more northern parts of the state. The straight-sided hills, the peaked and angular ridges, and the narrow valleys tell you that this part of Cattaraugus County was spared the grinding and leveling effects of the Wisconsin glacier more than 12,000 years ago. The topography is angular and deeply dissected by many little streams.

But the Allegheny River itself did not escape the glacier's effects. Before the Pleistocene Ice Age, when the glacier advanced over New York, the Allegheny River system was much different from what it is today. Instead of flowing south into Pennyslvania and into the Ohio River as it does now, the preglacial Allegheny River drained northward. The river's headwaters started in Pennsylvania east

of what was then the Kinzua col (present site of the Kinzua Dam). It then flowed north through what is today Steamburg and into valleys of Conewange Creek and Cattaraugus Creek. Eventually it emptied into Lake Erie. During the post-glacial period, a high moraine was formed where Steamburg is today, and another at Gowanda. These moraines prevented the Allegheny River from flowing north; instead, it was diverted south into its present drainage system.

On the northern edge of the state forest is one of many peaked hilltops of this area. Unlike the others, this one has a name, Pine Hill, after which the state forest is named. The elevation of this hill is 2,135 feet.

In the state forest there are four unnamed hilltops. Three have the same elevation as Pine Hill, and one is higher, with an elevation of 2,162 feet.

These hills give the state forest a commanding status, providing wonderful views. There may be a few higher hills on the other side of Allegheny River in Allegany State Park, but no others on this side are higher than the ones in this state forest.

Oldro Hill Road runs through the state forest and past the highest hill. Perhaps this hill was once called Oldro Hill, named after a settler who homesteaded the hilltop.

Access. The Pine Hill State Forest can be reached from the Southern Tier Expressway (NY 17). Coming from either the east or west, leave the expressway at Exit 17, located about 10 miles west of Salamanca and about 14 miles west of Jamestown.

From Exit 17, turn north and travel 0.3 mile. Turn west onto NY 394 at the south end of the village of Steamburg, and drive 0.4 mile to where Oldro Hill Road intersects from the south. Turn here, and

drive uphill on the winding Oldro Hill Road for 3.4 miles, to where the state forest begins on the left side of the road. Park here.

Trail. At the starting point, you overlook the wide Allegheny River Valley to the east. This valley is a postglacial trough that carried water south from the melting glacier over 12,000 years ago. The valley is filled with postglacial outwash sediment released by the ice sheet during its meltback.

You start your hike by heading west on Oldro Hill Road. At the outset the road is level, and 0.3 mile brings you to

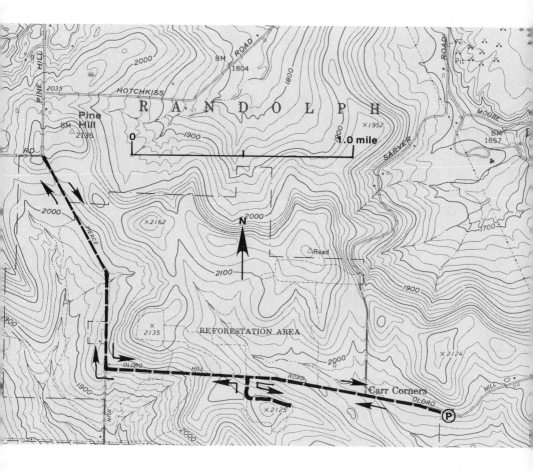

a small stream crossing. This is the outlet stream of a sizable pond that lies a short distance ahead, just off the right side of the road. Another 0.1 mile takes you to Sarver Road, intersecting from the north; this is known as Carr Corners. Just beyond is the man-made pond.

Here you encounter another problem with road names. A sign indicates that the east-west route on which you are traveling is called Carr Corners Road, but the official topographic maps insist on calling this route Oldro Hill Road.

In any case, continue hiking westward. The road begins to slope upward and becomes steeper the farther you go; at 0.6 mile a truck trail intersects from the south. Turn here, and in 0.2 mile you come to a pipe-gate barrier, prohibiting unauthorized vehicles. In 0.6 mile, this truck trail takes you to another barrier and to the top of the highest spot in the state forest; but unfortunately the tall trees obstruct views of the surrounding landscape.

Retrace your steps back to the main road; the elevation here is 2,100 feet. Continue westward. The road makes a steep descent, and in less than 0.2 mile your vertical drop is 100 feet.

From this point on, the road levels. An additional 0.3 mile brings you to an intersection with the north-south Pierce Run Road. Turn right here, and walk north on level terrain. The next 0.4 mile takes you over a west-flowing stream and then to a point where the road makes a slight turn to the northwest.

Continue in this direction for 0.4 mile. The state forest ends on the right side of the road but continues on left. The road begins to rise gradually, and an additional 0.2 mile brings you to a fork where Pierce Run Road meets Pine Hill Road coming from the north and Cross Road coming from the west. Pine Hill itself is 0.2 mile to the northeast.

At the crossroads you are greeted by attractive vistas in all directions. It is an excellent spot to rest awhile to enjoy the views and, if you brought sandwiches, a noon luncheon as well. The scenery here is exceptional. When you are ready, retrace your steps 2.6 miles back to your parked vehicle.

23

Bucktooth State Forest (Northern Section)

Hiking distance: 3.6 miles
Hiking time: 3½ hours
Vertical rise: 1,073 feet
Map: USGS 7½' Little Valley

The northern section of Bucktooth State Forest covers 557 acres of forested highlands, including a hilltop that anchors the eastern flank of Shutts Hill (elevation 2,400 feet), the area's highest spot. Running through this northern section, which on the map resembles a bent finger, is a hiking trail that connects two paved roads, Bucktooth Run Road in the south and the East Branch Bucktooth Run Road in the east.

This section of the hiking trail is part of the 648-mile-long Finger Lakes Trail (FLT). As the FLT journeys north, it passes through the state forest's southern (see Hike 24) and northern sections.

As the FLT goes from the southern section into the northern section, it crosses the paved Bucktooth Run Road, which acts as the primary access route to both these parts of the state forest.

The hike in the northern section is not long—only 3.6 miles round trip. But it is a demanding hike, since there is a sizable hill to climb going and coming. This means that by the time you complete your round trip, your vertical climb is 1,050 feet—and that's a lot of height to do in one hike. But for those who like a good climb in their weekend outings, this is the place to do it.

The high spot is a peaked hilltop, but its shape is obscured by the tree-cover. It is found at the midpoint of the 1.8-mile-long trail. Hence, it makes little difference which trailhead you select—the eastern one at East Branch Bucktooth Run Road or the southern one at Bucktooth Run Road. For this recommended hike, the latter trailhead is selected.

Access. To get to the trailhead, take the Southern Tier Expressway (NY 17) to Exit 20; turn east on Broad Street and drive east a short distance to the intersection with NY 353. Turn north on NY 353, and cross the bridge over the Allegheny River; two blocks north of the bridge, Washington Street intersects from the west on the left. Turn left, and follow Washington Street west for 1.6 miles to the intersection with Bucktooth Run Road.

Drive north on paved Bucktooth Run Road; 1.3 miles brings you to a fork. (The right leg is the paved East Branch Bucktooth Run Road.) Bear left onto Bucktooth Run Road and uphill into the state forest for 2.2 miles, where the Finger Lakes Trail crosses the road; signs on both sides of the road indicate where the footpath enters the wooded areas on the north and south side. Park here.

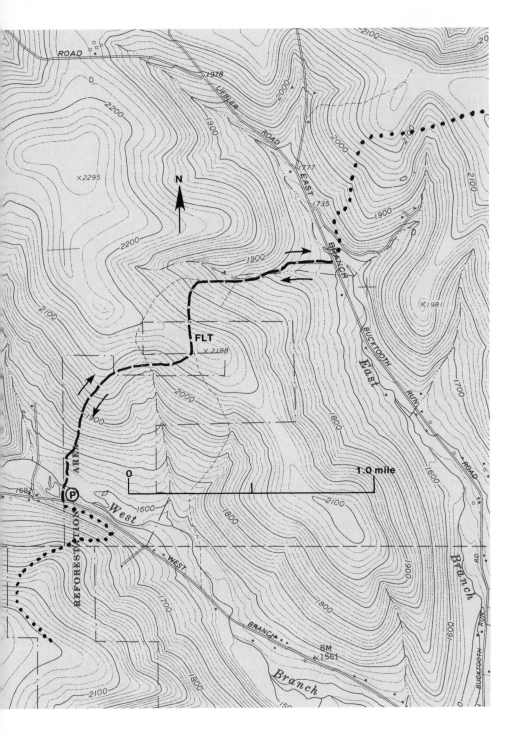

Trail. Your short hike takes you via the white-blazed FLT first in a northerly direction, and then in an easterly direction over a hilltop to East Branch Bucktooth Run Road. The road, not surprisingly, is named after a stream the road parallels, the east branch of the Bucktooth Run, which flows south on its way to join the Allegheny River. In this part of New York, the common term *run* refers to any stream smaller than a river.

You start your hike by making a short but steep descent at the road's edge to a low area, through which flows the west branch of Bucktooth Run; the stream has its origin in the state forest's western section (see Hike 25).

Once you reach the low area, the FLT follows the southern edge of the state forest boundary. Immediately on your left is a fair-size pond and a house, both on private land; the open area west of the state boundary includes a wide strip of fields.

Just past the pond you cross the narrow west branch stream, hopefully when it is low. Occasionally beaver homestead in this section of the stream and raise the water upstream to flood the foottrail's crossing spot. If this is the case, you may get your feet wet before you reach the other side.

In little less than 0.2 mile, the FLT turns right into the dense portion of the forest and heads uphill. You are now on a long, demanding climb, and you en-

Bucktooth State Forest

counter fairly steep sections as you pass through a thick section of pines and hardwoods.

From the west branch stream, it is 0.8 mile to a shallow gully as you near the top; here is the origin of one of the streamlets that flow south to feed the west branch. Your vertical rise to this point is 400 feet. An additional 0.2 mile uphill brings you to an old logging road, which passes on the left the area's high spot (elevation 2,188 feet), adding another 188 feet to your vertical rise.

Shortly thereafter, the FLT leaves the road by a left turn into an open area, then into a row of maple trees that some call the "Avenue of the Maples." The trail passes out of the state forest and through a plantation of pine trees as it again picks up the old logging road. Here you start your descent.

The road and the FLT turn east. As you head downhill, 0.2 mile brings you to a one-lane dirt road. Next to the road is a depression through which flows a streamlet; the road soon crosses the streamlet, which is racing downhill to feed into the east branch of Bucktooth Run. The length of the road to the junction with East Branch Bucktooth Run Road is 0.4 mile.

At the road's end, you leave the wooded area almost where the east branch passes under the paved highway. The FLT, of course, continues across the highway and steeply uphill to eventually cross the ridge called Bucktooth Hill.

But once you reach the paved highway, you are at your turnaround spot. You now reverse your route at the one-lane road that you just left. The road is nicely canopied by arching trees; retrace your steps uphill and you reach the midpoint, where the FLT passes the area's high spot. Your vertical rise to this point is 485 feet.

From here it is downhill for a mile where you cross the West Branch again, pass the pond on your right, and climb back onto the paved highway where your vehicle is parked.

Bucktooth State Forest (Southern Section)

Hiking distance: 4.8 miles
Hiking time: 2½ hours
Vertical rise: 1,108 feet
Map: USGS 7½' Little Valley

The vast region just north of Allegany State Park in Cattaraugus County is dotted with peaked hills, many reaching elevations of more than 2,000 feet. They are covered by a dense forest, which in summer makes an almost seamless blanket of green. Cutting through these forested hills are foot-trails, old logging roads, truck trails, and two paved highways. All this makes it a prime hiking territory, especially for those seeking a wilderness experience or an experience that can rival the high-peaks section of the Adirondacks.

This is where you find the 2,218-acre Bucktooth State Forest. Its somewhat odd name is taken from the Bucktooth Hill, a long high ridge that lies immediately east of the state forest. The origin of *Bucktooth,* however, has been lost in unrecorded history.

The state forest is part of and surrounded by a landscape of peaked hills—Jimmerson Hill (elevation 2,215 feet) in the south, Parker Hill (elevation 2,324 feet) in the southwest, Shutts Hill (elevation 2,400 feet) in the north, and of course, Bucktooth Hill (elevation 2,201 feet) in the east.

This area was once farmland, but from the turn of the century on it was increasingly abandoned. In 1930, the state purchased the abandoned farmland and converted it into Bucktooth State Forest.

Spruce trees were planted, but soon they were outgrown by the natural hardwoods native to this area, such as ash, cherry, and maple. But spruce trees can still be found near the trailhead. Hiking through this dense forest today, it is hard to picture it as once cleared and farmed.

In 1982, the state authorized a private logging company to selectively harvest trees in this state forest. At the trailhead is a landing where the logs were piled for loading onto trucks. As you walk south on the hiking trail you will see skid roads on which timber tractors, called skidders, dragged the logs to the landing.

You could spend days hiking the various trails in this general area, and you will surely want to spend a weekend on the trails and roads in the state forest itself. The physical layout is such that it is easy to divide the forest into three parts for hiking purposes—the southern, northern, and western sections. This hike is located in the southern section. Other hiking routes also are found in the northern section (see Hike 23) and the western section (see Hike 25).

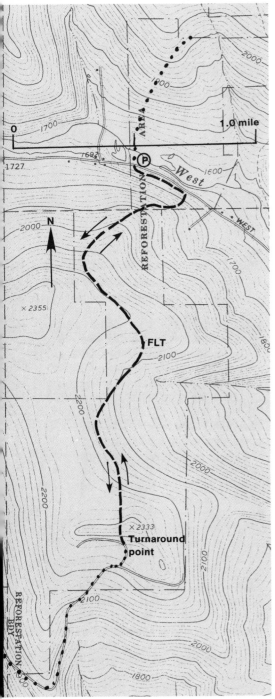

A small portion of the 648-mile Finger Lakes Trail (FLT) runs through the southern and northern sections of Bucktooth State Forest. The trail is marked with white blazes.

The hill country in which the state forest is located drains primarily to the south and southeast, and its brooks and streamlets eventually feed into Little Valley Creek in the east and the Allegheny River in the south. The spelling of names in this region initially may cause confusion, with names alternating between "allegany" and "allegheny." You find Allegany County and Allegany State Park, but adjoining the park is Allegheny River and abutting the park at the Pennsylvania border is Allegheny National Forest.

The hillsides in this area are steep, and climbing can be strenuous; look for routes with minimally steep ascents. In hiking the southern section, for example, you can start at a high point on the paved Bucktooth Run Road and head south to the end of the state forest, thereby avoiding the steep hill farther south. The paved highway parallels a small stream called Bucktooth Run. The term *run* is widely used in these parts to mean "creek" or "stream" and valleys are usually called *hollows*.

Access. You reach the trailhead by Bucktooth Run Road. This highway runs between NY 242 in the north and Washington Street in the south; Washington Street is located on the west side of the city of Salamanca. The Finger Lakes Trail, running in a north-south direction, passes through the entire length of state forest's southern section and northern sections, crossing Bucktooth Run Road in the process. Look for the trailhead at this crossing.

If you are coming from the east or west via the Southern Tier Expressway (NY 17), leave the expressway at Exit 20 and drive east to the intersection of

Broad Street and NY 353. Turn north, and drive on NY 353 over the bridge crossing the Allegheny River; two blocks north of the bridge, Washington Street intersects on the west. Turn here, and continue on Washington Street west for 1.6 miles, to the intersection with Bucktooth Run Road.

Drive 3.6 miles northwest on Bucktooth Run Road past the right fork (East Branch Bucktooth Run Road), to where you see signs at the forest's edge on both sides of the road announcing the crossing of the FLT. Park near here.

Trail. The FLT route takes you through the entire southern section of the state forest and some distance beyond, to Sawmill Run Road. A one-way trip to this road is 3.8 miles. This is plenty of walking, and you should have a friend leave a vehicle waiting for you on Sawmill Run Road. Without such a vehicle, the return trip back to Bucktooth Run Road is 7.6 miles, including a steep and strenuous climb for almost 2 miles. Hence, it is recommended for those who are making

View from Bucktooth State Forest

their first visit to this section of the state forest to walk south only to the point where the state forest ends and then return; this gives you a 4.8-mile round-trip hike with a few steep climbs.

At Bucktooth Run Road, the FLT goes up an embankment and then climbs gradually, paralleling the highway, for just over 0.2 mile. The trail then swings sharply to the right and continues uphill for 0.6 mile before reaching more level terrain; your vertical rise so far is 608 feet—a climb that keeps you puffing.

Once on the level area, you cover 0.3 mile before starting uphill again; initially, the ascent is gradual, but then it grows steeper until you reach a level stretch. The trail follows the same contour line along the side of the hill; on your left, the land pitches steeply downhill.

After walking on level terrain for 0.3 mile, you start uphill once again to reach a knob, the area's highest spot (elevation 2,333 feet). Once over the knob, the terrain pitches gradually downward for 0.2 mile where you reach a dirt road coming in from the right and running south. Follow it to an intersection with another dirt road running east and west, lying just north of the state forest's southern boundary. Here is where you can stop and reverse direction. If you go beyond this point, you soon experience an increasingly steep descent that tells you that you have left the state forest. In retracing your steps, you may find walking back north to be a bit easier than the route south. This is especially the case during the last 0.6 mile, in which you go downhill all the way to your parked vehicle on Bucktooth Run Road.

Bucktooth State Forest (Western Section)

Hiking distance: 5.2 miles
Hiking time: 3 hours
Vertical rise: 670 feet
Map: USGS 7½' Little Valley

The land that hosts Bucktooth State Forest blends level and tapered terrain. The western section of the forest differs physiographically from its next of kin, the steep-sided northern section (see Hike 23) and the hilly terrain of the southern section (see Hike 24).

The state forest is long and narrow, a little over 4 miles long but only a half-mile wide at its narrowest point. In the east and south the state forest is marked by peaked hilltops and rounded knobs that exceed elevations of 2,200 feet. The western section sits astride highlands overlooking plateau-like land that stretches to the north and west. At both ends, the land slopes, but the state forest's mile-long center portion is level, making for easy, flat walking.

Unlike the two other sections of Bucktooth, the western part contains no section of the Finger Lakes Trail, which runs the full length of both the southern and the northern sections. The walkable part of the western section is by a road that is barricaded at both ends to prevent road use by motorized vehicles. Your access to the western section is by truck trails that are restricted to official vehicle use only.

One of the barricaded routes is an east-west truck trail that runs through almost the entire length of the western section; it is an old route, still called Manley Hill Road on topographic maps, but it is no longer in public use. (If you take the road's name seriously, you can assume that the hill on which the state forest's western section sits has this unofficial name.)

The route tapers downward from the middle portion of the western section. Not far to the east from the trailhead at Manley Hill Road is another more recently constructed truck trail that goes south, more deeply into this portion of the western section; from the first barricade at the trailhead to the second barricade a mile away, the walking is all uphill, with only a short level stretch on which to catch your breath.

Your walk on Manley Hill Road is on a little-used route. The center portion of the road is grass-covered with the trees set back on each side of the road. This gives the route a friendly, open appearance inviting a stroll. In autumn, when the fall foliage is at its peak, the stroll can become something special—a fulfillment, a contentment, or just the sheer joy of being outdoors.

Here, too, you can find evidence of

forest management as done by the Divison of Lands and Forests of the state's Department of Environmental Conservation. Private logging companies were authorized by the state in 1978 and 1983 to selectively cut the area to thin out the trees so that younger growth could mature more rapidly.

The loggers cleared small areas near the main highway, Bucktooth Run Road. At these landings, logs were piled to await loading onto log trucks. Skid roads were cut to the landings and used by timber tractors, or skidders, to drag the logs to the landings. Signs on the road edge tell you where these landings can be found. One such site is on the north side of Manley Hill Road; another is a short distance east of the second truck trail. The third such site is located at the FLT trailhead leading into the southern section (see Hike 24).

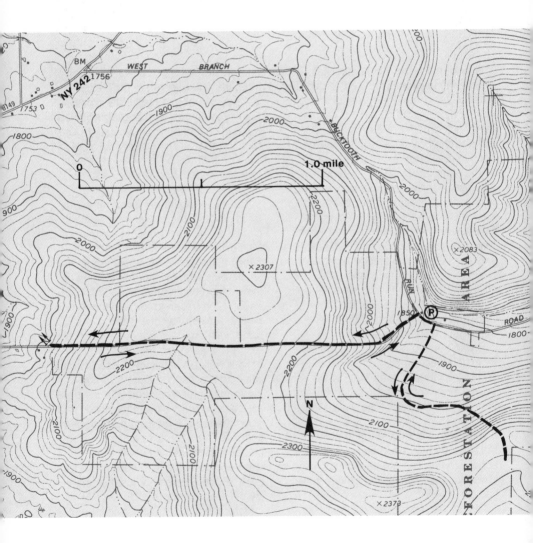

View to the west in Bucktooth State Forest

The cut areas reseeded themselves quickly, and the landing areas have grown back to grass and seedlings. Before the state purchased the land that is today Bucktooth State Forest, it was largely abandoned farmland. Today you will find a variety of mature trees: hard maple, red oak, white ash, red pine, and Norway spruce. This is also a place where white-tailed deer and black bear like to feed at the old landing areas, the deer on young twigs and the bear on berries.

Access. The villages of Randolph and Little Valley, located in the lower, western half of Cattaraugus County, are about 10 miles apart; running between them is NY 242, and Bucktooth Run Road intersects this route's midsection from the south. Bucktooth Run Road, a paved highway, takes you 2 miles into the western section of Bucktooth State Forest and to your trailhead at the intersection with the barricaded Manley Hill Road. Park here.

Trail. Beginning at the trailhead, your hike follows the grass-covered dirt route, Manley Hill Road. From the start, it is a steady climb west. After 0.5 mile, you encounter the first road barricade, a pipe-gate barrier. Your vertical rise to this point is already 380 feet—a respectable rise.

From the barrier westward, the land flattens to make walking easy. With the trees set back from the road, sunlight brightens your journey and welcomes you to this quiet forest.

From the barrier, it is 0.8 mile to where the land begins to slope downward, and an additional 0.3 mile brings you to the second barricade and to the end of the state forest. However, a short distance past the barricade is a fine view of the open area in front, the fields in the lowlands, and the forested hills to the west.

You are now ready to retrace your steps back to your vehicle. From your vehicle, walk east on paved Bucktooth Run Road about 0.1 mile, where a truck trail intersects from the south. It is also barricaded by a pipe-gate at the very beginning. Like your walk on Manley Hill Road, this route requires a climb at the very outset.

The first 0.3 mile is a fairly gradual ascent. The truck trail then turns left and becomes level as it goes east for little over 0.2 mile; then it starts a slow turn south and uphill again. The ascent is fairly demanding. By the time you reach the last road barrier, your vertical rise has been 410 feet.

Some distance to the east is one of the area's high spots (elevation 2,355 feet), and about 0.5 mile to the southwest is another (elevation 2,373 feet). In short, you are standing pretty much on the state forest's highest elevation; unhappily, the dense tree cover allows no vistas.

Now you can start your return trip. The fun of reaching the crest of a hill is that your return is an easy descent. Retrace your route via the truck trail and Bucktooth Run Road back to your parked vehicle.

Cattaraugus State Forest

Hiking distance: 5 miles
Hiking time: 2½ hours
Vertical rise: 240 feet
Map: USGS 7½' Cattaraugus

Cattaraugus State Forest is situated in the attractive landscape of rolling hills, open areas, and forested tracts so characteristic of west-central Cattaraugus County. Here the land ranges in elevation from 1,700 to more than 2,000 feet—high enough that the state forest provides commanding views of the land around it. Its many overlooks give the hiker some fine vistas, especially of the valleys, or *hollows* as they are called in Western New York. The hollows below Cattaraugus State Forest are near enough that they can be seen from the various overlooks in or near the state forest.

In fact, a long, almost circular valley surrounds the state forest, with a whole complex of streams. To the north, the circular valley begins east of the hamlet of Maples. Through it Mansfield Creek flows westward. About 1.5 mile east of the village of Otto, Mansfield Creek feeds into the south branch of Cattaraugus Creek. The south branch of the creek, in turn, itself passes through a narrow valley as it loops southward past Otto. Just 0.5 mile north of the village of Cattaraugus, it makes an elbow turn to the northwest, flowing through another valley called Skinner Hollow.

The eastern edge of the state forest pitches steeply downward, ending at the bottom of Jersey Hollow. Through Jersey Hollow, an unnamed creek flows north. In the southeast is the longer Toad Hollow, a narrow valley through which the headwaters of Little Valley Creek flow south.

To the south of the state forest is another semicircular valley. It begins east of the village of Little Valley and loops north to take in Linlyco Lake and its outlet stream. This in turn heads north past a long ridge of the west called Carroll Hill and then through the village of Cattaraugus to empty into the south branch of Cattaraugus Creek.

A little over 0.5 mile to the southwest lies the narrow, ravinelike Gowan Hollow, just over a mile in length.

All these valleys, streams, and rolling hills with their mix of fields and forests makes this part of Cattaraugus County a pleasure to visit and an eye-arresting place to hike.

The fall is a good time to hike the roads in and around the 1,058-acre state forest. The thickly forested state land with its changing scenery goes well with autumn's warm days and cool nights. This gives the foliage its brilliant color.

On a sunny day the landscape in late October is spectacular.

Although the state forest is on fairly high ground, it is level enough that the walking is easy. The high spot here is in the midsection, where a flattened hilltop reaches an elevation of 1,940 feet; from here the land drops gradually away on all sides of the state forest to reach low elevations in the surrounding valleys of little more than 1,300 feet.

Access. NY 353, from the north or south, brings you into the village of Cattaraugus. A mile south of the village, Lovers Lane Road intersects on the east. Turn here, and drive north for 0.1 mile to the intersection of Buehlow Hill Road on the right. Turn here, and drive east uphill for a mile through the intersection of Pepperdine Road on the left. The road now changes its name from Buehlow Hill Road to Smith Hill Road. In 1.0 mile on Smith Hill Road, you reach the intersection with a north-south road called State Land Road and, at the same time, you reach the southwest corner of Cattaraugus State Forest. The forest occupies the land north of Smith Hill Road and east of State Land Road. Park here.

Trail. You walk on dirt roads since the state forest contains no marked hiking trails. Start your hike by walking east from your parked vehicle on Smith Hill Road, which acts as a boundary between the state forest on the north side of the road and the private woodlands on the south side.

After walking 0.3 mile, you enter a denser forest area; now state land occupies both sides of the road. Another 0.3 mile brings you to an intersection with the north-south West Hill Road. Typical in this region, the name of the road changes to Krager Hill Road across the intersection.

Follow Krager Hill Road for just over 0.3 mile, to where the state forest ends.

Here open land begins, allowing you the enjoyment of vistas provided by this hilltop. If you look to the southeast you can see the forested peaks of Harry E. Dobbins Memorial Forest (see Hike 27). You also have a fine view of the open land in the northeast.

Retrace your steps to West Hill Road and turn north. The ground is level. After 0.4 mile, you will cross a brook that flows east and then north. In a little over 0.7 mile, you come to Potter Hill Road intersecting on the left. Another overlook lies straight ahead.

In just over 0.2 mile from this point, you reach the northern edge of the state forest, although woodlands continue for another 0.2 mile on the left side of the road. The terrain in front pitches downward, first gradually and then more steeply as it dips into the valley through which the south branch of Cattaraugus Creek flows. The land here is open, to give you an attractive view across the valley and to the hills beyond. Just ahead on the right side of the road is a small, old burial site, West Hill Cemetery. The names on the gravestones tell you who some of the early settlers were.

Retrace your steps to the Potter Hill Road intersection; turn right here and walk west. A little over 0.2 mile brings you to the western edge of the state forest ánd the beginning of private land. Continue on Potter Hill Road for 0.4 mile over level terrain; this route takes you through a wooded section and then past open land to the intersection with State Land Road.

At this point you can enjoy views to the north, west, and south, taking in the village of Cattaraugus, the south branch of Cattaraugus Creek, and, to the south, the narrow valley where the outlet waters of Linlyco Lake flow.

Turn left onto State Land Road, and follow it south for 0.4 mile. En route you

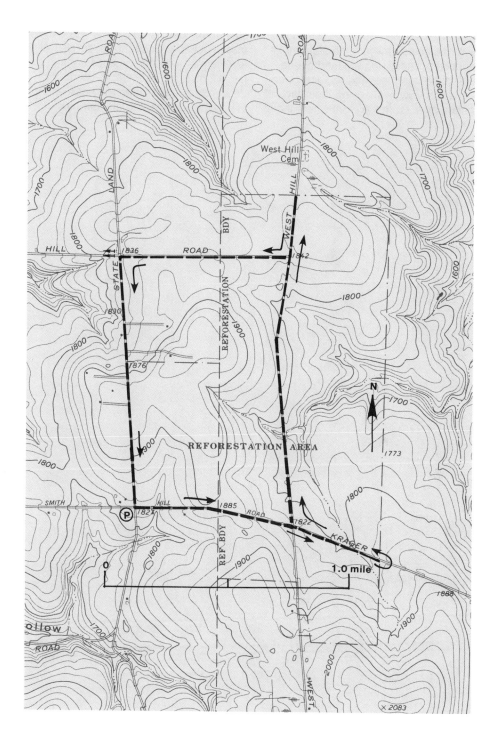

pass fields on the right and on the left. Now you come to where the state forest reappears, occupying the land on the left; on the right, the land remains open, with a fine view overlooking the village of Cattaraugus. From the point where the state forest begins on the left, it is 0.6 miles back to your vehicle over relatively level terrain, with the exception of the last 0.2 mile, where the road gradually descends to meet Smith Hill Road and the spot where you began your hike.

27

Harry E. Dobbins Memorial State Forest

Hiking distance: 5 miles
Hiking time: 2½ hours
Vertical rise: 380 feet
Map: USGS 7½' Cattaraugus

State forests are named in various ways. Sometimes the names are taken from local physiographic features, such as hills, hollows, or creeks; other times a forest is named after a person who served the area as a state forester. Such is the case with this state forest, named after the late Harry E. Dobbins.

Dobbins was the first district forester assigned to this area by the state in the early 1930s. His responsibilities were to purchase and develop the land tracts that eventually became today's forest areas. The practice of establishing memorial forests has been discontinued by the state, and the only other forest in this region named after a forester is the Edward J. Whalen Memorial State Forest in Chautauqua County (see Hike 15).

The Dobbins memorial forest straddles the high hills overlooking Little Valley Creek valley, about 2 miles south; Toad Hollow, a mile to the west; and Dublin Hollow, a mile to the southwest. Several of the hills can be identified by knobs that take on a peaked appearance, although the thick forest cover obscures the sharpness of their contours.

The highest peak is in the state forest's northern portion. It reaches an elevation of 2,283 feet—clearly the highest hilltop for miles around. The next highest hill (at 2,183 feet) is located in the forest's midsection; the third (at 2,158 feet) is really an elongated hilltop in the eastern corner of the state land. The last high spot (at 2,100 feet) is in the western portion. All these are located within a radius of less than 2 miles, which gives you some idea of the kind of land upon which the memorial forest is located—high and hilly.

Various parts of the state forest and of the private lands immediately adjacent provide ideal overlooks, allowing you to enjoy splendid vistas in all directions.

Access. Take the Southern Tier Expressway (NY 17) to Exit 20, at Salamanca. Drive north 6 miles via NY 353 to Little Valley, which can also be reached from the southwest and the northeast via NY 242.

Once in Little Valley, drive to the northern edge of the village on NY 353 to a cemetery on the west side. Across NY 353, a road turns right and runs past the fairgrounds on the left. As you leave the village and start uphill, this road becomes Kahler Hill Road.

From the fairgrounds, drive uphill on Kahler Hill Road for 1.4 miles. There you enter the northern section of the memo-

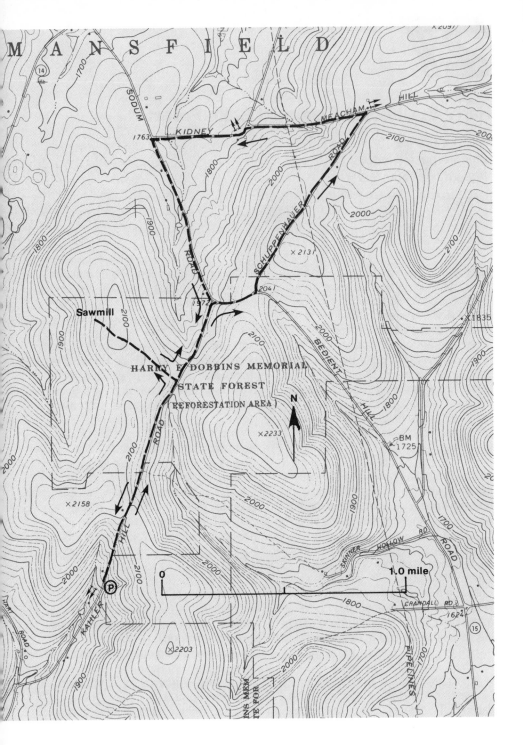

Dobbins Memorial State Forest

rial forest. Park here.

Trail. The memorial forest contains no marked hiking trails, but Kahler Hill Road, a dirt road, cuts through the western portion of the state land. The second access road is paved and allows you to reach the forest's northern section. For some of the finer vistas, you must leave the memorial forest once you reach its northern boundary and hike a loop over several dirt roads and a paved road.

Before you begin your hike through the memorial forest, turn around and walk south a few steps to where the forest boundary meets open fields. Looking south, you have a nice view of rolling hills sloping downward into the wide valley through which Little Valley Creek flows.

Start your hike by reentering the state forest and following Kahler Hill Road north. To your left, the land goes uphill; to your right, the terrain slopes downward, soon ending in a narrow ravinelike landform through which the headwaters of a streamlet flow south.

From your start on Kahler Hill Road, it is 0.4 mile to a truck trail intersection on the left. It takes you 0.5 mile to one of the forest's high spots (elevation 2,100 feet) and eventually to a turnaround. Before the state acquired the land, a sawmill was located here; it was used to cut the valuable white maple found on this hilltop.

After you have retraced your footsteps back to Kahler Hill Road, continue walking north on level terrain. From the truck trail intersection, it is a little over 0.3 mile to an intersection with a paved highway, Sodum Road. This road also acts as a boundary, marking the end of the memorial forest and the beginning of private land.

Turn right (east) onto the paved road, which soon takes you back into the memorial forest to a fork. The right leg, called Bedient Hill Road, is paved and runs downhill in a southeasterly direction; the left leg, called Schuppenhauer Road, is a dirt road; it runs a short distance uphill, where it leaves the state land.

This latter road continues for 0.3 mile from the fork, over a hilltop (elevation 2,131 feet), and then over a right-of-way for a gas pipeline. Although the land on both sides of the road is private, it is heavily wooded and contains several short-distance logging roads.

From the pipeline, the dirt road runs over level ground for 0.5 mile, where it intersects an east-west dirt road called Meacham Hill Road. The thick woods begin to disappear, replaced by fields, which give you an opportunity to view the hilly lands in the north.

Turn left (west) onto Meacham Hill Road. In the next 0.5 mile, the dirt road enters a woodlot which, while continuing on the north side of the road, gives way to a large open area on the south side. Because the road is going downhill, you have a wide and spectacular view of Toad Hollow and the knobby hills in the west.

Meacham Hill Road ends at its intersection with Kidney Road, which comes uphill from the north and then turns sharply to the west a short distance from Meacham Hill Road intersection.

Follow Kidney Road westward and downhill past open areas for a little over 0.3 mile, passing a small creek before reaching the intersection with paved Sodum Road. Turn left here, and follow Sodum Road uphill and past open areas for 0.7 mile to the intersection with Kahler Hill Road. The vertical climb on Sodum Road is 209 feet, a fair ascent in less than a mile. Continue south on Kahler Hill Road until you reach your vehicle.

Rock City State Forest

Hiking distance: 6.5 miles
Hiking time: 4 hours
Vertical rise: 1,079 feet
Map: USGS 7½' Salamanca

When strangers to this region first hear of Rock City State Forest, they are inclined to wonder how a state forest got mixed up with a metroplitan area. The confusion stems not from urban planning but from figurative speech. This state forest derives its name from a cluster of huge block-shaped boulders the size of ranch-style houses which have been arranged by nature to allow you to walk the "streets" between these immense rocks. The state forest was named Little Rock City because of this unusual feature, and this name has been officially sanctioned by state and federal topographic cartographers.

This unique "city" is located in the southern portion of the densely forested 2,905-acre Rock City State Forest, which lies in south-central Cattaraugus County, just 3 miles north of Allegany State Park.

Several factors account for Little Rock City: a massive resistant conglomerate bed, erosion of the conglomerate's weak shale foundation, and soil creep. The conglomerate bed here has its own geological designation, Devonian Salamanca conglomerate. With nothing to prevent this bed of rock from sliding downslope, the conglomerate has been carried slowly downhill by soil creep, and the downward inching has been going on for thousands of years.

As downslope movement takes place, the conglomerate bed breaks into huge, joint-bonded blocks to form something that looks like a building (given a little imagination). These "buildings" lean against each other and in various other directions, with enough space between them to form narrow passages, tunnels, and caves.

Little Rock City is only one of several sites where massive conglomerate beds crop out along the hillsides to form "rock cities." The best-known is Olean Rock City, south of Olean, formed from the Pennsylvania Olean conglomerate. Others include Thunder Rocks, also of the Pennsylvania Olean conglomerate, found in Allegany State Park (see Hike 35), and Panama Rocks, near the village of Panama and west of Jamestown, formed from the Wolf Creek conglomerate.

The 648-mile Finger Lakes Trail (FLT) passes through Rock City State Forest. From here, it journeys northeast, going through McCarty Hill State Forest (see Hike 29) and several other state forests before leaving Cattaraugus County for Allegany County as it heads for its terminus in the Catskill Forest Preserve.

Access. If you are coming from the Buffalo region, Rock City State Forest can be reached via US 62 which takes you south to Gowanda; 3.5 miles farther south on US 62 brings you to Dayton where NY 353 intersects on the left. Follow 353 southeast for about 10 miles through the village of Cattaraugus to the village of Little Valley.

From Little Valley, it is 4.4 miles to an intersection with a road with two different names. On the west side of NY 353, the road is called Woodworth Hollow Road and on the east side, Stone Chimney Road. Both of these roads follow the Finger Lakes Trail (FLT); the FLT is marked with white blazes. On the southeast side of the intersection is a golf course and country club.

If you are coming to this region via the Southern Tier Expressway (NY 17), leave at Exit 20 in Salamanca and head north on NY 353; 3.5 miles brings you to the intersection of Woodworth Hollow Road and Stone Chimney Road.

Turn onto paved Stone Chimney Road, and follow the white blazes east. After 0.7 mile, the road narrows to become a one-lane dirt road with grass growing down the middle. An additional 0.2 mile brings you to a short stretch of state land on the left side of the road. This belongs to a finger of Rock City State Forest pointing down from the north. Park here on the side of the road.

Trail. You now are parked at the first of two dirt roads intersecting from the north and, hence, from the state forest. The elevation here is 1,620 feet. From the first intersection, Stone Chimney Road continues a short distance past the second intersection to terminate quickly at a somewhat soggy (in spring) clearing. You are now on private land owned by International Paper Company.

The FLT, which has been following Stone Chimney Road up to this point, now crosses the clearing and enters the forest in an easterly direction on what is an abandoned single-lane road, the remains of an old horse-and-buggy route that once was a town road; this road has long since been washed out, exposing flattened stones and rounded boulders. The FLT follows this old road for 0.3 mile before branching off on its own.

The trail continues a gentle upward climb alongside a brook on the right; an additional 0.2 mile brings you to a bridge which crosses the brook that you have been following.

Probably built in the late 1800s, the bridge was erected with large squarish boulders, laid one upon another without benefit of mortar—a fair accomplishment in its own right. In addition, the bridge-builders somehow managed to create an arch, held together with hand-hewn keystones on either side—an unexpected sight for so small a bridge.

A short distance beyond the bridge, the old town road bends to the right, while the FLT bears to the left. From here it is 0.4 mile to the western edge of Rock City State Forest with a modest climb at first and a more demanding one later on. Soon, however, you emerge onto a turnaround that acts as the terminus of a state truck trail.

A little over 0.1 mile brings you to an intersection with another state truck road, called Salamanca Forest Road, coming from the south. Turn left (north) on this road and follow it for 0.2 mile where the FLT turns right off the road and enters the forest; 0.3 mile further brings you to an intersection with still another dirt road, Little Rock City Road.

Turn right (east) on this road and in a short distance you arrive at a large turnaround area; here and back along the road you find four small shelters each covering a single table, designed for those who wish to picnic. To the east

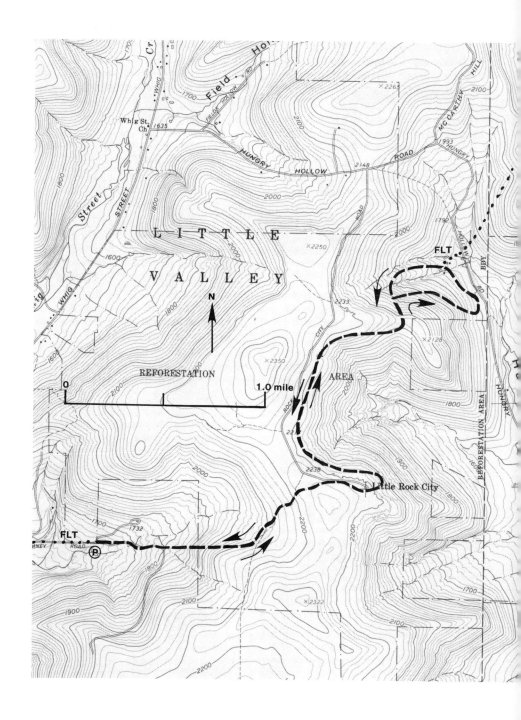

just over the lip of the road are broad, flattened tops of massive boulders. It is this huge cluster of boulders, many as large as a house, that constitutes Little Rock City itself.

The elevation here is 2,238 feet; you have climbed 618 feet to get to this spot; now you can explore this natural wonder. At the south end of the parking area is the beginning of a state-designed circular nature trail, marked by pink blazes. The trail takes you over, around, and through the several dozen block-like boulders, allowing you to walk through the "streets"—alleyways and corridors running between the boulders.

At the far end of Little Rock City, the trail forks. The pink-blazed nature trail goes to the left, while another footpath goes right. The latter is designated by several colored blazes—white for the FLT and pink and yellow for the state's loop trail. When you are ready, continue your hike on the loop trail which is part of the FLT. It follows a route that initially parallels Little Rock City Road which is located about 500 feet uphill on your left.

The road and foot-trail run west for almost 0.5 mile, where they then slowly bend to the right to head in a northward direction. The terrain at the start is flat, but that changes as the trail starts a descent; in 0.2 mile the trail starts a much steeper descent. An additional 0.1 mile brings you to a fork, the left leg of which is the terminus of a loop that begins on your right.

Turn here and follow the white-blazed FLT downhill. The trail runs on an old wagon or tote road, making your walk easy. The descent is gradual. From the fork to the bottom of the hill is 0.4 mile; the trail now turns sharply to the left to proceed on fairly level terrain through a stand of evergreens in a northeasterly direction of 0.2 mile.

Here you intersect a stone-lined walkway on your left; it leads to another such walkway. They were built during the construction of a Civilian Conservation Corps (CCC) camp in the mid-1930s and connected the several barracks used by the CCC workers. This is Camp Seneca.

As the last walkway ends, you step across a brook and emerge in a large clearing which serves as a picnic area (camping is not allowed). In the area's center is a shelter with four tables; tucked off along the clearing's edge is a circle of five more tables. If you brought a lunch, this is the place to have it.

A forest truck trail passes along the clearing's east side. The FLT, in turn, crosses the dirt road to enter the forest on its northeasterly route into the McCarty Hill State Forest (see Hike 29).

From the clearing the pink-blazed loop trail heads west uphill. A short distance from the clearing brings you to a small pond with an anchored wooden bench overlooking the pond. Continue past the pond; a steady uphill climb brings you in 0.4 mile to a left turn in the trail and then the completion of the loop as you intersect the FLT you walked earlier.

You now are on your return leg. Follow the trail back to Little Rock City and continue on the FLT to Salamanca Forest Road and then downhill to Stone Chimney Road and your parked vehicle.

McCarty Hill State Forest

Hiking distance: 5 miles
Hiking time: 3 hours
Vertical rise: 449 feet
Map: USGS 7½' Ellicottville; USGS 7½' Salamanca

In the McCarty Hill region, you will find some of the most picturesque hill country in Western New York. The early settlers of this part of Cattaraugus County must have been inspired by the scenery that greeted them, especially the many winding valleys and the rugged peaked hilltops, because they gave a name to virtually every hill, ridge, and valley found in these parts.

Some of them have fairly common names, like Bartlett Hill, Watson Hill, Somerville Valley, Porter Hollow, and Hinman Valley. Others, however, are a bit unusual, such as Fish Hill, Poverty Hill, Murder Hill, Mutton Hollow, and Hungry Hollow. Still others have an ethnic flavor, such as McCarty Hill, Irish Hill, and Dublin Hollow.

McCarty Hill (elevation 2,323 feet) and its namesake, McCarty Hill State Forest, occupy the high ground that overlooks much of this country. The northern face of the hill itself is fine for downhill skiing, one of the popular sports in this part of Western New York. Skiers come here from as far away as Cleveland, Pittsburgh, Washington, D.C., Philadelphia, and New York City. There are several ski resorts here, and a few are for members only; The Holiday Valley Ski Center, how-ever, is open to the public.

The village of Ellicottville sits in the valley at the foot of McCarty Hill, and in winter, the village is transformed into a skiers' mecca. In recent years, condominiums and townhouses have sprung up on the hillsides and throughout the broad valley in and around Ellicottville. When the snow comes, the village population soars, and streets, shops, restaurants, and bars are full of customers.

In summer, however, the scene changes. The village is quiet, almost sleepy, with a population of mostly local year-round residents. Occasionally, a hiker, traveling east or west on the Finger Lakes Trail (FLT), stops in the village for supplies. The FLT passes a mile west of Ellicottville, en route either to Allegany State Forest to the south or to Allegany County next door and east to the Catskill Forest Preserve.

Summer is a good season to follow the FLT through the 3,109-acre McCarty Hill State Forest. From the summit of McCarty Hill you can look down the hill's east side to the long ski slopes that now sport their summer dress, a soft green mat of grass. About the only things moving in the valley are golfers on their carts and swimmers in the resort's pool. The

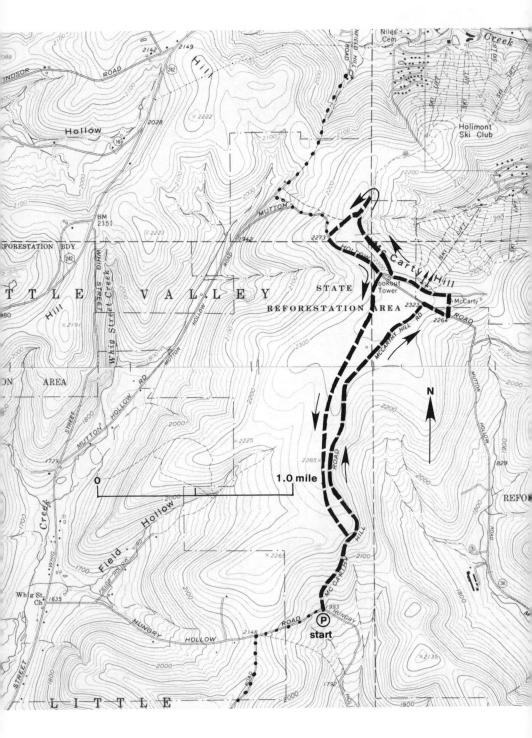

rest of the country belongs to the hiker.

The state land in this region is extensive, as Rock City State Forest (see Hike 28) to the south adjoins McCarty Hill State Forest. The line of division between them is Hungry Hollow Road, which cuts through a southern chunk of McCarty Hill State Forest and the northern tip of Rock City State Forest. Together, these two state forests total 6,014 acres, giving hikers a lot of room for foot-travel.

The several roads (all state truck trails) running through McCarty Hill State Forest intersect often enough to allow you to combine some of these roads along with the FLT to form easy walking loops that bring you back to your starting point. On the other hand, if the preference is that of a one-way route, a car shuttle can be set up if several hikers come in their own vehicles. The recommended hike here is that of a loop, covering a round-trip of five miles.

Access. Take the Southern Tier Expressway (NY17) to Exit 21. Drive into Salamanca. In the city drive north across the Alleghany River and then east to the intersection with NY 219. Follow NY 219 north for 10 miles to Ellicottville.

From the north, NY 219 passes through Springville at the southern edge of Erie County. From here it is 15 miles south on NY 219 to Ellicottville.

Once in Ellicottville, turn west on NY 242 and drive uphill out of the village; 2.6 miles brings you to the top of Fish Hill and past the spot where the FLT crosses the highway in a north-south direction. From Fish Hill, continue south on NY 242 for 1.4 miles to a dirt road, Whig Street, intersection on the left.

Turn onto Whig Street and drive south into McCarty Hill State Forest; the steep hill on your right has the sinister name of Murder Hill. From the beginning of Whig Street, it is one mile to the intersection with a paved road, Mutton Hollow Road,

coming from the northeast.

Continue south on Whig Street (now paved) for 0.7 mile; enroute you pass a pond on the left, cross Whig Street Creek, and pass a cluster of houses in the narrow valley before you reach Hungry Hollow Road, intersecting from the east at Whig Street Church.

Turn onto Hungry Hollow Road (a dirt road) and drive east uphill. A little over 0.2 mile brings you to Field Hollow Road intersecting on the left (north); an additional 0.9 mile on Hungry Hollow Road takes you to an intersection with Rock City Road on the right (south). Continue on Hungry Hollow Road for an additional 0.4 mile where a truck trail (called CCC Forest Road on some state maps) intersects on the left (north); a metal pipe gate (which may be open or closed) is found here. Park your vehicle at this junction.

Trail. You start your hike here and return to this spot via a loop made up of state-maintained truck trails and a section of FLT. In this region, the FLT in its eastward route runs through Rock City State Forest (see Hike 28), and then passes through McCarty Hill State Forest in a northeasterly direction that eventually takes it past Ellicottville, then into Allegheny County, finally ending in the Catskills.

Walk past the gate and head uphill on the state truck trail (CCC Forest Road). It is a steady uphill climb for the next 0.4 mile; here is where the FLT crosses the road, the route you will use on your return. From your start to this point, the vertical rise is 207 feet.

Continue north on the tree-lined truck trail. After a small rise of land just ahead, the terrain flattens to allow for easy walking for the next 1.2 miles; here you pass another metal gate just before intersecting a dirt road, Mutton Hollow Road, which in this section of the state forest runs in a northwesterly-southeasterly direction. You are now at the highest point of McCarty Hill (el. 2,333 feet).

Turn right on Mutton Hollow Road and follow it downhill for little over 0.1 mile where a barricaded road intersects on the left (north). Follow this little-used road north and uphill for 0.1 mile to the top where it intersects another little used road, running east-west. In getting here you walked through a small piece of state land and then onto private land belonging to the Holiday Valley ski resort.

Turn left (west) onto the east-west road (which in winter-time serves as a cross-country ski trail) and head west through a forest which covers the top as well as the northern slope of McCarty Hill; 0.2 mile brings you to a building housing machinery for a chairlift. This, of course, is the spot where skiers leave their chairs and take off downhill on one of the ski trails found on the right and left of the building.

View from McCarty Hill State Forest

A short distance westward puts you back into McCarty Hill State forest; from here it is 0.2 mile through a mixed forest of hardwood and evergreens to the base of a lookout tower which is no longer in use. However, at the tower's base, enclosed by a high wire fence, is found a large propane gas tank and small wooden building housing emergency communication equipment.

The FLT, coming from the south, crosses the road at this point, passing close to the tower on its west side. Take this portion of the FLT. As the trail re-enters the state forest, it turns gradually in a northwesterly direction. After walking 0.4 mile on the FLT, you intersect an unused road running in a north-south direction.

Turn here and follow the road north; in a short distance the FLT turns off the road into the woods on the left. Continue north on the road, and in 0.1 mile you come to the end of the state forest and to a clearing ahead. In the clearing is a fair-sized pond used in winter to make snow for the ski slopes that belong to the private Holimount Ski Club.

Retrace your steps to where you initially intersected the road via the FLT. Continue south on the road past this point; an additional 0.2 mile brings you to an intersection with Mutton Hollow Road. You now are ready to start your return trek.

Turn left (east) on Mutton Hollow Road and follow it in a south-easterly direction for almost 0.4 mile to the lookout tower you visited before. Pick up the white-blazed FLT across the road (south); follow the trail as it takes you over the flat terrain and through the mixed hardwood-evergreen forest for 1.3 miles where the FLT crosses the CCC Forest Road you walked earlier. Turn right onto the road and follow it downhill for 0.4 mile to your parked vehicle.

30

Golden Hill State Forest

Hiking distance: 4.5 miles
Hiking time: 2½ hours
Vertical rise: 320 feet
Map: USGS 7½' Humphrey

Golden Hill State Forest meanders over the highlands in southeastern Cattaraugus County, surrounded by hills of all shapes and varieties. Some of them are round, some are peaked, and still others are strung together to form lengthy ridges. Most are without names, but a few have names, such as Pierce Hill (elevation 2,270 feet) and Laidlaw Hill; the latter is actually a 2.5-mile-long ridge, topping out at 2,280 feet. But no hill is called Golden Hill.

In the southern portion of the 2,281-acre state forest is a Golden Hill Road—a road that does in fact pass over a hill. Perhaps it was this hill that someone had in mind when they named the road, or perhaps the name was taken from some early settler who built his homestead on this hill. But no matter; the state forest in this area is a beautiful place to hike.

For administrative purposes, the state has divided this huge tract of public land into two parts—the rectangular-shaped northern section (1,176 acres) and the irregularly shaped southern section (1,105 acres). No clear demarcation separates these two sections, other than Golden Hill Road, which runs over the southern area's highest spot, with an elevation of 2,090 feet.

Fire Lane Road runs through the entire length of the northern and southern sections. The state forest also contains other roads that, combined with Fire Lane Road, allow the hiker to cover the top of a fairly wide ridge without any hill climbing.

Mixed in with the state land is also private land. The variety in size and type of trees in this area make it an ideal place for bird-watching or, as the more sophisticated would say, for some serious "birding." This activity can be enjoyed in any season, but especially during nesting time in late spring and early summer.

Different birds can be seen depending on the season, and also according to the height of vegetation, from grasses and low shrubs to tall trees. State forests offer combinations of open fields with young growth, developing forests of seedlings and saplings, woods of pole-size trees with shallow canopies, and mature forests of saw-timber-size trees supporting thick canopies.

In the low growth are the ground feeders and nesters, including wild turkey, ruffed grouse, rufous-sided towhee, song sparrow, field sparrow, and yellow-throat warbler. Those that feed in the foliage above the ground include the chestnut-

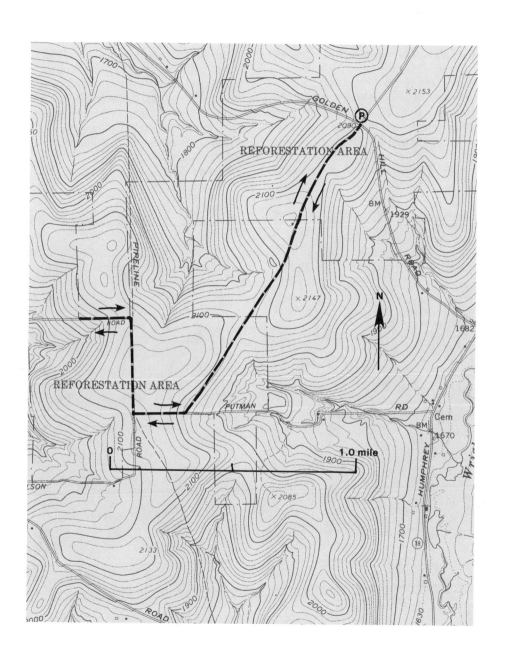

sided warbler, rose-breasted grosbeak, and gray catbird. At medium height (10 to 24 feet) in the more dense canopies are the ovenbird, red-eyed vireo, and black-capped chickadee. Still higher (50 to 60 feet) in the hardwood-hemlock forests are the bark-drilling group: the downy woodpecker, hairy woodpecker, and pileated woodpecker; the tops of trees provide food for the black-throated green warbler, blackburnian warbler, solitary vireo, barred owl, and red-shoulder hawk.

If you know where birds like to feed and nest, you can improve your chances of sighting and identifying them. So look low, high, and in between to match the bird species with the height of the vegetation.

The land on which Golden Hill State Forest is located is rolling and knobby, but its high sections are surprisingly level. At the edges, the land tapers sharply downward into Forks Creek valley in the west, Ischua Valley in the east, and Wrights Creek valley in the south and southeast.

Access. NY 98, which runs between

Hikers in Golden Hill State Forest

the village of Great Valley in the southwest and Franklinville in the northeast, almost touches the western edge of Golden Hill State Forest. This state route provides the best access to your trailhead.

Great Valley can be reached via US 219 running north out of Salamanca at Exit 21 of the Southern Tier Expressway (NY 17). Franklinville can be reached from the north or south via NY 16.

From Great Valley it is 5 miles on NY 98 to where Golden Hill Road intersects on the right; coming the other way from Franklinville, 8 miles will bring you to the intersection with Golden Hill Road. Once on Golden Hill Road, drive uphill in a southeasterly direction for 1.2 miles. Here you find the western edge of Golden Hill State Forest. Continue driving uphill an additional 0.6 mile to the intersection with Fire Lane Road. Park here.

Trail. Your hike starts initially on top of the hill (elevation 2,090 feet) and follows Fire Lane Road in a southwesterly direction. The terrain here is as level as a tabletop and continues so for little over 0.3 mile; then the road slopes gradually upward for 0.2 mile, bringing you to the end of the state forest. As you follow Fire Lane Road past private land, the area opens up; 0.4 mile brings you back into

the state forest again, and the road begins to pitch gradually downward. The pitch, however, is so slight, you hardly notice it.

Again the road flattens, staying level for just over 0.4 mile, where it intersects Putman Road, running in an east-west direction. Turn right onto Putman Road and walk west; Putman Road acts as a boundary with state forest land on the north side of the road and private land on the south side. Here the habitat changes again.

An additional 0.2 mile over relatively level ground brings you to the intersection with Wilson Road, running in a north-south direction. Turn, and walk north. There is a slight rise in the road at the beginning, but it slowly changes to a slight downward pitch as you reach the road's left turn.

Follow Wilson Road west for about 0.1 mile, where the road suddenly dips in a sharp descent. Here you find a nice view to the west, looking first downhill to Forks Creek valley and then next at the forested hills on the far side. There is a cut in these hills called Haines Hollow; it is easy to see from your position.

You are now ready to retrace your steps; just over 2 miles brings you back to your parked vehicle.

31

Boyce Hill State Forest

Hiking distance: 7.2 miles
Hiking time: 3 hours
Vertical rise: 460 feet
Map: USGS 7½' Ashford

Four hilltops in Cattaraugus County run in a straight line from northeast to southwest. They form a forested ridge over 2 miles long. The official name of this ridge is Boyce Hill, and this is also the name of the 971-acre state forest that occupies the middle portion of this ridge.

The region is true hill country, and early settlers who set up homesteads here quickly named the many hills and ridges. South of the state forest is Crosby Hill, while to the north is Tug Hill; to the northwest is Canada Hill, and to the southwest, Bryant Hill.

The ridges all run in the same direction and reach about the same height, ranging between 2,000 and 2,200 feet. The valleys, several hundred feet below the hilltops, are not deeply cut; most have elevations of between 1,600 and 1,700 feet. This is an effect of the Wisconsin glacier 12,000 years ago.

Running the entire length of Boyce Hill State Forest are the white blazes and maintained footpath of the Finger Lakes Trail (FLT). The 648-mile FLT connects Allegany State Park in the southwest and the Catskill Forest Preserve in the southeast.

Access. The western edge of the state forest touches NY 242, a state route that runs between the intersection with NY 394 just east of East Randolph and NY 16 just south of Lime Lake. East Randolph is located in southwest Cattaraugus County and Lime Lake is in the northeastern part.

You can reach NY 242 from the north or south via NY 219, which runs through the middle of the county. NY 219 intersects NY 242 in Ellicottville, where you turn northeast on NY 242. Continue north on NY 242 for 4 miles to the hamlet of Ashford Junction, where NY 240 intersects from the north.

Continue on NY 242 for an additional 2.6 miles to the hamlet of Devereaux. From here, it is 0.55 mile to Phillips Road, intersecting from the southeast. Touching this road is the western tip of Boyce Hill State Forest. The trailhead with a sign at the edge of the state forest tells you that you have found the FLT route into the state forest.

Trail. Starting at an elevation of 1,716 feet, the FLT parallels Phillips Road as it gradually climbs through a dense stand of spruce. At the 0.5-mile mark, Phillips Road turns southeast, while the FLT turns east.

The ascent becomes more pronounced when the FLT reaches an ele-

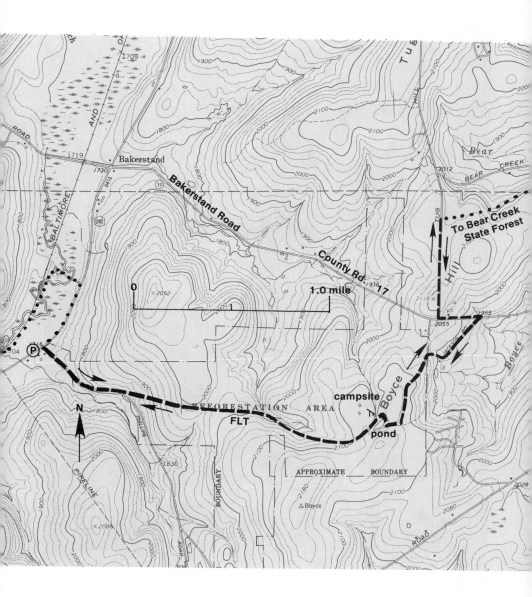

vation of 2,000 feet; from here it continues east on level ground. The vertical rise to this point is 284 feet.

For the next 0.6 mile through the forest, the FLT continues over flat terrain. On the left you pass the headwaters of a streamlet flowing west through a gully. This streamlet will eventually head downhill, passing through several ponds before finally emptying into the Devereaux Branch of Great Valley Creek.

The FLT now begins a gradual climb again; an additional 0.2 mile brings it to a broad, level area containing a fair-

Boyce Hill State Forest

sized pond. Once around the pond, the trail continues in an easterly direction along the edge of the pond into a stand of evergreens at the pond's eastern end.

Here you encounter a side trail intersecting on the left. It is a short trail leading to a campsite near an old spring at the edge of the state property. To make this short trip, follow the blue blazes heading north to the campsite. Here you may wish to stop for a lunch break or brief rest. When ready, return to the pond or continue your hike on the FLT.

Once back in the evergreen stand, follow the white blazes of the FLT to the state access road; a short distance on this route takes you to the beginning of Jackson Road. Turn left onto Jackson Road, and head northeast for 0.4 mile, where you leave the state forest. Jackson Road now turns to the right (east) for a short distance, then again follows a northeast route; an additional 0.3 mile brings you to the intersection with Bakerstand Road (County Route 17).

Turn left (west) onto Bakerstand Road and follow the white FLT blazes along the road for 0.2 mile, where Tug Hill Road intersects from the north. Turn onto Tug Hill Road, and in less than 0.1 mile you reach one of the area's highest points (elevation 2,118 feet). The land, while high, is comparatively level to the east; this is also true for a short distance on the west, after which the land dips gradually downward for the next two miles until it reaches the Devereaux Branch of Great Valley Creek.

The white-blazed FLT continues north on Tug Hill Road for 0.5 mile, where it leaves the road and turns right (east) into the woods. This is your turnaround point. The FLT, of course, continues eastward through the woods for another mile, where it enters Bear Creek State Forest. If you have time, you can add to your hiking distance by including Bear Creek State Forest in your day's outing.

If, on the other hand, you are confining your hike to Boyce Hill State Forest, reverse direction and head south on Tug Hill Road the way you came; 3.6 miles brings you back over the short road system and the longer woods trail to NY 242 and your parked vehicle.

32

Bear Creek State Forest

Hiking distance: 2.8 miles
Hiking time: 2 hours
Vertical rise: 450 feet
Map: USGS 7½' Franklinville

Bear Creek State Forest is small compared with other state forests in Cattaraugus County. Its small rectangular shape covers only 547 acres. But good things come in small packages, and Bear Creek State Forest is one of them. It is a delightful place to do some easy walking at a leisurely pace.

A small stream flows diagonally through the state forest from the southwest to the northeast. Its name is Bear Creek. Running parallel to the creek is a road that, not surprisingly, is called Bear Creek Road.

The southern portion of the state forest occupies high ground, including three sizable hills. The highest reaches an elevation of 2,052 feet. The hills are strung out in an east-west row to form a forested ridge. These hills slant down to form a shallow valley, through which Bear Creek and Bear Creek Road pass.

Just south of this road and creek and over the southern ridge runs a portion of the Finger Lakes Trail (FLT). The north side of the valley is not as steep as the south side, but nonetheless, it reaches an elevation of 2,000 feet. More than a mile from the state forest, by way of the FLT, lies Boyce Hill State Forest (see Hike 31), and 5.5 miles to the east on

the FLT lies Bush Hill State Forest (see Hike 33). A short distance to the north, it takes you to Farmersville State Forest (see Hike 34).

Two joint state routes, NY 16 and NY 98, pass through the village of Franklinville, located just over a mile to the southeast. Franklinville sits in a broad valley, called Ischua Valley, through which flows a wide stream, Ischua Creek. After Bear Creek comes out of the state forest, it flows into Ischua Creek north of Franklinville.

Access. The state forest can be reached from the north or south via NY 16; in the north, NY 16 ties into the Southern Tier Expressway (NY 17) at Exit 27.

From the south, drive to Franklinville on NY 16. From the center of Franklinville, it is 2.2 miles to where NY 16 and NY 98 part. Bear left and continue north on NY 16 for an additional 0.5 mile, where Bear Creek Road intersects from the south.

Turn onto Bear Creek Road and drive 1.2 miles to the intersection with Upper Bear Creek Road. The state forest begins here. Park here.

Trail. Combining Bear Creek Road with the FLT, you can walk a 2.8-mile loop and cover this relatively short distance in about two hours.

Your hike begins at the northeast corner of the state forest. The FLT enters the forest there, south of Bear Creek Road, close to your parking spot. A double white blaze tells you that the FLT leaves the road to enter the wooded area; just off the road, you also see a large FLT sign at the trailhead.

Walk through this state forest slowly, with an eye of a naturalist. How and where you look will be affected by the

season. In early spring, the transition between winter's whiteness and late spring greenery gives the woodlands a gentle stillness. Bare of foliage, the trees let in the light and allow you to see deep into the forest. This is the time to look for the movements of birds, especially those passing through in northward migration.

In summer, when the forest's upper story is a canopy of green, your sight should be shorter and lower. Now is the time to study the forest floor—the green mosses on rocks and logs and the many

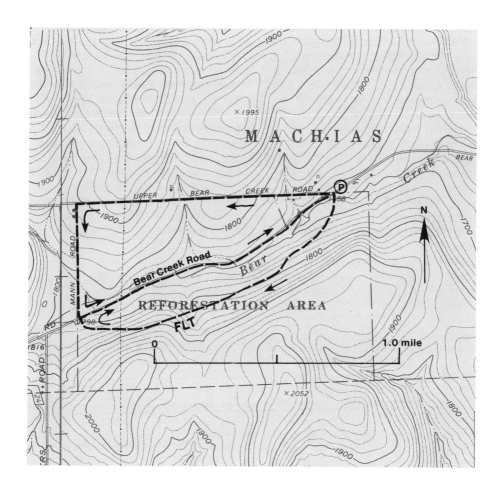

varied ferns. In fall and early winter, gaze up again and be awed by the explosion of fall foliage at its brightest. Later, when the leaves have dropped, look for the birds of winter: the white-breasted nuthatch, red crossbill, black-capped chickadee, purple finch, and if you move slowly, perhaps the pileated woodpecker.

So pick your season, and then come to Bear Creek State Forest. Walk with measured steps. Listen to the creek flowing beside the road. Stop from time to time and look about you and read the forest's natural signs.

Soon after you enter the forest on the FLT, you come to Bear Creek. Once across the creek, you go through a moist, boggy area and then start uphill. Your climb is gradual, and soon you reach the top of the ridge where the land levels to form a fairly flat area about a mile wide and a mile long.

The FLT follows the ridge for just over 0.5 mile, with a few minor ups and downs, passing through mixed stands of hardwoods and evergreens as well as larches. You come to an open grassy area, where you find a right-of-way of an electric power line. Here, too, you will find a variety of lichens, wildflowers, and ferns.

Leaving the open area, you reenter the forest and start a gradual descent along the north side of the ridge until you reach the southeast corner of the state forest. The FLT ends at Bear Creek Road at the point where Mann Road intersects from the north. Turn right (east) onto Bear Creek Road. The road slopes ever so gently downward. Bear Creek flows on the north side of the road. At the 0.5-mile mark, the stream crosses under the road, then turns to follow the road on its southern side. Along the way, you encounter two streamlets that flow off the north ridge into Bear Creek. From the stream crossover, it is 0.7 mile to where your vehicle is parked.

You can end your hike at this point, or you can walk still another loop. This loop starts close to where your vehicle is parked at the intersection of Bear Creek Road and Upper Bear Creek Road. Turn onto the latter road, and head west. A mile of minor ups and downs brings you to the intersection with Mann Road. (Upper Bear Creek Road forms the state forest's northern boundary, and Mann Road its western boundary.) Turn south on Mann Road, and walk gradually downhill for 0.5 mile to the intersection with Bear Creek Road. You can now return to your vehicle, either by Bear Creek Road or by the FLT.

33

Bush Hill State Forest

Hiking distance: 5 miles
Hiking time: 2½ hours
Vertical rise: 540 feet
Map: USGS 7½' Freedom; USGS 7½' Rawson;
* USGS 7½' Delevan; USGS 7½' Franklinville*

Hills are so plentiful in this corner of Cattaraugus County that little effort has been made to give them names. But, Bush Hill is an exception, and it can be found by that name on official topographic maps.

Bush Hill is a landform that is peaked more than most hills hereabouts. It tops out at an elevation of 2,201 feet. The nearby state forest takes its name from this officially designated hill. But the hill maintains its own independence, occupying the high ground on private land a little over a half-mile north of the state forest.

Bush Hill State Forest actually lies south of Bush Hill itself. Although it is large, the 3,108-acre state forest has an odd shape; it is two large tracts joined by a narrow strip of state land—0.3 mile wide and almost 1.5 miles long.

Two roads run east-west through the southern section: Clark Road and Palmer Road. The northern section is accessible by Peet Hill Road and a state-maintained truck trail running east-west through the length of the state forest.

In Cattaraugus County the Finger Lakes Trail (FLT) passes through a number of state forests, including Bear Creek State Forest (see Hike 32), about 5 miles to the west of Bush Hill, and Farmersville State Forest (see Hike 34), about a mile north of Bush Hill. It enters Bush Hill State Forest from the southwest and crosses Kingsbury Hill Road a little over a mile south of NY 98 and 3 miles south of Farmersville. If you wish to lengthen your walk, you can follow the FLT from Kingsbury Hill Road for a little over 2 miles to where it enters the state forest. In another 0.5 mile, the FLT intersects with Peet Hill Road, which is the starting point of the hike described here.

In the state forest's western end is half-mile-long Harwood Lake, which is used extensively for fishing. There is also a state boat launching site here. The lake and some of the surrounding land make up the state forest's 298-acre multiuse area. All this is located across the road from the hamlet of Farmersville.

The northern section of Bush Hill State Forest occupies the highland overlooking Farmersville, Harwood Lake, and NY 98. Drainage off this highland is to the south, where you find the headwaters of the east-flowing Caneadea Creek. Topping this portion of the state forest is an unnamed hilltop (elevation 2,149 feet), one of the high spots in the state forest.

Access. Take the Southern Tier Ex-

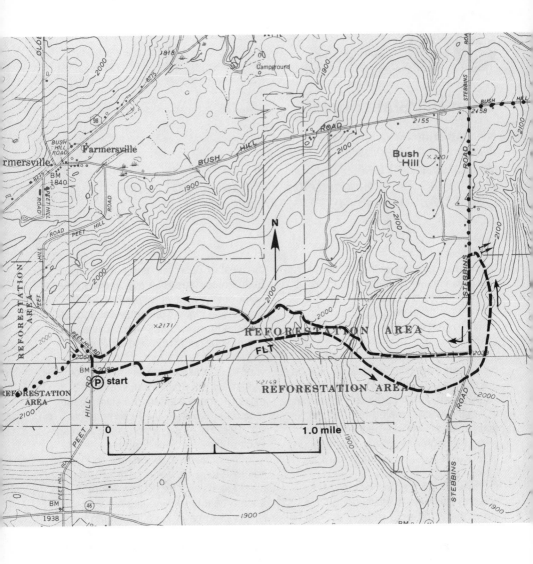

pressway (NY 17) to Exit 27 and get on NY 16 going north to Franklinville. Once in Franklinville, drive north on NY 98 for 2.5 miles, to where NY 16 goes north and NY 98 goes northeast; 4 additional miles on NY 98 bring you past Harwood Lake on the right and into Farmersville. In Farmersville, Bush Hill Road intersects from the east. Turn here, and drive 0.2 mile to where Peet Hill Road intersects

from the south. Follow the latter road south for 0.8 mile, where a sign and white blazes tell you that you have found the FLT.

The FLT crosses Peet Hill Road just past the intersection of Peet Hill Road and an unnamed state-maintained truck trail. You can park at the intersection or along Peet Hill Road, near the spot where the FLT crosses the road.

Trail. Hiking in Bush Hill State Forest is an up-and-down affair, although the ascents are not very demanding. Nonetheless, on your return trip, you must climb a rise of 240 feet in a little over 0.5 mile.

Begin your hike at the junction of Peet Hill Road and the truck trail. This is at an elevation of 2,058 feet, indicating that at the start of your hike you are already on high ground.

The trail begins on the left side of Peet Hill Road, at the point where you find single white FLT blazes on both sides of the road. Enter the pine plantation, and head east up the hill. Initially, the FLT follows an overgrown logging road, passing a large campsite frequently used by scout groups.

For a short distance, the dirt truck road is visible through the trees on the left. Then the FLT veers away from the road and enters a stand of beech and maple trees. The trail soon comes to a small creek; here it turns south for a short distance, then swings sharply to the east and heads uphill to the top of a ridge.

The trail now follows the ridge, and you encounter several spots that provide nice views of the surrounding landscape. Then the FLT leaves the ridge and begins a long and sometimes steep descent. It takes you into a gully, where you come to a junction of two creeks that you must cross. After the creek crossing, the FLT turns right and follows a circular route until it crosses north-south Stebbins Road. Here is an attractive forest with a mix of hardwoods and evergreens, swales of ferns, and in early spring, an explosion of wildflowers.

Bush Hill State Forest

At Stebbins Road, turn left. Walk a short distance north, to the point where the FLT reenters the forest and turns north, paralleling Stebbins Road. The trail stays in the forest on its northward route for 0.8 mile; it then swings left (west) and leaves the forest to intersect again with Stebbins Road. This is the northern edge of the state forest; beyond is private land.

This is your turnaround point, although the FLT continues north on Stebbins Road for 0.7 mile to the intersection with Bush Hill Road and 0.6 mile east on the latter road to enter Farmersville State Forest.

At your turnaround spot, you have excellent vistas to the east, where the land slopes downward into a valley, only to rise again in a series of hills that shape a 1.5-mile-long ridge. Turn about here and head south, following Stebbins Road past a large plantation of tall spruce trees on your right.

After walking 0.4 mile, you reach a truck trail intersecting on the right. A pipe-gate barrier may or may not be in place; in the summer it is usually open to motorized vehicles. This is the same truck trail that you encountered at the beginning of your hike.

Turn west onto the truck trail, and follow it back to Peet Hill Road. As you head back, you have to make a fairly long and sometimes steep ascent. It brings you to an elevation of 2,171 feet, one of the high spots in the state forest. The climb is somewhat demanding for hikers and especially for cross-country skiers. If you come to Bush Hill in winter for Nordic skiing, you will find the downhill run on this section of the truck trail a thrilling experience. Once you are over the hill's crest, you have a short downhill journey to the intersection with Peet Hill Road and your parked vehicle.

34

Farmersville State Forest

Hiking distance: 5.2 miles
Hiking time: 4 hours
Vertical rise: 929 feet
Map: USGS 7½' Freedom

This state forest takes its agricultural name from the locale. A little over a mile to the southwest of the state forest is the hamlet of Farmersville, and 1.5 miles to the northwest is the fair-size community of Farmersville Station. A train-stop once gave that village a mark of importance. These small communities constitute the Town of Farmersville (in New York state, "town" is the equivalent of "township" in other states).

This is farm country and it was almost inevitable that the state forest would end up with one of the most prominent names in the area.

Farmersville State Forest is perched on top of a high ridge that runs in a northeast-southwest direction for almost 4 miles. Cream Ridge, as it is called, rises from a high plateau; nonetheless, this uneven, hilly countryside fluctuates in elevation from several hundred feet in the valleys to over 2,000 feet on the hills.

The elongated state forest is on this ridge; its right shoulder touches the boundary separating Allegany County on the east side and Cattaraugus County, in which the state forest is situated, on the west side.

The ridge drains in all directions, but most of the streamlets eventually come

together to feed either Elton Creek to the north or Caneadea Creek to the southeast.

Running through the full length of the state forest is a section of the Finger Lakes Trail (FLT). In its northward, then eastward journey, the FLT passes through several state forests in this region, including Bush Hill State Forest (see Hike 33), just a mile to the southwest of Farmersville State Forest, and Swift Hill State Forest (see Hike 50), 5 miles to the northeast. You can use the FLT not only to walk within these state forests but to get from one to the other.

Access. Farmersville State Forest lies a mile south of the intersection of NY 98 and NY 243. NY 98 runs between Arcade, 9 miles to the north, and Franklinville, 10 miles to the south. NY 243 runs southeast from its junction with NY 98 past Rushford Lake to intersect with NY 19 in the east.

Once you have reached where NY 98 and NY 243 meet, drive east on NY 243 for 1.01 miles to an intersection called Fairview. Unhappily, some name changes cause confusion. On the north side of Fairview, the road is called Fairview Road and on the south side, Huyck Road. Turn onto Huyck Road and drive

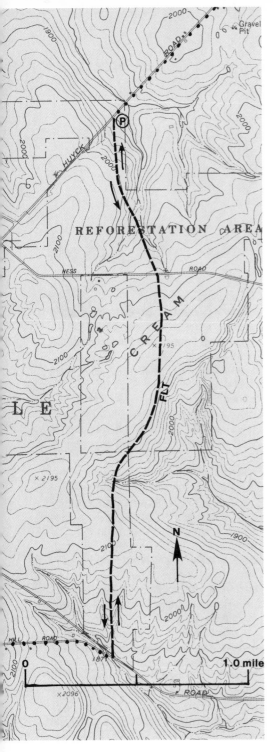

south for 1.01 miles to the northern edge of Farmersville State Forest.

A short distance farther, you cross a creek and then arrive at the trailhead where a footpath, heading south, takes you into the state forest. Look for a sign at the forest's edge to locate this section of the white-blazed FLT. Once you find it, park your vehicle nearby.

Trail. The FLT, running the length of the state forest, is 2.6 miles long; a round-trip hike amounts to 5.2 miles—a good afternoon's hike. Given the area's rolling terrain, you will have some moderate climbing. Your total vertical rise will be over 900 feet—enough to make you aware of the terrain's unevenness.

Your hike, beginning at an elevation of 1,900 feet, starts uphill immediately. The ascent for the next 0.2 mile is steep, but then the trail flattens. A short distance through the forest, the foot-trail begins to descend, dropping steeply for a short distance into a gully through which flows the beginnings of a streamlet.

Once over the gully, the FLT starts uphill along the streamlet and continues the ascent for the next 0.3 mile, where it intersects a dirt truck trail, Hess Road. At this point you have reached the top of Cream Ridge.

The FLT crosses Hess Road and continues south in a gradual descent. The climb here, however, is less demanding than it was before, and in 0.3 mile, you reach the area's high spot—a knob with an elevation of 2,195 feet.

Once over the knob the trail heads downward, gradually for the first 0.5 mile, then steeply for the next 0.2 mile, where you enter another gully and the origin of a streamlet flowing east. Another fair climb brings you in 0.2 mile to the top of another hill (elevation 2,100 feet).

Once again, the trail heads downhill for the next 0.5 mile. The descent at first is gradual, but at the halfway mark it becomes increasingly steep. When you emerge at West Branch Road, your vertical drop has been 129 feet.

This now becomes your vertical rise as you turn around and head back on the FLT. Much of the next 1.5 miles is pretty much hill climbing, but after that, you begin your descent, which eventually brings you back to Huyck Road and your parked vehicle.

Road trail in Farmersville State Forest

35

Allegany State Park (Quaker Lake Area)

Total hiking distance: 20.8 miles (3 days)
Total hiking time: 14 hours
Vertical rise: 1,952 feet
Map: USGS 7½' Red House; USGS 7½' Steamburg;
  Allegany State Park Map

Allegany State Park is a hikers' mecca. It contains 135 miles of marked trails and almost twice as many miles of unmarked routes—old railroad grades, long-forgotten wagon roads, former hiking trails, and other little-used paths. Add the park's road system—both gravel and paved hardtop—and you have enough miles to keep even the hardiest hiker walking for months.

Allegany State Park stands out from other state lands in several respects. Size, rugged terrain, dense forests, scenic beauty, and miles of hiking trails certainly are some of its more striking attributes.

The park covers 62,000 acres in southern Cattaraugus County. It is the largest park in New York State and resembles a wilderness park. Its size and its natural beauty have led the state to speak of Allegany State Park as the "matriarch" of New York's park system.

To appreciate this, remember that the state distinguishes between state parks and state forests. State parks are usually small and generally used for picnicking and swimming; moreover, they are managed by the state's Office of Parks, Recreation, and Historical Preservation. On the other hand, the state's other lands,

such as the Adirondack Forest Preserve and the Catskill Forest Preserve, are very large and managed by the Department of Environmental Conservation. Allegany State Park is not the state's largest piece of real estate, but it is nonetheless the most impressive of the state's parks in physical dimensions.

The park is especially designed to accommodate a variety of recreational pursuits. Of special interest to hikers is the park's hiking trail system, which contains 18 specially designated, groomed, and marked walking trails, covering 53 miles in some of the finest hiking territory in Western New York. In addition, there are 27 miles of cross-country ski touring trails and 55 miles of snowmobile or horseback trails that hikers also use.

All the hiking trails have names for easy identification, and the park provides maps showing where they can be found. They range in distance from a half-mile to 18 miles. The 18-mile trail is part of the Finger Lakes Trail (FLT); it runs from the Pennsylvania border (where it ties into the Keystone Trail system in the Allegheny National Forest) to Exit 19 of the Southern Tier Expressway (NY 17), located 2.7 miles west of the park's Red House Lake.

At all trailheads are signboards with encased topographical maps (USGS 7.5-minute series), on which the trail section is clearly shown in black ink. The hiking trails, in turn, are marked with large blue metal discs with an image of a hiker with a walking stick. Markers for ski touring trails are orange discs showing a figure of a skier. Snowmobile trail markers show a white snowmobile on a red background outlined in white; horseback trails, in turn, are marked with a yellow disc with a horse and rider in black.

The Finger Lakes Trail (FLT) is marked by both blue metal discs and white blazes painted on trees. On the park map, the FLT is identified as the North Country Trail (NCT). The federally sanctioned but privately managed NCT, still in the development stage, makes use of existing trail systems, such as the FLT. When completed, it will run from Crown Point, New York, through New York state over the FLT, and then through Pennsylvania, Ohio, Michigan, Wisconsin, Minnesota, ending in western North Dakota.

The park contains two sizable lakes, Quaker Lake in the southwestern section, and Red House Lake in the central section (see Hike 36). The Quaker Lake area has 230 cabins and a dozen or so campsites, open from early April through mid-December; also near Quaker Lake is the newest site, Cain Hollow Camping Area, with 164 tent and trailer sites. The Red House Lake area contains 144 cabins, 80 of which are winterized for year-round use, and 134 campsites for tents and trailers.

The lakes are ideal for swimming, boating, canoeing, and fishing. Both lakes are stocked with rainbow and brown trout. On the south side of Red House Lake are biking trails, picnic areas, and playfields.

Cutting through the park's midsection are two main highways. One of these, identified as ASP 1, enters the park's northern section from Salamanca, located across the Allegheny River; it runs south to Red House Lake, then southwest to the park's southern end, to intersect another highway, ASP 3, running east and west. From Red House Lake another highway, ASP 2, also runs south, but some distance east of ASP 1; it, too, intersects ASP 3 just a short distance north of the Pennsylvania border.

These hardtop, two-lane highways also attract hikers. Trees and other growth have been cut back from the highways to provide wide, grass-covered shoulders to serve as hiking routes paralleling the roadways.

The land over which the highways run has a distinctively rugged, angular appearance—the telltale sign of a land that escaped the scouring and leveling effects of the Wisconsin glacier. Only part of what is now the state park was spared the effects of the glaciation.

Additional information about the park's landforms, geological features, and wildlife and plant species is found in the introduction to the section on the Red House Lake Area (see Hike 36).

It takes time to come to appreciate the park's many features and scenic beauty. Plan your visit to cover at least two days, or even better, a three-day weekend, including campouts at either the Quaker Lake or the Red House Lake area. If you plan to hike extensively in these areas, your visit should be extended to six days or a week.

In the Quaker Lake area is a network of foot-trails connected by roads and highways. By combining these, you can form hiking loops to cover three days of walking. Use the Diehl Tent and Trailer section in the Quaker Cabin Area as your base camp; from here, it is possible to hike three loops, each starting and

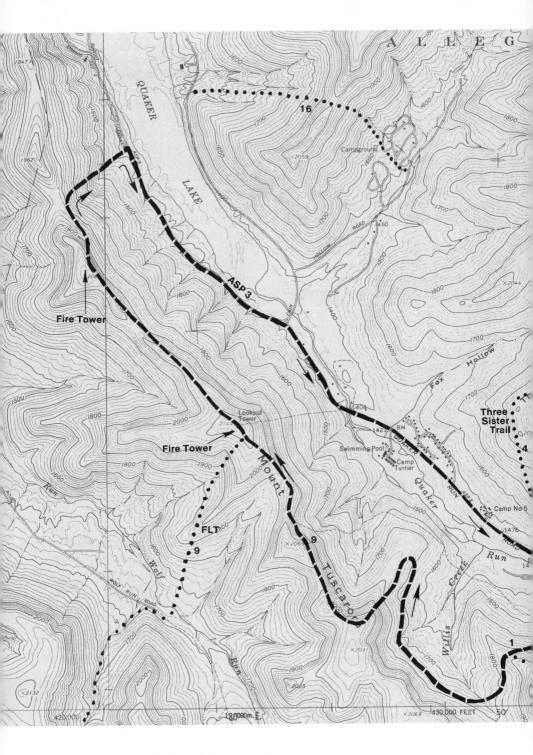

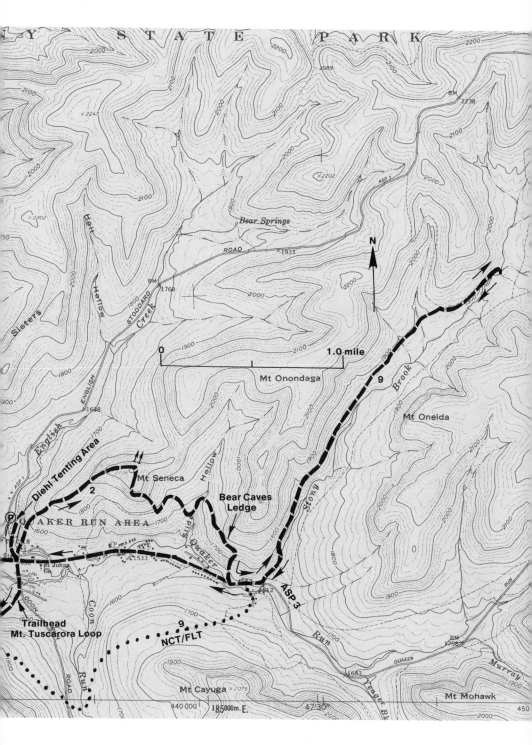

ending at your campsite.

If you prefer a cabin, you can rent one. But from June to Labor Day, cabin reservations must be made for a minimum of seven nights; reservations for the rest of the year must be made for a minimum of two nights. The per-night fee ranges from $7 to $9.50.

Access. Allegany State Park can be reached from the east or west via the Southern Tier Expressway (NY 17) and from the north (Buffalo–Niagara Falls area) via US 219, to where it intersects the Southern Tier Expressway at Exit 21. From the park's southeastern entrance, it is 5 miles to Bradford, Pennsylvania, which can be reached via US 219 from Du Bois, near the Pennsylvania Turnpike.

For those using the Southern Tier Expressway and coming from the east or north, follow the Expressway around the northern portion of the state park to Exit 18 on the park's west side; those coming from the west on the expressway, use the same exit. Leave the expressway at Exit 18 and turn onto NY 280; drive

south on NY 280 for 4 miles, where you enter park land. Here the park uses its own route designation, ASP 3; an additional 1.5 miles on ASP 3/NY 280 brings you past the southwestern part of Quaker Lake (on your left) to the park's entrance booth.

Continue driving southeast on ASP 3 for 3.5 miles to the rental office building on the left, across the highway from the Quaker Inn and store. After checking in to obtain your campsite (or cabin), drive a few hundred yards past the intersec-

tion with ASP 1 for 0.5 mile to Diehl Trail (access roads to camping areas are designated "trail" rather than "road"); turn north on Diehl Trail, and 0.2 mile brings you to your site. Many trails radiate from this spot.

Trails. From your base camp, you easily can find the trailheads of four hiking trails: the Bear Caves–Mount Seneca Trail, the Three Sisters Trail, the Mount Tuscarora Trail, and the North Country (Finger Lakes) Trail. When these trails are combined with the area's road sys-

Quaker Lake

tem, several hiking loops suggest themselves; hence, the recommended hikes can be divided into three days of walking. The recommended routes are the Mount Tuscarora–ASP 3 loop (7.5 miles); the Mount Seneca–Stony Creek–ASP 3 loop (7.8 miles); and the Thunder Rocks loop (5.5 miles).

Day One (Mount Tuscarora–ASP 3 Loop). From your campsite, walk south 0.2 mile to ASP 3. Cross the highway, and continue south on a dirt route, Coon Run Road, and over Quaker Run (creek) for little over 0.1 mile to an intersection. On the right are the trailhead and the trailhead signboard containing the marked topographic map. The elevation at the trailhead of the Mount Tuscarora Trail is 1,466 feet.

This part of the trail carries two markers—the blue discs for the Mount Tuscarora Trail (designated Trail 1 on the park map) and the white blazes for the North Country Trail (Finger Lakes Trail, also designated Trail 9 on the park map). The portion of the trail carrying the double markers only runs a mile; the trails then split and go their own way.

The Mount Tuscarora Trail (Trail 1) immediately heads southwest into the wooded area and starts uphill a short distance, then crosses one of the cabin area access roads. The gradual ascent continues for an additional 0.1 mile, and the upward pitch becomes more noticeable. In the next 0.4 mile, you climb 300 feet. There this portion of the trail intersects the main trail route, which carries the combined designation of Trail 1 (blue discs) and Trail 9 (white blazes). Turn right at the intersection and head west through the forest. In a short distance, the trail turns left, following the side of the hill to the south for 0.2 mile and then downhill for 0.1 mile to cross Willis Creek.

A short but steep uphill climb on the other side of the creek brings you to a point where the trail flattens as it goes northwest along the hillside for 0.5 mile. Then the trail turns north and makes a gradual descent for the next 0.4 mile. There it makes a sharp turn left, to head uphill in a southerly direction.

The next 0.5 mile is all uphill and becomes steeper until you reach the crest of Mount Tuscarora, an elongated hill that runs in a northwest-southeast direction, parallel to Quaker Run valley, a mile to the north. Your climb in the last 0.5 mile has taken you up 300 feet, to an elevation of 2,000 feet.

Your walk now continues in a northwesterly direction along the top of Mount Tuscarora ridge. At the 1.1-mile mark, a trail intersects on the left. This is the white-blazed Finger Lakes Trail (Trail 9 on the park map). Continue along the ridge on the Mount Tuscarora Trail; an additional 0.1 mile brings you to an abandoned lookout (fire) tower.

The trail continues its level course for an additional mile, to another unused lookout tower. Then the trail begins a gradual descent, turning a little to the left and then to the right as it heads downhill for the next 0.4 mile. Here you cross your last knob (elevation 2,064) with a good view to the northwest; the trail now turns sharply to the right (northeast) to start its steep descent. Another 0.5 mile of downhill walking brings you to forest's end and to park highway ASP 3. Turn right onto the highway, which heads southeast. Like all the park's highways, ASP 3 is an attractive route to walk. On your left is Quaker Lake, its blue waters attractively framed by the peaked hills to the north. A thin line of trees runs along the lake's southern edge, and on the north side is a beach and swimming area, as well as the road from the southeast. On your right, the forested hillside

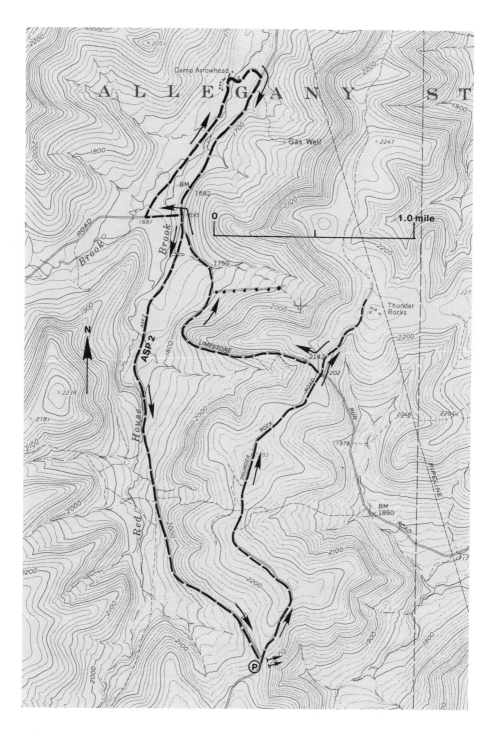

rises steeply for 600 feet to Mount Tuscarora ridge.

A little over a mile of level walking on ASP 3 brings you to a paved route, Cain Hollow Road, which intersects on the left. The road crosses Quaker Run (a creek that flows into Quaker Lake) and then forks. The left route takes you to the beach area, and the right to the newly built Cain Hollow Camping Area, a mile to the north.

As you continue your hike along ASP 3, you pass a small cluster of cabins in the woods well off the road; stands of pine and spruce grace both sides of the highway. In the next mile you pass Quaker Run Chapel on the right, cross over Quaker Run, and pass Camp 6 (a cluster of cabins) a short distance to your right.

An additional 0.7 mile brings you to the road leading to Camp 5 in the north; 0.3 mile more brings you to a road on your left that takes you to the park's maintenance area as well as to a cluster of cabins. To the left of these cabins is the trailhead of the 2.5-mile Three Sisters Trail, a loop that brings you back to this spot.

A few more steps brings you to the park's rental office on the left and the Quaker Inn and adjoining store on the right. An additional 0.4 mile takes you past ASP 1 on the left to Diehl Trail, which leads you back to your campsite.

Day Two (Mount Seneca–Stony Creek–ASP 3 Loop). Leave your campsite and head for ASP 3. Just before you reach the park highway, turn left (east) onto a camp road. A few steps brings you to the trailhead and signboard showing you the route over Mount Seneca. The park identifies this route as the Bear Caves–Mount Seneca Trail. This hike falls into what the park calls a "tough" climb, meaning that your total

vertical rise in the 4-mile hike is 900 feet—demanding, but not overly strenuous.

This region contains peaks named after the six nations of the Iroquois Confederacy. Mount Seneca is one of these; a mile to the north is Mount Onondaga, and a mile to the east is Mount Oneida. Several miles to the south is Mount Mohawk, and 1.5 miles to the west is Mount Cayuga. Several miles from the latter peak, in the northwest, is Mount Tuscarora.

The Bear Caves–Mount Seneca Trail (Trail 2 on the park map) begins to climb as soon as it enters the wooded area by the trailhead. It initially takes you into the edge of the camping area, but turns gradually away and to the right as you climb.

As you continue your ascent, the trail becomes steeper. From the trailhead, you hike 0.4 mile, then the trail levels a bit as you reach the top of the first knob. But once over the knob, the trail steepens more sharply for the next 0.2 mile, where you reach the summit of Mount Seneca (elevation 2,106 feet). Your vertical rise to this point is a respectable 700 feet, and the top of Mount Seneca provides a reward—a spectacular view to the north.

From here the trail takes you downhill in a southerly and then easterly direction for 0.8 mile, where you encounter a gully called Slide Hollow. Once across the footbridge, the trail heads uphill again, steeply at first, then less so. The trail curves around the hillside to reach a conglomerate rock ledge. You find two small caves near the top of this tall and elongated outcrop; the third cave is midway along the bottom. The whole outcrop is the Bear Caves section of this trail. The origin of this geological phenomenon is the same as that of the Thunder Rocks (see below) in this park and of Little Rock City in Rock City State Forest (see Hike 28).

Stay on the trail, which passes along the southern edge of the Bear Caves outcrop. The trail turns right and heads downhill; in 0.2 mile, you reach the hill's base and ASP 3.

Turn left on ASP 3, and walk east a little over 0.1 mile to where the FLT (North Country Trail or Trail 9, white blazes) crosses the highway and enters the woods on the highway's north side. This trail follows Stony Brook north for 4.6 miles, but the recommended portion of this hike goes only 2 miles; then you turn around and retrace your steps.

The Stony Brook section of the FLT is a most pleasant hiking route. It is relatively level and has only a few short uphill climbs as it heads north on the west side of the babbling, fast-flowing brook. Nonetheless, the trail does climb, if ever so gradually. The elevation at the trailhead is 1,612 feet, and at your turnaround point 2 miles north, the elevation is 1,900 feet, for a vertical rise of 288 feet.

Once on this trail inside the woods, you turn right and climb a small embankment, to bring you to a short road leading to a cabin. The trail continues past the cabin, following Stony Brook. At the 0.2-mile mark, the trail climbs 80 feet along the hillside, which drops steeply into a gully, through which Stony Brook flows.

The trail hugs the hillside for the next 0.8 mile, where the land becomes more level. After crossing two streamlets that feed into Stony Brook, the trail brings you to an abandoned foot-trail intersecting on the left and then to an open area stretching eastward from the brook. The trail now almost touches the edge of the brook; if you look closely along the trail, you may discover an abandoned foot-trail crossing the brook to intersect the trail you are walking.

This spot also is your turnaround point. Retrace your steps 2 miles to the highway where you started earlier. Turn right (west) and follow ASP 3 for 1.6 miles to the road that takes you back to the Diehl Tent and Trailer Area.

Day Three (Thunder Rocks Loop). This hike is worth a special effort to see an unusual rock outcrop called Thunder Rocks. This geological formation can be reached by a dirt road–highway loop, which is open to both vehicular and foot traffic; hiking is far more interesting and is the mode of travel I recommend.

To get to the loop, drive east from your campsite on ASP 3 for 6.5 miles, where ASP 2 intersects from the north. Turn onto ASP 2, and drive north for 1 mile, where you find a fork and an overlook on your right. Pull off the road and park here.

From this highpoint (elevation 2,160 feet), you have a fine view to the east. Look across the forested valley, to the headwaters of the east-flowing Limestone Brook; beyond the valley are peaked hills that on a sunny day are deep blue.

At the fork, the paved highway follows the left route; a single-lane dirt road goes to the right. Follow the dirt road as it heads uphill for 0.4 mile. There it flattens as it travels northeast on top of a ridge for 0.4 mile; then the road takes a shallow dip and continues north on the ridge and over a knoll for an additional mile. It then intersects another unnamed dirt road at one of the area's high spots (elevation 2,202 feet).

Cross the intersection and continue north over level terrain for 0.5 mile to a turnaround area. On your right, a few hundred feet uphill and into the woods are the rock outcrops of Thunder Rocks. Take a little time to wander about the tall rock conglomerates, and appreciate a geological manifestation seen only in a few other places in New York. If you brought a snack, enjoy a break in what may be called a "rock city."

Thunder Rocks are a cluster of tall, square boulders as tall as two-story houses. They were formed out of the conglomerate outcrop that was exposed by the erosion of the surrounding soil. As erosion continues to undermine its weak shale foundation, the massive conglomerate outcrop is slowly being carried downslope by soil creep. As this occurs the outcrop breaks into huge, joint-bounded blocks that look somewhat like "buildings," and narrow passages, or "streets," separate the blocks. More than a dozen such blocks form this "rock city"; walk through it for a closer inspection.

Once you have completed your tour of Thunder Rocks, retrace your steps to the intersection, and turn right on the unnamed dirt road. This road takes you downhill, gradually at first, then more steeply, for 0.7 mile, where the road turns right. From here the descent is not so steep; 0.5 mile brings you to the highway, ASP 2.

Turn right, and walk north a short distance to where a dirt road intersects on the left. Then turn west onto the dirt road called France Brook Road for a short distance, to where the road crosses a stream. This is the north-flowing Red House Brook, which empties into Red House Lake 5 miles north of here.

You can add 2 miles to your hike by taking a side trip to Camp Arrowhead, a cluster of rentable cabins. To do so, continue west on France Brook Road for a little over 0.1 mile, to where another unnamed road intersects on the right. Turn here, and walk north to the single-lane road under a canopy of trees. This is not only an attractive route, but on a hot, sunny day, it is a very cool walk.

In the next 0.8 mile of flat walking, you parallel Red House Creek on the right and cross two streamlets that feed into the creek. At the 0.8-mile mark, the forest recedes, giving way to a large open area resembling a field. On your left is a semicircle of cabins.

Follow the road past the cabins, to where it ends at a footbridge over Red House Creek. Cross the bridge and continue east across the open area to the park's highway, ASP 2.

Turn right on ASP 2 and head south; 0.7 mile brings you over level land to the intersection with France Brook Road (the one you walked earlier). Continue south on ASP 2 for an additional 0.6 mile, to where a streamlet crosses under the highway. At this point (elevation 1,740 feet), the terrain gradually pitches upward. Over the next 1.4 miles, the uphill climb becomes a little steeper. When you reach the overlook (elevation 2,160 feet) and your parked vehicle, the vertical rise has been 420 feet—a respectable climb.

From here you can return to your campsite to conclude your three-day outing in the Quaker Lake Area. You may also wish to visit and hike the Red House Area (see Hike 36); it, too, offers a number of hiking routes.

Allegany State Park (Red House Lake Area)

Total hiking distance: 16.1 miles (3 days)
Total hiking time: 9 hours
Vertical rise: 2,288 feet
Maps: USGS 7½' Red House; USGS 7½' Limestone;
  Allegany State Park Map

The Red House Lake Area is located in the north-central part of 62,000-acre Allegany State Park, the largest park in New York. The park is well endowed with recreational facilities to satisfy all tastes. Surrounding 110-acre Red House Lake are tennis courts, a swimming and beach area, picnic areas, bike trails, a boat-rental site, seven camping areas with cabins, and a large tent and trailer area.

Fine hiking trails radiate from the Red House Lake Area. Four of these are loop trails that return you to the trailhead where you start. A fifth trail, in the Bova area, ties into a network of ski touring trails (excellent hiking trails in summer); and a loop trail can be formed by combining two ski-touring trails in this section of the park.

The Red House Lake Area is one of three major recreational areas in Allegany State Park; the others are the Cain Hollow Camping Area and the Quaker Lake Area; both are located in the park's southwestern section. In the Quaker Lake Area are five named, groomed, and marked hiking trails (see Hike 35).

Red House Lake is the smaller and older of the park's two man-made impoundments; it is 0.7 mile long and 0.6 mile wide—big enough, however, to allow you to fish for rainbow and brown trout without feeling crowded by boaters.

The Red House Lake Area is only a couple of miles southwest of the park's Art Roscoe Ski Touring Area, which contains six individually named ski-touring trails, totaling almost 30 miles, all of which can be used for hiking during spring, summer, and fall. The hiking trails, in turn, range from 2 to 6.5 miles. When all the park's trails are combined, they total 135.5 miles of walking routes—including 53.5 miles of groomed hiking trails, 27 miles of ski-touring trails, and 55 miles of snowmobile or horseback trails.

When you hike in Allegany State Park you become part of the cultural and natural history of this area. The park's varied cultural history includes the legacy of the Erie, Susquehanna, and Seneca Indian nations, which occupied this part of Western New York for hundreds of years before the coming of the white man. The Senecas, called the "Keepers of the Western Door," were part of the Iroquois Confederacy. Today the Seneca Indian Reservation partially encircles the state park. In the reservation's northern portion is Salamanca, the only city in the United

States located wholly in an Indian reservation.

During the nineteenth and early twentieth centuries, the land that today makes up the state park was homesteaded by those who hoped to farm the land—a largely unfulfilled aspiration, because of the land's rugged terrain. But a community of the Society of Friends, better known as Quakers, managed to settle here; and it is in memory of this community that the Quaker camping area and Quaker Lake were named.

The origin of Red House is also an interesting bit of history. Red House is believed to have taken its name from a small Indian community located on the south side of Allegheny River; this community was named after a house with a door painted red by its Indian owner.

For a period of ten years, ending in 1930, the Ferndale School, an educational institution for African-Americans, operated within the park boundary. But only the overgrown foundation of the school building remains today. The state park was established with 7,000 acres of land by legislative act in 1921.

The most attractive structure in the Red House Lake Area is the three-story Tudor-style administration building. It was built in 1928 with hand-hewn timbers, greystone brick, and stucco. Today it houses the rental, park police, business offices, museum, restaurant, and gift shop.

Man-made Red House Lake was constructed between 1929 and 1930. Besides swimming, boating, and fishing during the warm months, ice skating is permitted in winter. Eighty of the 144 cabins in Red House are winterized, allowing year-round use. Campsites are available from April 1 to December 15.

There also is a lot of history underfoot. The Allegany State Park region is the only part of the state that has strata of Mississippian and Pennsylvanian bedrock, laid down over 325 million years ago.

The region is rich in oil, the production of which contributes more than $55 million to the state's economy. Oil and gas wells are located in the state park and throughout the southwestern part of New York. Some of these wells are dry, but there are enough active wells to add a substantial amount to the state's income. Oil was discovered in New York in 1627 at a spot that today is called Seneca Oil Spring; the "burning spring" was originally located on the southern edge of Cuba Lake. The first oil well in New York was drilled in 1865, near the village of Limestone at the southeastern edge of the state park. Most of the natural gas wells are active, and those that are not have been used to store gas imported from other states. The oil comes from the permeable sandstone in the late Devonian Conneaut and Canadaway group.

In this region, too, are conglomerate rock beds of the late Devonian Conewango group, the Mississippian Pocono group, and Pennsylvania Pottsville group. Out of these groups "rock cities" rise—clusters of large stones formed when the conglomerate beds break into huge, joint-bounded blocks carried downslope by erosion and soil creep. In the state park, such conglomerate outcrops are located at Bear Caves on the Seneca Trail and at Thunder Rocks in the southern half of the park (see Hike 35).

The park is also unique in having escaped the bulldozing effects of the Wisconsin glacier. During the Pleistocene Era or Ice Age that began two million years ago, four major glacial advances and retreats occurred. In the last advance, the Wisconsin glacier, a mile-high ice sheet, covered all of New York except the land that now makes up Allegany State Park. The park's preglacial landscape displays a more rugged terrain and more angular-shaped hilltops than that of the rest of Central and Western New York. This park is the most northerly region of unglaciated terrain in eastern North America.

Virtually the entire state park is thickly wooded, giving it a wilderness appearance. The park lies in a transition zone, where mixed oak-hickory forests and northern hardwoods are both evident.

Trees growing on the park's east- and south-facing slopes are typical of the northern hardwoods: American beech, red and sugar maple, and black and yellow birch; also found on these slopes are Eastern hemlock, white pine, quaking and big-tooth aspen, black cherry, and white ash. Trees found on the south- and west-facing slopes include such southern species as white, red, and black oak; chestnut and pine oak; shagbark, bitternut, and pignut hickory; and cucumber trees and tulip trees of the magnolia family.

More than 160 species of birds are found in the park's forests and lakes. Commonly seen waterfowl include mallard, wood duck, blue-winged teal, American coot, common gallinule, horned grebe, hooded merganser, greater scaup, double-crested cormorant, great blue heron, and even the whistling swan. Among the predator birds are barred owl, screech owl, great horned owl, barn owl, goshawk, broadwinged hawk, Cooper's hawk, red-shouldered hawk, red-tailed hawk, rough-legged hawk, sharp-shinned hawk, and turkey vulture. Game birds include wild turkey, ruffed grouse, and ring-necked pheasant.

The park also contains white-tailed deer, black bear, opossum, beaver, muskrat, cottontail rabbit, raccoon, woodchuck, long-tailed weasel, porcu-

pine, striped skunk, gray and red fox, and red, gray, and flying squirrel.

The timber rattlesnake also makes a home here. This snake is shy and is usually found in rock crevices and thick underbrush, locations not usually frequented by humans. But in late spring and late fall, the rattler, like other snakes, comes out to warm its body—a time when most sightings are reported. Among the nonpoisonous snakes in the park are the rat snake, northern water snake, brown snake, and common garter snake.

It takes several days to become familiar with the Red House Lake Area and its hiking trails. A three-day weekend is ideal, allowing you to hike all or most of the marked trails in the area. For a weekend stay, you can pitch a tent in the Red House Tent and Trailer Area, which can serve as your base camp. This camping and tenting area is located 0.5 mile south of Red House Lake on the west side of the park highway, ASP 1; a general store is situated across from the tent and trailer area.

Hiking trails radiate from all sides of the lake. On the north side is Osgood Trail (Trail 7 on the park map), a loop trail that runs 2.5 miles. On the south side is the 6.5-mile Beehunter Trail (Trail 6 on the park map). On the west side are two trails—the 2-mile Red Jacket Trail (Trail 8), which also serves as self-guided nature trail, and the 4-mile Conservation Trail (Trail 10); the trailheads for both are found together behind the administration building.

A mile east of Red House Lake is the Bova Area and the trailhead to the Patterson Ski-Touring Trail (Trail 11), which is a fine route for summer hiking. By combining Patterson with another ski-touring route, Snowsnake Run Trail (Trail 18), you can hike a 5.6-mile loop over some of the ground that cross-country

skiers use in winter.

Seven Nordic ski trails are found in the park's Art Roscoe Ski Touring Area, the south end of which is only a mile east of Red House Lake. The starting point of all theses trails is at an intersection on the park's highway, ASP 1, leading into the Summit Cabin Area. At the intersection is a skier's warming hut and check-in point. From here, the Nordic trails run to the north, east, and south.

The park's hiking trails are marked with large round blue-metal discs that depict the silhouette of a hiker. Markers for the ski-touring trails are orange discs with a silhouetted skier.

At each hiking trailhead is a signboard with an encased topographical map (USGS 7.5-minute series), on which the trail is marked in black ink.

Access. Allegany State Park can be reached from the east or west by the Southern Tier Expressway (NY 17) and from the north (Buffalo–Niagara Falls area) via US 219. Exit the Expressway at Exit 21, and follow the signs south to the park. Those coming south on US 219, follow the route through Salamanca, across the Allegheny River, and past the Expressway's Exit 21; then follow the signs directing you to the park's entrance.

Inside the park boundary, the route signs change to ASP 1; follow this route south 1.5 miles to the entrance booth. From here, it is 4.5 miles to the intersection with ASP 2 at the northern tip of Red House Lake. Continue south to the administration building on ASP 1 to register for a tenting site in the tent and trailer area. From the administration building, drive south on ASP 1 for another 0.5 mile to the entrance to the tent and trailer area and your tenting site.

Trails. From your base camp, it is a short walk to the various trailheads around Red House Lake. The Bova Area and the trailhead for Patterson Trail are the farthest away.

The recommended hiking routes are the Conservation Trail (Trail 10), 4 miles; Beehunter Trail (Trail 6), 6.5 miles; and the Patterson and Snowsnake Run Trails (Trails 11 and 18), 5.6 miles. During a three-day stay, you can hike one of these each day.

Day One (Conservation Trail). From your campsite at the tent and trailer area, it is 0.6 mile to the park's administration building. Walk to the back of the building and up a short flight of stone stairs to a path. A short distance on the path brings you to the intersection of two trails. Maps on the signboards identify the two trails. The one to the right is the short Red Jacket Trail (Trail 8), and the one to the left, which immediately heads into a wooded area, is the Conservation Trail (Trail 10).

Take this route; it is marked with blue-metal discs and blue blazes. The Conservation Trail is all uphill.

Walk uphill from the intersection behind the administration building. In a few hundred yards, you encounter a new water control structure. Stay on the upper side of the cleared area. The trail now heads uphill in a southwesterly direction, becoming steeper. At the 0.8-mile mark, the trail levels somewhat as you cross a knoll. From here, it is a gradual ascent for the next 0.3 mile, where a snowmobile trail intersects on the right; this at one time was part of Trail 9. (Now the snowmobile trail runs north into a valley, finally emerging near the Red House entrance booth.)

Continue on the Conservation Trail; the climb becomes steeper for the next 0.2 mile. At 1.5 miles, the trail forks into two routes. Both are part of Conservation Trail. Each route brings you in 0.7 mile to intersections with the white-blazed Finger Lakes Trail (Trail 9; also identified as North Country Trail).

Take the route on your right; this part of the Conservation Trail is marked with orange blazes and blue-metal discs. The trail follows a gradual uphill course for the next 0.4 mile, where the forested terrain flattens; an additional 0.3 mile takes you to an intersection with the FLT.

Turn left (south) onto the FLT. From here it is a steady and steep climb for the next 0.2 mile to the summit of an unnamed hill with an elevation of 2,174 feet, the trail's highest spot. The vertical rise from your starting point (elevation 1,460 feet) to here is 774 feet—a fair climb.

The FLT now heads downhill, fairly steeply at first, then more gradually for 0.3 mile, where you encounter a log lean-to at an intersection. The right route is the continuation of the FLT, while the left puts you on the blue-blazed east branch of the Conservation Trail.

Turn left onto the latter, and in a short distance, you cross an old wooden footbridge. After a short but gradual climb, the trail becomes level as it runs on top of a ridge for 0.4 mile; here you start a gradual descent.

It is now a short distance downhill to the intersection you encountered before when you turned onto the west branch of the Conservation Trail. From here you merely retrace your steps 1.5 miles to the rear of the administration building and back to your campsite.

Day Two (Beehunter Trail). Leave your campsite for the park's highway, ASP 1. Follow it north to the intersection with ASP 2A at the southwest corner of Red House Lake. Turn right onto ASP 2A, and walk east along the lake's southern shore for 0.4 mile to the first Beehunter trailhead, just south of the highway; this will be your exit point when you com-

plete the hiking loop. Continue east for an additional 0.1 mile, where you come to the second Beehunter trailhead, also located south of the highway. Although you can begin your hike at either trailhead, the second one puts you on an easier route; its initial climb is less demanding.

The park classifies this trail as intermediate in difficulty and hence not as rugged as the Conservation Trail you just completed. Nonetheless, there is climbing on this trail, and some of the ascents demand a fair effort.

At the start, you cross a level, open area with playfields on your left. In 0.2 mile, the trail crosses Beehunter Creek and then heads slightly to the left as it starts a gradual climb to the Beehunter Cabin Area. Here it crosses the area's loop road to a signboard with a topographical map showing the direction of the Beehunter Trail.

The trail now heads east, steeply uphill, crosses a small open area, and then enters into a forested area covering the steep hillside. From here it is a fairly demanding climb for the next 0.2 mile, where the trail turns to the left and becomes more level.

From this point, the trail follows a half-circle route and then heads south, continuing its ascent but more gradually. An additional 0.4 mile brings you to the crest of a knob, one of the area's high spots (elevation 2,010 feet).

Your hike continues now on top of a long ridge for the next 0.8 mile, where the terrain suddenly becomes more rugged. From here, the climb becomes steeper as you work your way up the hillside for the next 0.3 mile. The vertical rise over this distance is 240 feet. You cross from one knob onto another, higher ridge, which allows level walking for the next 0.3 mile.

The trail now makes a short but steep

descent before leveling as it curves around the side of a peaked hill. This half-circle route brings you around the base of the hill and heads you in a northerly direction. You are now at the halfway point; from here, the trail heads north in the direction of Red House Lake.

After running 0.2 miles due north, the trail turns slightly to the left and heads gradually downhill. An additional 0.3 mile brings you to a place where an abandoned foot-trail crosses the Beehunter Trail. From here the descent is steeper as you enter a narrow valley, through which flows one of the headwater branches of Beehunter Creek.

Once over the creek, you come in 0.1 mile to a second abandoned foot-trail, which also crosses the Beehunter Trail. From here you gradually climb for 0.2 mile, where you encounter a gully. Through it flows the second branch of Beehunter Creek.

The trail now climbs steeply. In 0.4 mile you reach a knob (elevation 1,958 feet). From here the land pitches downward. The descent is gradual at first, then becomes steeper for the next 1.2 miles, where you reach the hill's base and the park's highway, ASP 2A, the spot you passed en route to your starting point. From here you can return via ASP 2A and then by ASP 1 to your campsite.

Day Three (Patterson–Snowsnake Run Loop). From your campsite, it is 2.4 miles to the Bova Area, where there is a cluster of cabins (Camp 8). You can either drive or walk to the trailhead. Either way, leave your campsite for ASP 1, and follow it north to the intersection with ASP 2A at the southwestern edge of Red House Lake. Follow ASP 2A around the lake's southern shore, to where you intersect ASP 2. Turn right onto ASP 2; 0.5 mile brings you to where a dirt road

intersects on the left. Turn here, and follow the dirt road 0.6 mile to its end.

Here are the signboard and trailhead to Patterson Trail. The signboard shows you the route of this ski-touring trail, which takes you north into a network of Nordic ski trails (the Art Roscoe Ski Touring Area). All are ideal hiking trails during the warm months.

From the Bova Area, the Patterson Trail follows a moderate uphill route over what was formerly a narrow-gauge railroad bed. The markers on this trail are orange discs with a skier in black. From the trailhead, this route enters the woods and starts a gradual climb. At the 0.3-mile mark, an abandoned walking trail intersects on the left. The Patterson Trail continues a short distance, where it dips to cross one of several streamlets found in this sector, all of which drain into Bova Creek.

Once over the streamlet, the trail becomes steeper for a short distance until it comes to a fork. The right leg is the southern portion of another ski-touring trail, Ridge Run Trail, which ends here, while the left leg is the continuation of Patterson Trail.

Follow the latter trail north; at the 0.8-mile mark, it crosses a second streamlet feeding Bova Creek. Just beyond the streamlet, Snowsnake Run Trail intersects on the left; this is the spot where you will come out on your return loop.

Continue north on Patterson Trail, which now follows a level grade alongside the hill for the next 0.8 mile. Here an old abandoned foot-trail angles off to the right. A short distance farther on Patterson Trail brings you to a dip over another streamlet.

The trail now heads uphill for a short distance, then levels as it follows the side of the hill for the next 0.3 mile. There it crosses still another feeder stream.

The trail's upward pitch now becomes more pronounced, and in the next 0.2 mile, your vertical rise is 200 feet. Here you encounter an intersection where Patterson Trail meets the Ridge Run Trail on the right (north) and Snowsnake Run Trail on the left (south).

Patterson Trail continues straight ahead for a little over 0.1 mile, where it intersects the park's highway, ASP 1. Across the highway is a large parking area, a warming house for Nordic skiers, and a skier's check-in point. Reverse direction, and return to where the three trails intersect.

Turn right onto the Snowsnake Run Trail, which heads south and uphill. The climb is a fair one, with a vertical rise of 200 feet before the trail loops north on level ground. At the 0.6-mile mark, the trail loops again, heading south on a level stretch alongside a steep hill that pitches downward on the left. The trail continues on this level course for 0.8 mile, where again it loops north, still on level ground. In another 0.4 mile, the trail gradually turns in a westerly and then southwesterly direction. From here, it is 0.4 mile to where the trail starts a steep descent and turns, one more time, in a northerly direction.

In a little over 0.2 mile, the trail crosses a streamlet that flows south to feed into Bova Creek, a mile south. At this point the trail is actually running parallel to its earlier route, except at a lower level, as it travels first southeast and then due north for a mile, then loops one more time south.

From the top of this loop, the trail heads downhill, steeply at first for 0.2 mile, then on more level terrain for 0.3 mile, and finally gradually downhill for an additional 0.2 mile, where it turns left.

It now crosses a feeder stream flowing into Bova Creek. Then it climbs uphill for 0.2 mile, where it intersects the Patterson Trail at the point you passed earlier. It is now just a matter of retracing your steps south on Patterson Trail to the Bova Area. From here, it is 2.4 miles back to your campsite to conclude your three-day visit to the Red House Lake Area.

Southwestern Region:
Allegany County

37

Bully Hill State Forest

Hiking distance: 7.6 miles
Hiking time: 4½ hours
Vertical rise: 1,250 feet
Map: USGS 7½' Alfred

"Bully Hill" appears to have been a popular name for hills in upstate New York. Another hill with the same name is located on the west side of Keuka Lake in the Finger Lakes Region; from a vineyard there comes a regionally known wine that bears the hill's name. But Bully Hill State Forest encompasses 3,512 acres of forest-covered state land in Western New York. One of the larger parcels of state forestland, it covers much of east-central Allegany County.

This elongated, thickly wooded state forest occupies the highland that rises between the Canisteo River and Karr Valley Creek. The land culminates in three unnamed hills. One of these peaks has an elevation of 2,203 feet; the second rounds off at 2,167 feet, and the third at 2,038 feet.

A groomed, well-marked footpath runs from one end of the state forest to the other. This trail is part of the white-blazed Finger Lakes Trail (FLT). It passes over the southern slope of the first peak and over the top of the third. Bully Hill's portion of the FLT treats you to a varied landscape—steep slopes, forested hills, narrow valleys, deep gullies, and numerous small streams and creeks. The state forest also contains a network of dirt roads and state-maintained truck trails, some of which are part of the FLT.

Access. From the north or south, take NY 36; from east or west, take the Southern Tier Expressway to Exit 34 and drive north on NY 36 for 2 miles into Arkport. In the village, North Almond Valley Road (County Route 67) intersects from the west. Turn onto North Almond Valley Road, and drive west 5.6 miles. A dirt road that intersects on the left (south) is Bush Road, which from the paved road runs straight south past several buildings on the right. Turn onto Bush Road, and cross the Canisteo River. Continue south over flat, open land. En route you see white blazes on the trees along the road, indicating that this is the route of the Finger Lakes Trail, coming from the north.

From the highway, it is 0.4 mile on Bush Road to the edge of the wooded area on the left side of the road, the northern boundary of Bully Hill State Forest. Park here.

Trail. Follow the Finger Lakes Trail, which uses the beginning part of Bush Road on its route south. At 0.1 mile, the FLT turns left into the forest and heads straight uphill in a steep climb for the next 0.2 mile. Then it begins to level off

Among the trees in Bully Hill State Forest

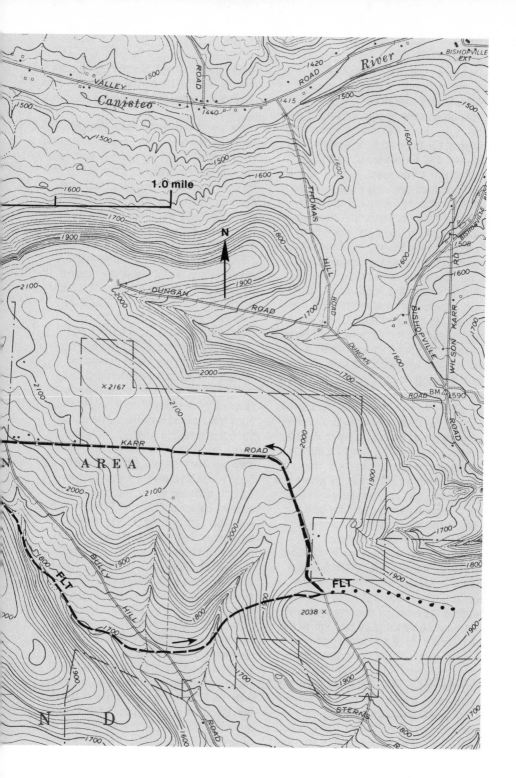

as it follows the slope of the hill. On the left, the trail overlooks a gully through which flows a streamlet.

It soon crosses this streamlet 0.6 mile from Bush Road and climbs steeply for the next 1.5 miles up a vertical rise of 160 feet. The terrain levels and in another 0.1 mile you reach a truck trail. The FLT turns right onto this truck trail and follows it straight south and gradually uphill for 0.2 mile. There the truck trail bends slightly to the right, continuing south on level ground for 0.4 mile. It now bends to the left and, in a short distance, intersects another dirt road. (On the USGS map, this road, which forms a loop, appears to have two names; the western leg is called Mike Dixon Road and the eastern leg Andrew Ferry Road.)

At the intersection there is also a jeep trail heading west and the Mike Dixon Road heading south. On your return trip, you'll be taking the jeep trail. Take the FLT's left turn on the road and continue along its route straight east for 0.5 mile, where the road turns sharply to the south and becomes Andrew Ferry Road. En route from the intersection, you make a gradual climb for 0.25 mile, to where the road levels. You now are nearly at the top; a short distance north through the forest is the area's highest spot, a knob with an elevation of 2,203 feet.

Finally, at the 0.5-mile mark from the earlier intersection, the FLT leaves the road and heads straight east into the forest. At first, the downhill route is gradual, but then the descent becomes steeper as it enters another gully through which the headwaters of a feeder stream flow south to eventually reach Karr Valley Creek. Here you meet still another road, Bully Hill Road, which, coming from the south, forms a loop and then turns south to intersect Andrew Ferry Road.

At the road's loop, the FLT turns south to follow a route that runs alongside the feeder stream that flows through a narrow ravine. The hill on the west side is extremely steep; the one on the east less so.

The vertical drop en route through the ravine is 310 feet, to the point where the FLT turns left away from the stream to cross first a streamlet and then Bully Hill Road at an intersection of a truck trail heading north. The FLT continues east of Bully Hill Road along the side of a hill for 2.5 miles, where it crosses still another gully and feeder stream.

From here the climb for the next 0.4 mile is steep, and it becomes steeper as you near the top, the forest's third highest hill, with an elevation of 2,038 feet.

At the top, the FLT levels and in a short distance intersects a truck trail. This is your turning point. The FLT crosses the dirt road and continues eastward. You, however, turn left onto the truck trail and head north over level terrain for the next 0.7 mile, where the truck trail, called Karr Road, bends to the left and heads west.

The terrain here is quite level, rising only gradually as you proceed westward. Soon Karr Road meets a dirt road intersecting from the south, the one you passed earlier at Bully Hill Road. You are now approaching the southern slope of the second-highest hill of the state forest; its elongated knob, at 2,167 feet, lies 0.2 mile north of Karr Road. From this point, the road heads downhill past private property and houses on your right; the left side is still state forest.

The point where Karr Road reenters the state forest is also the spot where it intersects the northern loop of Bully Hill Road; a short distance on the Bully Hill Road loop brings you to the intersection with the FLT on the part you walked earlier. Continue west on the FLT through the forest for 0.3 mile, to the intersection of Andrew Ferry Road cominig from the south. The road and the FLT now run west for 0.5 mile over the same route you walked earlier to the junction of Mike Dixon Road, the truck trail, and the jeep trail.

Follow the jeep trail west as it gradually climbs uphill and then descends abruptly. From the last junction it is 0.7 mile by the jeep trail to Bush Road. Turn right (north) here, and follow Bush Road downhill for 0.8 mile to your parked vehicle.

38

Slader Creek State Forest

Hiking distance: 6.2 miles
Hiking time: 3½ hours
Vertical rise: 436 feet
Map: USGS 7½' Canaseraga

Slader Creek State Forest is located on top of a sizable hill. In fact, you have to engage in some hill climbing, or what the British call "fells walking," to get to the state forest. At the northeastern edge of the state forest are two hills side by side, North Hill (elevation 1,850 feet) and Miller Hill (elevation 1,980 feet). The highest spot in Slader Creek State Forest is a hill with an elevation of 2,080 feet. The highest hill in this highland area has an elevation of 2,140 feet.

An unusual feature of this state forest is its natural ponds, impoundments, and wetland areas. These are located not in the valleys below but, somewhat surprisingly, on one of the highest spots in the region. The water accumulates here because the top of the hill contains a large, level area with several shallow depressions. Moreover, the bedrock is so close to the surface that the water cannot seep into the ground. The result is a clutter of 20 ponds, some natural, some man-made, some quite small, others of fair size, scattered over the two-mile-wide level top of the hill.

Slader Creek originates in this flat hilltop and can be located by the hiker quite easily. The hill is a natural geographic divide as streamlets rush from some of these ponds and wetlands, through gullies, on their way down the hill, draining to the north and south. The waters that drain northward become the headwaters of Slader Creek. This creek flows north downhill, turns east, follows a narrow valley for some distance, then turns north again and eventually empties into Canaseraga Creek.

To the north of the divide is the 1,132-acre Slader Creek State Forest; to the south is the 2,612-acre Klipnocky State Forest (see Hike 39). There are no distinguishing markers to tell you where the Slader Creek forest begins and Klipnocky ends, so the drainage divide serves as a rough approximation.

One way to reach Slader Creek State Forest is by way of the Finger Lakes Trail (FLT), which passes through the state forest. The FLT approaches from the north, following NY 70 through the hamlet of Garwoods. There it turns into a straight southerly route to Slader Creek State Forest.

The FLT takes you past several ponds and impoundments. The white-blazed trail can be combined with several of the dirt roads to allow you to cover a good portion of the state forest and observe several of the features of this area.

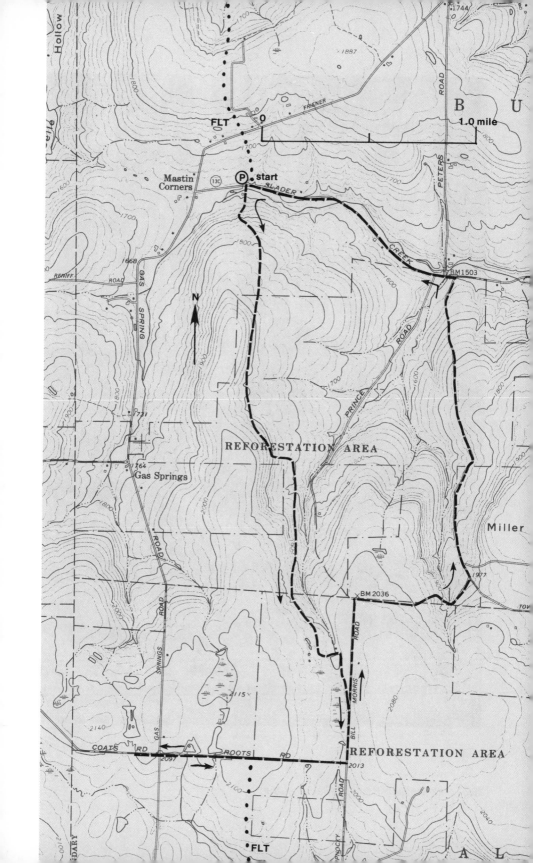

Hikers in Slader Creek State Forest

Access. Your starting point lies north of the state forest on Slader Creek Road, which runs parallel to Slader Creek through a narrow valley about 2 miles south of the village of Canaseraga. The village is located in the northeastern corner of Allegany County on NY 70, about 8 miles north of Arkport and 9 miles north of Exit 34 of the Southern Tier Expressway (NY 17); this exit is about halfway between Arkport and Hornell.

In the center of Canaseraga you find County Route 13, also called South Valley Road, intersecting NY 70 from the south. Turn onto South Valley Road (County Route 13) and drive south 1.4 miles to the second intersection on your right (west). This is Slader Creek Road (County Route 13C). Turn west and follow Slader Creek Road for 3.2 miles where the north-south Finger Lakes Trail crosses the road. Look for the white blazes, which take you to an iron gate and a small unpainted barn building on the south side of the road. This is your trailhead. Park here.

Trail. Your hike begins at an elevation of 1,580 feet and takes you across Slader Creek, over open fields, and immediately uphill. Once over the creek and past the farm building, you begin a fairly steep ascent, which as you advance becomes more gradual. Ahead of you is the edge of the forest, the northern boundary of Slader Creek State Forest.

From your starting point, it is 0.5 mile to the forest's edge. As you enter the forest, the trail levels off considerably at an elevation of 1,900 feet as you follow along the side of the hill for 0.7 mile. Then the trail turns east and makes a short but steep descent before turning south again. You are now in a small valley; soon you come upon a small feeder stream flowing down the hillside. The trail continues uphill alongside the

stream for a mile where the land levels. Here the trail turns sharply to the left (east) and crosses a dam that impounds a small pond, the source of the feeder stream you encountered earlier.

You now have arrived at the hill's large, level area, and a score of ponds and impoundments lie within a mile of where you are walking. The elevation here is 2,020 feet, which means you have climbed the vertical distance of 440 feet from your starting point.

Past the pond, the trail turns south again, and in a few steps you emerge from the forest onto a dirt road, called, rather strangely, Bill Morris Road. Follow this road south, and in 0.1 mile you pass a sizable pond on your right (west). An additional 0.1 mile brings you to a much smaller pond and to Roots Road intersecting from the right (west). At this point you have passed over the hill's divide; now the water drains to the south.

Walking west on Roots Road for 0.7 mile, you come upon two more impoundments, all draining to the south. Just north of the larger pond, however, is a wetland area that sits on the divide and drains both to the north and the south. About 0.3 mile farther west, just past Gas Spring Road, is one of the larger ponds in the area. This one drains north and, like the wetland, feeds Slader Creek. You have now identified the main sources of Slader Creek. Turn around and return to Bill Morris Road.

Back on Bill Morris Road, you can follow the road northward to begin your return. This route takes you back to your starting point via several dirt roads, which generally are well shaded on a sunny day. From the intersection with the Finger Lakes Trail, it is 0.3 mile to a sharp turn in the road; follow this road east. It runs downhill gradually at first, and then more steeply in about 0.3 mile as it eventually crosses the upper reaches of still another streamlet, which, too, flows into Slader Creek at the bottom of the hill.

The road now turns to the left and goes uphill, turning gradually southwest, where it serves as a boundary line for the state forest on the left. On the east side, the land rises to form Miller Hill. The road runs alongside Miller Hill as it descends for the next mile.

The descent becomes more pronounced as the road passes through a large stand of white pines. Soon the road intersects Slader Creek Road at the hill's bottom. Turn left here, and proceed west on Slader Creek Road for 1.2 miles to your parked vehicle.

Klipnocky State Forest

Hiking distance: 6 miles
Hiking time: 4 hours
Vertical rise: 1,064 feet
Map: USGS 7½' Alfred; USGS 7½' Canaseraga

Klipnocky State Forest meets its next of kin, Slader Creek State Forest (see Hike 38), at the highest spot in this part of the Cattaraugus Hill Region. The two contiguous state forests abut each other without any discerniable features to separate one from the other; without a properly marked topographical map, it is impossible to tell where the two meet.

But no matter. When you reach the summit of this huge highland area, you meet conditions that are not customary for the top of a hill—small ponds, large impoundments, marshy areas, and a swampy section—all of which feed a score of streamlets that run off the hilltop in all directions.

These ponds and wetlands are found at the impressive elevation of 2,125 feet. But why all this water here, of all places? For several reasons: This portion of the hill is flattened out and is even slightly depressed, so it acts as a shallow, saucerlike collecting area. The slow seepage from the ground collects there because the bedrock lies so close to the surface and prevents the water from soaking into the earth.

The result is a cluster of 20 ponds and impoundments where Klipnocky State Forest and Slader Creek State Forest

merge. This meeting place amounts to a natural divide; drainage from the many bodies of water flows downhill from here—to the north to Slader Creek, and to the south into the Canisteo River.

The highest spot (elevation 2,145 feet) is in the western section of Klipnocky State Forest. This unnamed high spot is really a flat, tree-covered area that provides no spectacular peaked summit.

Passing close by this high spot is a dirt road with the unusual name of Gas Spring Road. This tells you something else about the region—it contains a score of gas wells. The wellheads are enclosed with a large blue-painted housing—very conspicuous when first seen, especially in a nearby tract called, not surprisingly, Gas Spring State Forest.

Still another of Klipnocky's attractions is the groomed, well-marked section of the Finger Lakes Trail (FLT), which runs the entire length of the state forest. The section of the trail in Klipnocky runs south from Slader Creek State Forest by way of the hamlets of Swain and Garwoods next to NY 70 through to Bully Hill State Forest (see Hike 37) and eastward beyond the town of Hornell.

To hike Klipnocky, you make use not only of the hiking trail but of several

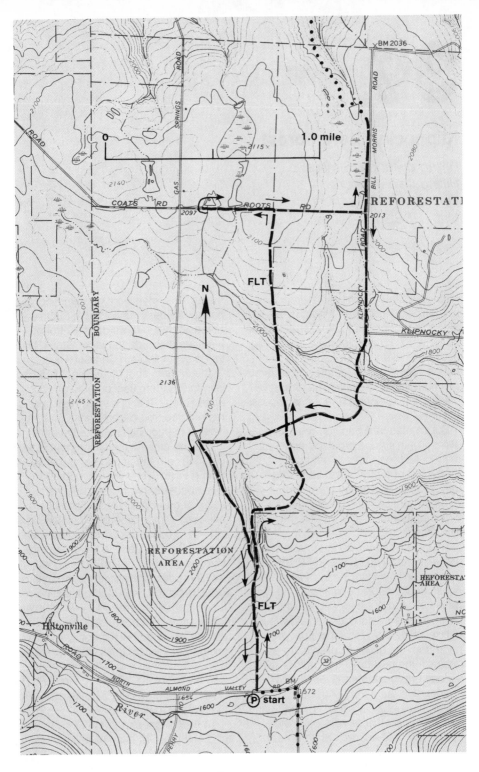

truck trails to form a nice loop. This allows a good view of the hill's flora and a good feel of the changing terrain.

Access. Klipnocky State Forest is most easily reached from Arkport, which lies about 4 miles north of Hornell and 1.5 miles north of the Southern Tier Expressway (NY 17). Get off the Expressway at Exit 34, and drive north to Arkport. In Arkport, you pick up Steuben County Route 67 going west; this route changes to Allegany County Route 32 once you cross the county line. Another name for this route is North Almond Valley Road, but when it reaches the Bush Road intersection near your starting point, the name changes to Hiltonville Road.

From Arkport, it is 8 miles to Bush Road, intersecting from the south; an additional 0.2 mile on Hiltonville Road brings you to Gas Spring Road intersecting from the north. Park here.

Trail. At this intersection, white blazes mark the portion of the Finger Lakes Trail that runs south on Gas Spring Road to Hiltonville Road, where it turns east to reach Bush Road, then south on Bush Road to reach Bully Hill State Forest.

Your hiking route is northward and uphill on Gas Spring Road. From your vehicle, which is parked at an elevation of 1,572 feet, to the high spot in Klipnocky State Forest, at elevation 2,145 feet, is a rise of 573 feet. The uphill climb to the top of the state forest is demanding!

From your starting point, 0.3 mile brings you to the southern boundary of Klipnocky State Forest; it is on the left (west) side of the road. An additional 0.4 mile brings you to the state forest's right (east) side boundary; you now are fully in Klipnocky State Forest.

At this point the FLT veers to the right, leaving the road as it enters into the forest and follows the state forest boundary northward.

The trail parallels the boundary line for about 0.1 mile. Then it continues uphill through the forest and turns sharply to the right (east) and again follows the boundary line for a little over 0.1 mile. Here the trail turns gradually northward; an additional 0.2 mile brings you finally to more level terrain, which continues to flatten as you approach and cross an unnamed dirt forestry road. From your starting point, you now have come 2.2 miles.

Cross the road, and continue north on the hiking trail for 0.3 mile. You begin a short but steep descent into a gully. You cross a streamlet that drains from several ponds to the north and higher elevations.

Once over the streamlet, the trail ascends once again, climbing fairly steeply at first, then more gradually. You cover the next 0.6 mile to reach another level area and a road running east-west. This is Klipnocky Road, but in a most confusing fashion, several sections here have been given other names. The one you intersected from the hiking trail is called Roots Road; farther west, another section is called Coats Road, and just beyond that section, it again is called Klipnocky Road.

If you turn left (west) on Roots Road, 0.3 mile brings you to two impoundments, north of and just next to the road; the first one is fairly large, the second smaller. Both drain south into the streamlet you crossed a half-mile back. You have now reached the hilltop's level area, where all the ponds and wetlands are found.

Retrace your steps to where the hiking trail intersects the road; from this point, continue eastward on Roots Road, which is also the FLT route. Follow the white blazes, and after 0.4 mile, you come to an intersection with another dirt road. To add to the confusion, the section running south is called Klipnocky Road and the section running north is called Bill Morris Road.

Walk north on Bill Morris Road for 0.2 mile. Here you find two more impoundments; the first is quite small, and the second is very large. Retrace your steps to the dirt road intersection, and head south on what is now Klipnocky Road. This route takes you gradually downhill for a little over a half-mile, where Klip-

nocky Road turns left (east); an unnamed forestry road, however, continues south. Follow this latter route downhill to where the road makes a steep descent and crosses a streamlet flowing south through a gully.

A few more steps bring you to a second streamlet that, a short distance downstream, merges with the first. Once over the streamlet, the uphill route becomes fairly steep for the next 0.3 mile;

Hikers in Klipnocky State Forest

the road now veers gradually to the right (west) as you reach a level section.

For the next 0.7 mile, walking is fairly easy as you proceed over relatively level terrain to the intersection with Gas Spring Road. En route you pass the point where the north-south FLT crosses the road, the route you hiked earlier. Here you have reached an elevation of 2,100 feet. The area's high point is about 0.3 mile north on Gas Spring Road and a short distance to the west of the road. Here the forested land's elevation is 2,145 feet.

On reaching Gas Spring Road, turn left (south) and head downhill. The hiking now becomes easy as you continue your descent for 1.2 miles, where you reach the bottom and your parked vehicle.

Jersey Hill State Forest

Hiking distance: 3.5 miles
Hiking time: 2 hours
Vertical rise: 449 feet
Map: USGS 7½' West Almond; USGS 7½' Alfred

Jersey Hill is the highest spot in this gentle, rolling, and ever-changing landscape. There is nothing showy or spectacular about the terrain, but the unpretentiousness of this hill makes it ideal for leisure walking or steady hiking.

The 1,088-acre Jersey Hill State Forest rises gradually from the Black Creek valley in the west, the Canisteo River valley in the east, and Karr Valley in the south. The top of this hill has been designated on topographical maps as Jersey Hill, with an elevation of 2,240 feet—a level area a mile wide and a half-mile long. The only unusual characteristic of the hill is that it doesn't look like a hilltop. Also unusual is that the hill's high point is privately owned; completely surrounding it, however, is state-owned land.

The state forest is inconspicuous, partly because of its farming past. A goodly portion of the state land is in transition, changing from its former agricultural status to an expanding wild forest. It also blends in with other state holdings. All the state forests hereabouts are joined together in one large crazy-quilt pattern. Hence, it is virtually impossible to tell where one state forest begins and another leaves off.

Jersey Hill State Forest abuts Karr Val-

ley Creek State Forest (see Hike 41) in the southwest, and that forest in turn touches the northeast boundary of Palmers Pond State Forest (see Hike 43). To the north, Jersey Hill State Forest runs along the western edge of Hiltonville State Forest. The latter is only a stone's throw from Gas Springs State Forest, which in turn touches the western boundary of Slader Creek State Forest (see Hike 38). This forest joins Klipnocky State Forest (see Hike 39) to the south.

To let Jersey Hill State Forest win you over on its own subtle way, hike this hill area on a bright spring day or on a warm autumn afternoon; the ascents and descents will make a lasting impression, and that's the hill's unexpected surprise.

Access. Jersey Hill State Forest can be reached by the Southern Tier Expressway (NY 17). If you are coming from either the east or west, leave at Almond (Exit 33), just west of Hornell. Drive into the village of Almond to the intersection with NY 21; turn north on NY 21 and drive to Karr Valley Road, intersecting on the left. Turn here, and drive west on Karr Valley Road for 5 miles to Camp Road, intersecting on the right. Turn onto Camp Road, and head northwest for 2.4 miles where it intersects Jer-

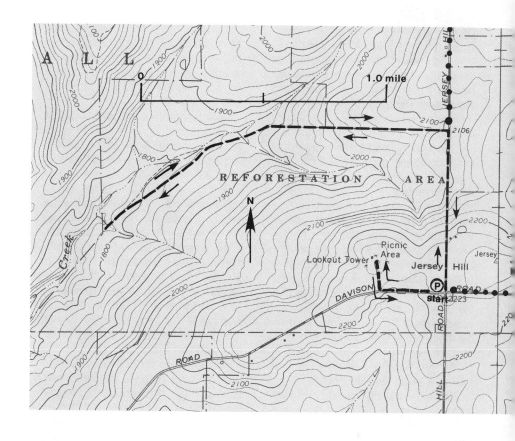

sey Hill Road. Turn, and drive a mile north on Jersey Hill Road to the intersection with Davison Road. Park here.

Trail. Your parking site is at the top of the area's highest hill, Jersey Hill (elevation 2,240 feet). Just over 0.2 mile to the west of the intersection is the old fire tower and picnic area, where you'll stop on your way back.

If you look northeast across Davison Road, you see the open area that makes up the rectangular parcel of private land and the true summit of Jersey Hill. But the wide, flat hill extends about a half-mile in all directions from here.

You start your hike by heading north on Jersey Hill Road. On the right is pri-

vate property and open area; on the left is a mature forest. For the first 0.2 mile, the road is level, but it slopes downhill to a noticeable degree, then reaches a level stretch. This stretch continues north for a little over 0.2 mile, where a truck trail (a state-maintained dirt forestry road) intersects on the left.

Turn onto the truck trail and walk straight west. The forested land on the left (south) belongs to the state forest; the open fields and woodlots on the right are privately owned. The truck trail descends gradually for the first 0.5 mile. Now the land on both sides of the road belongs to the state; you find here an open area containing young growth, indicative of the area's earlier farm use.

The road continues its descent another 0.2 mile; it now slowly turns to the left and crosses a stream-fed gully to head in a southwesterly direction along the edge of the gully. In the wet season, a streamlet flows through it to feed into Black Creek, a couple miles to the west. The road continues its downward route to the southwest for another 0.5 mile, passing through a large open area of new growth before crossing another shallow gully with its streamlet. Just beyond the gully is the turnabout, where you reverse direction and head back. You have walked 2.1 miles with a vertical descent of 443 feet—a sizable drop.

The walk back, of course, is all uphill, although the first 0.8 mile is not all that steep, rising only 80 feet. After the road crosses the gully, you become aware of the more demanding ascent, and in the next 0.8 mile you climb for a vertical rise of 206 feet. Soon you return to the intersection with Jersey Hill Road.

Continue retracing your steps, heading south on Jersey Hill Road. After a level stretch, the road begins a fairly steep incline for 0.2 mile before again leveling off. When you reach the intersection with Davison Road, turn right (west) here and head along the level Davison Road for 0.6 mile past the road on your right that leads to the fire tower site and picnic area.

Just beyond the 0.5-mile mark, the trees give way to an open area that allows you to view the scenery to the south. Turn about here, and head back to the old fire tower road; turn here and walk north about 0.1 mile to the circular turnabout at the old fire tower site and the picnic area. This is a good spot to relax and enjoy the snacks you have brought. When you have finished, you can continue to retrace your steps to your parked vehicle.

If you want to put in a longer day of hiking, you can follow the local dirt roads in a loop or choose any of the hikes through adjoining state forests (see Hikes 38, 39, 41, and 43).

To make a 4–5-mile loop for this longer hike, you will actually follow the form of a rectangle. Start at the intersection of Jersey Hill Road and Davison Road, where you parked your vehicle. Continue east from Jersey Hill Road on Davison Road for a mile, to the first intersection with Dobson Road. Turn north here, and walk along Dobson Road on level terrain for 0.9 mile. At this point the road pitches steeply downward, dropping 260 feet in less than 0.4 mile.

This 1.45-mile distance on Dobson Road brings you to the intersection with Sullivan Road. At the outset, Sullivan Road passes over a gully and then goes uphill. The first 0.15 mile is fairly steep, but as you continue, the road begins to flatten more and more until you reach a level stretch after a mile of uphill walking just before intersecting with Jersey Hill Road.

Turn south on Jersey Hill Road. You have a short climb at the start, but the road is level for the next 0.5 mile, where you reach the truck trail (which you walked earlier) running west. Continue south on Jersey Hill Road for 0.6 mile to the intersection with Davison Road and your parked vehicle.

Karr Valley Creek State Forest

Hiking distance: 4.2 miles
Hiking time: 2½ hours
Vertical rise: 412 feet
Map: USGS 7½' Alfred; USGS 7½' West Almond

Karr Valley Creek State Forest is located in the Cattaraugus Hills in east-central Allegany County, sandwiched between several of the state forests that make this region a hiker's mecca. One of the area's pleasant attractions is Karr Valley, which the state forest's southern section encompasses.

In the northern section is the highest spot—a hill with an elevation of 2,232 feet and a width of almost a mile, which makes it look more like a ridge. From this lofty position, the state forest commands a fine view of Karr Valley.

The thickly forested valley also contains a stream, not surprisingly, called Karr Valley Creek, which flows southeast and then east and eventually feeds into the Canisteo River, near Hornell. The creek's headwaters are in a wooded swampy and marshy area just west of the state forest's boundary. Here, too, begins Karr Valley; it is wide and flat at this point, with low hills set back a good distance. As the creek flows through the valley, however, steep hills on both sides close in on it, as the valley narrows.

The state forest reflects well the many characteristics of the Cattaraugus Hills, which are high, rounded, and usually elongated. The valleys tend to be nar-

row, and many have been cut by streams. Also the long slopes of these hills are marked by gullies where the headwaters of larger streams such as the Canisteo River in the north and Karr Valley Creek and McHenry Valley Creek in the south are found.

Karr Valley Creek State Forest adjoins Jersey Hill State Forest (see Hike 40) in the north and touches the northeast corner of Palmers Pond State Forest (see Hike 43) in the south. These are only two of more than 15 state forests clustered in the east-central part of the county.

Karr Valley Creek State Forest is blessed with a number of roads running alongside or through it. So, by combining several paved and unpaved county roads, state truck trails, and a red-marked hiking trail, you can walk a loop through virtually the entire state forest. This route also allows a close look at the forest's main features, including various types of trees, open fields, high hills, the central valley, streamlets, creeks, gullies, and streambeds.

Access. Coming from either east or west, the best route to reach Karr Valley Creek State Forest is the Southern Tier Expressway (NY 17). Leave the Expressway at Almond (Exit 33), just west of

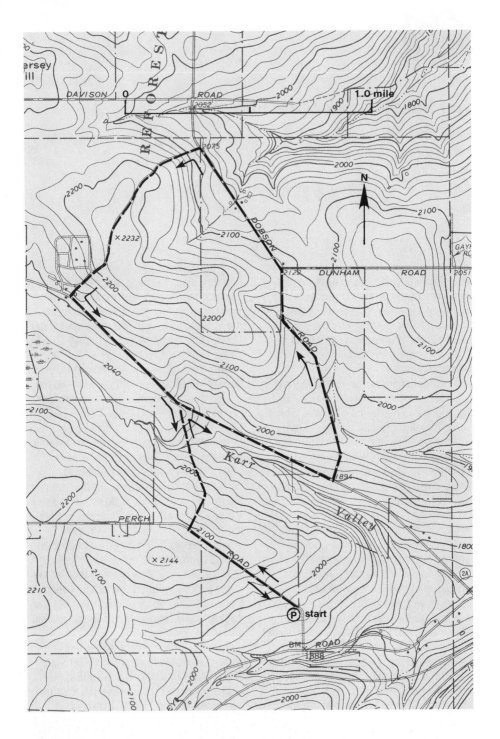

Hornell. Drive into the village of Almond to the intersection with NY 21; turn north on NY 21 a short distance to Karr Valley Road intersecting on left. Turn here, and drive west on Karr Valley Road for 5 miles past Camp Road intersecting on the right. Continue on Karr Valley Road; from Camp Road it is 0.8 mile to the next intersection on the right (north). This is Perch Road.

Turn here, and drive uphill on Perch Road 0.15 mile, where the road turns left and brings you immediately to Karr Valley Creek State Forest on the right side of the road. Park here.

Trail. The state forest contains only

The Author admiring the view in Karr Valley State Forest

0.6 mile of trail that is designated exclusively as a walking path. The bulk of your hike is on a combination of county roads and truck trails.

You begin your hike on Perch Road. From your parked vehicle it is a gradual uphill walk for the first 0.5 mile. There you find the path intersecting on the right, shortly after you pass a state forest boundary on the left. This boundary marks the northeast corner of Palmers Pond State Forest.

Turn right onto the path, which is marked with red discs, and head downhill through the forest. The terrain slopes downward for the next 0.35 mile. There you reach Karr Valley Creek, flowing southeast. After crossing the wooden bridge, the trail begins a gradual climb; 0.1 mile brings you to paved Camp Road.

Turn right here, and walk southeast on level Camp Road for 0.65 mile to where Dobson Road intersects on the left. Turn onto Dobson Road, and head uphill through the southeastern section of the state forest. With trees on both sides, the road is usually well shaded, to make your hike comfortable even on the sunniest day.

As you walk northwest through the state forest, the road levels. About 0.5 mile from Camp Road, the woods show signs of younger growth, and another 0.1 mile brings you to a spot where the state forest ends on the left, although it continues for another 0.25 mile on the right. Sloping uphill on your left is open land.

Dobson Road bends to the right slightly and then heads straight north for a short distance to Dunham Road, which intersects from the right. Here the state forest ends; you are now walking past private land.

From the intersection with Dunham Road, Dobson Road veers northwest, moving gradually downhill through open country. After 0.4 mile, you come to a cluster of farm buildings and a streamlet. From here it is a level walk for 0.3 mile, to where the road reenters the state forest. At this point you also come to a truck trail intersecting on the left (west). From your starting point, you have now hiked 3.6 miles.

Turn onto the truck trail, which immediately starts uphill. The upward pitch is fairly pronounced for the next 0.2 mile, then it levels out. You walk on flat terrain for the next 0.5 mile. Surprisingly, the highest spot in the state forest is an L-shaped hilltop here, just about a mile in length, with an elevation of 2,232 feet.

Continue downhill on the truck trail, leaving the hilltop. The trail soon loops to the right to reach a large maintenance area operated by the state's Department of Environmental Conservation. However, stay on the truck trail, which bypasses the maintenance area and leads back to Camp Road.

Turn left onto the paved Camp Road, and head southeast for 0.7 mile, where you encounter the footpath intersecting on the right; this is the same footpath you walked earlier. Turn onto the red-marked hiking trail, and retrace your steps a mile back to your parked vehicle.

Phillips Creek State Forest

Hiking distance: 8.6 miles
Hiking time: 4½ hours
Vertical rise: 880 feet
Map: USGS 7½' Alfred; USGS 7½' West Almond

Phillips Creek State Forest lies quietly during the summer, when only a handful of hikers use its trails. When the snows come, however, especially on weekends, the parking area fills with cars, and cross-country skiers crowd the Phillips Creek Trail System.

This trail system is the area's big draw. All kinds of trails await the Nordic skier in winter—several beginner trails, several intermediate, and one expert trail. In summer, hikers find a blue-marked hiking trail set aside for them. It allows you to do quite a bit of walking in this thickly forested state land.

This part of Allegany County is rugged; the hills are numerous, with well-defined peaks, mostly at elevations of more than 2,100 feet. The terrain is quite irregular, cut by narrow, deep gullies along the base of steep hills. Climbs of 500 to 700 feet are common, and most foot travel is through vast acreage of forestlands.

This environment is especially noticeable in the county's northeastern section; the state owns almost half the land there. Although settled and farmed during the nineteenth century, the hilly terrain in this part of the county made farming difficult. When the Industrial Revolution replaced

agriculture in the twentieth century, farming began to decline in the hill communities and with the Great Depression of the 1930s, farming virtually disappeared. The state purchased marginal and abandoned farmlands, and today it manages 17 state forests in the northeastern portion of the county, amounting to over 60,000 acres of prime woodland—certainly enough land to keep the hiker going for weeks.

Holding down the southern flank of all this state land is Phillips Creek State Forest, which covers 2,708 acres in the east-central part of Allegany County, just 4 miles west of Alfred. Several small streams that traverse the hiking trails make up the headwaters of Phillips Creek, which flows southwest to the Genesee River, located 10 miles to the west. The state forest owes its name to these small streams, which are the source of water for Phillips Creek.

Access. NY 244, which runs from Alfred in the east to Belmont in the west, passes through the heart of Phillips Creek State Forest, and provides direct access to the parking area and trailhead located on the north side of the highway. A site sign tells you when you have reached the state forest and its parking area, which is located 4 miles west of Alfred and 9 miles east of Belmont. The trailhead is about a quarter-mile north of the parking area.

Trail. Within the 4-square-mile area is an extensive, interconnected trail system designed for cross-country skiing. The trails are color coded with yellow, red, and blue markers. The blue markers designate a hiking trail.

To find the trailhead of the blue trail, leave the parking area and walk northeast for a little over 0.2 mile. The intersecting trail on the left is the beginning of the blue-marked trail. A short distance farther, where the road bends to the right, you'll find the start of the yellow-marked beginner Nordic trail and the red-marked Nordic intermediate trail on your left—in the event you want to return in winter for skiing. For hiking purposes, begin your walk on the blue trail.

This trail starts by running in a northwesterly direction for a short distance and then turns sharply to the right heading due north. You are on high ground at the very start. The elevation at the trailhead is 2,275 feet. As you head north through the woods, the terrain pitches gradually downward. In about 0.2 mile you come to a footbridge and a short distance downtrail you cross another. The water here drains to the west to form the first of two branches of Phillips Creek that originate in this state forest.

For the next 0.3 mile you make a gradual climb and then a fairly abrupt drop to a low area, through which the second beginning branch of Phillips Creek flows. The creek, which you now cross on a third footbridge, originates in a small pond 0.7 mile to the east of the blue trail.

Once over the footbridge, the trail turns left through the forest, passing a lean-to on the right, and then heads

northwest along the north side of Phillips Creek. At the 0.3-mile mark, the trail turns north; 0.1 mile more brings you to Lockwood Road, a narrow dirt road that runs in an east-west direction.

Going north but downhill now, a little over 0.1 mile brings you to a fourth footbridge. It crosses the main branch of Phillips Creek. Here you'll find a yellow-marked trail forking to the right; you, however, continue north. From the creek you climb gradually for 0.4 mile to the intersection with another dirt road, Stewart Road. On the north side of the road is a parking area.

Turn right (east) on Stewart Road and head uphill for a little over 0.3 mile; now the road descends for 0.1 mile, then heads uphill after crossing a small feeder streamlet. About 0.1 mile from the streamlet, the road veers gradually to the left and heads uphill in a northeasterly direction. At the turn, a yellow-marked Nordic ski trail intersects from the right; at this point the red-marked expert Nordic trail also begins, following the road for a while, then turning east to begin a 1.85-mile loop, which returns it almost to its starting point.

But you continue on the dirt road for another 0.1 mile, where the red expert trail crosses, going south on its return loop. The road now begins to bend still more to the left, until finally you are again heading due north. For the next half-mile you are climbing gradually until you reach an open area, which is also the high point of your hike—2,240 feet. The highest point in this general area is a hill with an elevation of 2,303 feet, located a half-mile to the southwest. A short distance to the west of the road is the second-highest spot, with an elevation of 2,276 feet.

The road continues in a northerly direction, first turning slightly to the left as it crosses a level area, then heading

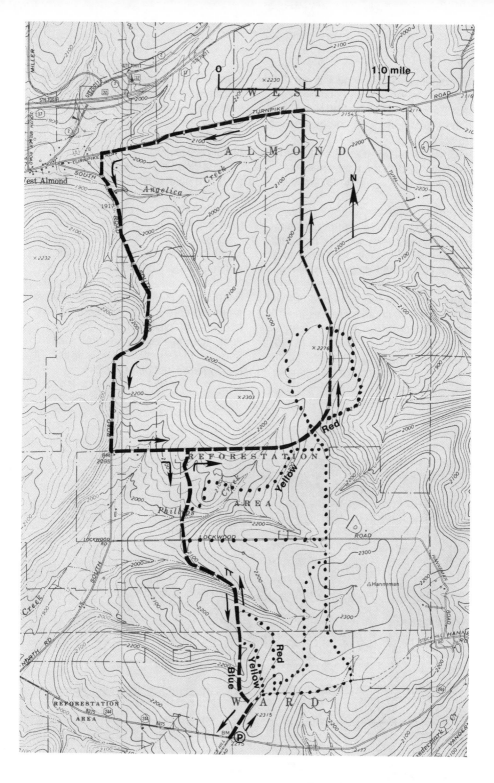

north again as it goes downhill out of the forest into an open area to finally intersect Turnpike Road. From the high spot in the south to the road, the distance is 1.3 miles.

State land extends across the Turnpike Road and to the east where the 4,744-acre Turnpike State Forest is located.

Turn left (west) on Turnpike Road; 1.2 miles of downhill walking through fairly open country brings you to a dirt road intersecting on the left. Turn here, and head south a short distance to where you intersect another road coming from right (west). This is South Road; turn left and follow it south as it crosses the headwaters of Angelica Creek, then starts climbing for the next mile to cross into Phillips Creek State Forest.

The vertical distance of your uphill route is 300 feet—a fair climb in a walk of just under a mile. To the right of the road is a shallow gully. Drainage is to the north, and when the rains come, the water flows downhill to eventually reach Angelica Creek.

South Road now turns to the right, angling in a southwesterly direction for little over 0.2 mile over level terrain before turning south. In a short distance, the road begins to pitch downward, at first gradually and then more steeply. Within a half-mile you reach Stewart Road, which intersects on the left.

Turn here, and walk east on Stewart Road for a half-mile, where you come to a parking area on your left and the entrance to the blue hiking trail on the right. You can now retrace your steps back 1.7 miles to your vehicle in the parking area just off of NY 244.

Entrance to Phillips Creek State Forest

Palmers Pond State Forest (Northern Section)

Hiking distance: 10 miles
Hiking time: 5 hours
Vertical rise: 594 feet
Map: USGS 7½' West Almond; USGS 7½' Alfred

The northern section of Palmers Pond State Forest presents a host of natural and man-made features that stand in sharp contrast to those in the same state forest's southern section (see Hike 44), including, among other things, miles of marked and groomed hiking trails. As a matter of fact, just over 10 miles of trails are found here and managed as a multi-purpose trail system. This means that in winter, the trails are used for cross-country ski touring, while in summer, hikers enjoy short and long walks over a diverse and attractive landscape.

New York's Southern Tier Expressway (NY 17) not only cuts through the middle of the state forest but succeeds in separating two physiographically and ecologically different sections. The northern section is high, with the elevation topping 2,100 feet, but is generally flat compared with the southern section, and it is largely unforested, being used instead for crops and pastureland.

Miller Road divides the upper portion of the northern section into two separate ecological zones. West of Miller Road, where the large parking area and trailheads are found, the terrain is high and level, with a mix of open grassland and immature woodlots. There, young hard-

woods and evergreens compete to achieve dominance upon maturity. On the east side of the road, however, reforestation has been in place a good many years, and virtually the entire area contains mature hardwoods.

The trail systems on either side of Miller Road also differ. The west trail system forms an elongated loop with the outgoing and incoming sections running parallel. In contrast, the east trail system is more circular but also more irregular, following the contours of the rolling terrain.

To the first-time visitor, this well-managed trail system comes as something of a surprise, tucked away as it is in the heart of the Cattaraugus Hill Region, remote and removed from civilization. But that is the key to its charm and attraction; it's a place to enjoy a wild forest experience, winter or summer.

Access. Palmers Pond State Forest is located halfway between Almond and Hornell to the east and Angelica to the west. It may be reached by the Southern Tier Expressway (NY 17) or by Karr Valley Road. Those coming on the Southern Tier Expressway should exit at West Almond onto Karr Valley Road and drive east for 2 miles to Camp Road intersecting from the north. Those traveling west on Karr Valley Road from Angelica should continue past West Almond for 2.4 miles to the intersection with Camp Road. Those coming east on Karr Valley Road from Almond or Hornell will find Camp Road 0.7 mile from the hamlet of Karrdale.

Drive northwest on Camp Road for 2.5 miles to where it turns sharply southward. Jersey Hill Road intersects from the north shortly after the turn, but continue on Camp Road for 0.3 mile to a fork. Bear left onto Miller Road, and continue due south past open farmland and gradually uphill for 0.7 mile to where Kelley-Perch Road intersects from the east; there is a large parking area on both sides of the road.

Trail. The trail system is divided at the parking area. One system runs west for 4.96 miles, and the other loops east for 5.12 miles. All the trails are groomed and marked, and all begin and end at the parking lot. While you can start with either the east or west trail, I recommend the west loop for openers. The trailhead is quite visible from the parking lot.

Once you enter the woods, the trail forks; stay to the right. In about 0.1 mile, the trail starts a gradual descent; at the 0.3 mark, the trail turns right and continues downhill for another 0.1 mile. Here it turns left and levels out. You have been walking through an immature woodlot, but now you enter a thicker, more mature forest.

As you proceed, the trail goes uphill, gradually at first, then more steeply, and finally levels at the mile mark, near this section's highest spot (about 1.0 mile to your left), with an elevation of 2,200 feet. Since your starting point was at 2,157 feet, your vertical rise to this point has been only 140 feet.

Entering a more open area, the trail starts downhill and keeps descending

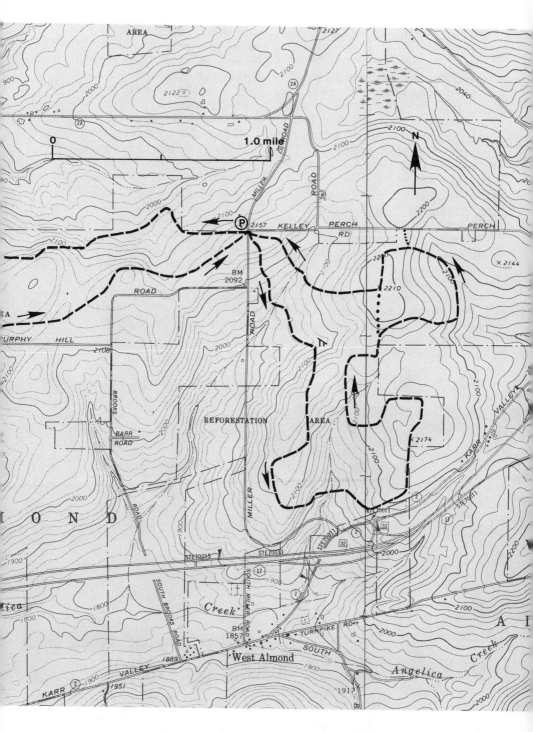

for the next 0.5 mile, until it reaches the beginning of a streamlet. In midsummer it will be dry, but during spring and late fall or after a heavy rain, quite a bit of seepage will fill the streambed with running water. Across the streamlet, the trail flattens out and follows the level contour of the hill, which pitches sharply downhill through a thick stand of trees.

A slight distance ahead, you come to the 2-mile mark and start a short but fairly steep climb to the top of the hill, the 2.2-mile mark. The trail turns right and goes downhill again for the next 0.6 mile. Here it turns sharply left and loops back uphill. This is really your turnabout; from here on, you'll be traveling west back to the parking area.

This section of the hill contains young growth, with hardwoods and evergreens filling in the thick grassy meadow. Soon you reach the top of the hill where the terrain flattens, making your walk through this level section of new growth easy. Even though this area is level and high, there is nonetheless seepage, which makes the area wet during most of the late spring and early summer months.

This condition continues for the next mile, where you encounter a fire lane intersecting on the right. This short lane runs south to Murphy Hill Road. Another 0.4 mile brings you slightly uphill to another high spot, which quickly gives way to a gradual descent, allowing you to pass through a thick stand of trees. Then it goes through a section of young growth and finally exits at the parking area.

Across the road is the entrance to the east trail section. Stay to your right as you enter a stand of young growth,

Palmers Pond State Forest

which gives way to a much older forest. The trail immediately starts downhill for the first 0.3 mile, where it crosses a brook flowing southwest. It may dry out during the summer, but most of the time it is full.

Once across the brook, the trail heads uphill for the next 0.3 mile, where it turns right (south) at the site of a lean-to; this is an ideal spot to stop for a rest or to eat lunch. From here, the trail continues uphill for 0.2 mile to a short, flat area in the forest, the top of the hill at 2,160 feet.

Just beyond this point, you start a short descent, which ends when the trail turns right. It follows a level area to the west for little over 0.1 mile. It then turns left to head south again; at the turn you have reached the 1.1-mile mark. After a short distance on this level section, you come to a left turn, where the trail starts a sharp descent for 0.2 mile to cross another brook. Both brooks in this section of the state forest make up the headwaters of Angelica Creek, located just south of the expressway. Angelica Creek flows west to the Genesee River.

Once over the brook, the trail starts uphill through the forest, turning a little to the south before looping through a section of young growth to go north back into the forest. You reach this section's highest spot, at an elevation of 2,174 feet, just beyond the 2-mile mark.

Continue north a short distance over level terrain until you turn left and start a gentle descent to the same brook that you crossed upstream a short time ago. At the brook, the trail turns north again through a shallow depression and past a swampy area on the right.

Beyond the swamp, the trail turns first right and then, in a short distance, left to again head north. In less than 1.0 mile, the trail reaches the 3.3-mile mark, and a trail intersects from the north at the point where the main trail turns right. This is a connecting trail that runs north a little over 0.2 mile to join up with the main trail.

Continue east to stay on the main trail. It makes a large loop, running first east, then north, finally circling back in a westerly direction. At the 4.1-mile mark, another trail intersects from the north; this 0.1-mile footpath is an access trail from Kelly-Perch Road. A little over 0.1 mile from the intersection, the main trail turns left and heads south over a level area which marks the top of another hill, at 2,210 feet.

Soon the trail turns right and again heads west, gradually descending 100 feet to reach the first brook, which you crossed when you started your hike. After crossing the brook, the trail heads uphill northwest for 0.3 mile. It leaves the forest, passing through a stand of young growth, and finally arrives at the parking area and your waiting vehicle.

Palmers Pond State Forest (Southern Section)

Hiking distance: 4½ miles
Hiking time: 2 hours
Vertical rise: 1,500 feet
Map: USGS 7½' West Almond

Palmers Pond State Forest sits regally astride some of the highest hills in this part of Allegany County, rivaled only by its next-door neighbor, Phillips Creek State Forest (see Hike 42), in providing some of the best views of the surrounding Cattaraugus Hills, whose many peaks rise well above 2,000 feet.

These peaks, the narrow, steep-shouldered valleys, and the thick forests blanketing the hills give this part of New York its rugged appearance. Its beauty makes hiking here a delight. The southern portion of Palmers Pond State Forest is an excellent place to experience the wild forest feeling of Allegany County's Cattaraugus Hills.

The 3,645-acre state forest runs in a north-south direction and is shaped like a huge T. At one time, several roads allowed travel the length of this state forest without difficulty. But the Southern Tier Expressway (NY 17) cut the roads and, in effect, divided the state forest into two roughly equal parts: the northern section and the southern section.

The state forest was named after Palmers Pond, which is a highlight of this hike. It is a surprisingly large, circular pond, about 0.1 mile wide. A picnic area on its southern fringe provides a wel-

come place for hikers to stop for a break and, perhaps, lunch.

The dammed pond is fed by a brook that starts about a half-mile away in the eastern part of the state forest. The pond's overflow moves down a slight depression in a southwest direction, becoming the headwaters of the north branch of Phillips Creek, which feeds into Black Creek, then Angelica Creek, and finally to the north-flowing Genesse River.

The southern half of Palmers Pond State Forest occupies the highlands that rise between two attractive valleys. NY 244, running from Alfred in the east to Belmont in the west, is on the southern edge of the state forest. On the northern edge is the county highway, Karr Valley Road, which runs from Almond in the east to Angelica in the west. Karr Valley Road runs parallel and close to the Southern Tier Expressway, a major roadway with exits for Almond, Angelica, and West Almond.

Between NY 244 and Karr Valley Road are 11,097 acres of state forest. This huge chunk of real estate is divided into three contiguous, but individual state forests—Palmers Pond, Phillips Creek, and Turnpike.

Access. Palmers Pond State Forest can be approached from either the north or the south. The easiest is from the north, which takes you from West Almond on Karr Valley Road to the state forest's Palmers Pond Road. The West Almond exit of the Southern Tier Expressway also takes you there. From Angelica in the west or Almond in the east, you can take either the Expressway or Karr Valley Road.

The intersection of Karr Valley Road and Palmers Pond Road, a dirt roadway, serves as your trailhead and the place to leave your vehicle. This intersection is 0.6 mile west of West Almond. Coming from the west on Karr Valley Road, the intersection is 3.4 miles east of the point where Karr Valley Road crosses over the Southern Tier Expressway.

Trail. No extensive footpaths in the state forest serve as hiking trails; instead, Palmers Pond Road, which runs north-south through the entire southern half of the state forest, serves as your route.

Your trailhead at the intersection of Palmers Pond Road and Karr Valley Road is on high ground, with an elevation of 1,951 feet. Nonetheless, from here it is a steady climb of almost 250 feet for the first half-mile before you reach the first high spot, a level area at an elevation of 2,200 feet.

The area around the trailhead is thickly wooded on both sides of Karr Valley Road. In the forest, a short distance south on the right side of Palmers Pond Road lies a small pond. Beyond this point, the forest gives way to open area on the left side of the road, then closes in with forestation again as you near the top of the hill.

Once you've reached the top, the road levels while continuing due south, allowing you to enjoy an easy walk along the tree-lined roadway. The forest extends

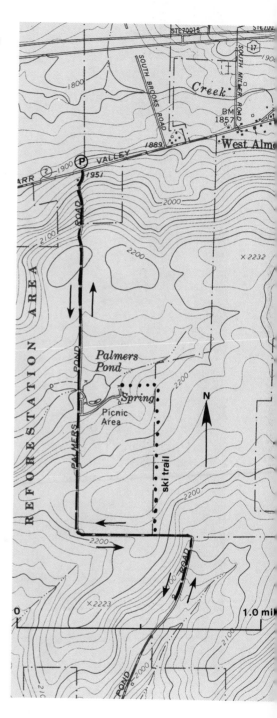

Palmers Pond State Forest

for several miles both east and west from the road. On a sunny day, the trees provide enough shade to make your hike comfortable, especially in the morning or afternoon, when the angle of the sun's rays is low.

When you reach the half-mile mark, the road pitches downward gradually for about 0.25 mile. Here you come upon Palmers Pond, on your left close to the road. A pulloff area abuts the pond, and there is a picnic area on the south side. Just below the pulloff, a short road runs east into the picnic area for 0.2 mile and ends after making a short loop north at a spring.

Here, too, a ski trail coming from neighboring Phillips Creek State Forest terminates; you will use it later to form a short loop. Across the main road, just before the pulloff area, you'll find a trail running west into the forest immediately north of the pond's outlet. This short trail, about 0.1 mile long, takes you to a small pond.

At Palmers Pond, take the picnic area road to its terminus at the spring. In the summer you can expect to find quite a few local people enjoying the pond and picnic area. It is a nice place to seek relief from summer's heat.

The ski trail should not be very hard to find. Follow it as it runs from Palmers Pond east about 0.1 mile, where it turns sharply to the right and heads straight south. A little over 0.5 mile past an open area on your left, you come to the intersection with Palmers Pond Road, which has turned and is now running due east.

If you have difficulty locating the ski trail, return to the main road and continue to hike south. The road now pitches upward for a gradual climb of about a quarter-mile; it is flat for the next quarter-mile, then turns left to head due east.

In about a half-mile, after passing an open area on your left, the road again turns, this time heading south in a gradual descent. In about 0.2 mile, you will see a small pond near the road on your right; another 0.2 mile brings you to a spot where the trees are set back from the road on your left, allowing you to enjoy a fine vista to the south. You'll be looking down upon the hamlet of Phillips Creek, a half-mile away, situated in the valley through which NY 244 passes.

To the east of the hamlet and across NY 244 is the southern section of Phillips Creek State Forest. Still farther south, about 2 miles, but hidden by the hills in front of you, is Vandermark State Forest. The spot where you are now standing marks the end of Palmers Pond State Forest on the left side of the road, although it continues for almost 0.4 mile before ending on the right side.

After you have enjoyed the sights from this overlook, retrace your steps uphill, past Palmers Pond and the picnic area, and finally downhill to your parked vehicle.

Gillies Hill State Forest

Hiking distance: 6.6 miles
Hiking time: 3½ hours
Vertical rise: 460 feet
Map: USGS 7½' West Almond; USGS 7½' Birdsall

Gillies Hill State Forest, occupying the central section of a three-mile ridge, has a commanding view of the Black Creek valley to the east and Baker Creek valley to the west.

This long, tree-covered ridge contains three knobs, each about a mile apart. They are too low to have names, but collectively they form the high ground that locals call Gillies Hill. The highest spot of this land mass, at 2,184 feet, is located in the middle of the ridge and in the central portion of the state forest. The second highest knob, at 2,180 feet, is in the south and outside the state forest land. The third, at 2,128 feet, is located in the north, also outside the state forest. The differences in height are hardly noticeable, and to the human eye the ridge looks like a straight line running in a north-south direction between Black Creek and Baker Creek.

From the ridge the land pitches downward steeply almost 600 feet in the east and south into the narrow Black Creek valley. Much of this steep hillside is state forest land. On the western side of the ridge, the land is more level for a while, then it, too, drops abruptly for 369 feet into Baker Creek valley.

Astride this highland is the 2,332-acre state forest, occupying the east central portion of Gillies Hill. A narrow 1.5-mile finger of state forest land extending north points toward a lowland area that, a short distance to the east, becomes the combined Keaney Swamp State Forest and the Keaney Swamp State Wildlife Management Area.

Draining from the ridge in the east, seven streamlets flow west through this narrow strip. These streams are the headwaters of the south-flowing Baker Creek.

Gillies Hill State Forest is on the northwestern flank of a phalanx of 14 state forests in northeastern Allegany County. This part of the county's rugged highland drains mainly to the southwest and west, with streams running to the north-flowing Genesee River, which cuts through the county from the southeast to the northwest.

Other state forests are located near Gillies Hill. Less than a mile to the east is Jersey Hill State Forest (see Hike 40), and several miles to the south are the northern section of Palmers Pond State Forest (see Hike 43) and Bald Mountain State Forest.

Access. Gillies Hill State Forest can be reached by roads from the northeast

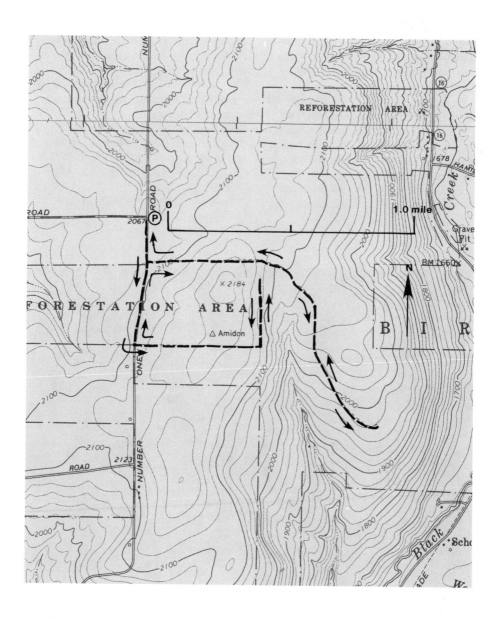

and southwest. From the north, NY 70, which begins at the south end of Letchworth State Park, runs southeast toward the village of Canaseraga. About 2.5 miles west of Canaseraga, County Route 15B intersects NY 70 from the south.

Follow County Route 15B for 4.5 miles to the hamlet of Birdsall; here the road turns north onto County Route 16 and almost immediately turns west onto Gillies Hill Road. This road takes you in 1.3 miles to the intersection with Number

One Road. Turn here, and drive south on Number One Road for 1.7 miles to the intersection with Carson Road. Park here.

From the south the best approach is via the Southern Tier Expressway (NY 17), which passes through the village of Angelica. Leave at Exit 31. The off-ramp road takes you a short distance north to the main street of Angelica.

Turn west here and follow this street through the village, where it becomes County Route 16. From the center of the village, it is 1.6 miles to the intersection with County Route 15. Turn north on County Route 15, and drive 3.2 miles to the hamlet of Aristotle, where the road forks. Take the right leg, which is Old State Road; drive 2 miles north to the intersection with Carson Road. Turn here, and drive uphill on Carson Road for 2.4 miles to the intersection with Number One Road. Park here.

Trail. The area at the intersection is

Raccoon in Gillies Hill State Forest

fairly open, with young growth dominating; it is also level, and the land pitches gradually downward as you face north but remains level as you face south. There you can see the main stand of mature forest.

You begin your hike by heading south on Number One Road. This dirt road in the parlance of state officials is called a truck trail within the boundaries of the state forest. From your parked vehicle, 0.2 mile brings you to another truck trail intersecting on the left (east). You will take this road later; for the present, continue south on Number One Road on level terrain for 0.3 mile, where you encounter a third truck trail intersecting on the east.

Turn here, and follow this dirt road; it runs straight in an easterly direction for 0.5 mile, moving at first gradually uphill into the heart of the forest and then gradually downhill. At the half-mile mark, the road turns sharply to the north and runs over level ground for 0.25 mile to a turnabout, where the road ends. You have come a total of 1.4 miles. To your left about 0.1 mile is the highest spot of Gillies Hill, a knob of land that rounds off at an elevation of 2,184 feet. Through the forest a short distance north of the turnabout is the truck trail you passed earlier on Number One Road.

But the recommended hiking route is to retrace your steps to Number One Road and return north to the intersection with the first truck trail. Turn right here, and follow it eastward. Here again you enter a thick, mature forest as the road runs gradually uphill for 0.4 mile, then heads gradually downhill. Just past the half-mile mark, the road gradually turns to the south. The terrain is now quite level and remains so for about 0.4 mile. At this point the road heads downhill, gradually at first, then more steeply, as it reaches its end at a turnabout. Your total hiking distance so far is 3.6 miles.

You are now at a spot where the land begins to pitch downward. About 0.1 mile from the turnabout, the land drops precipitously into narrow Black Creek valley; the vertical descent here is 360 feet. You now are ready to retrace your steps. From the turnabout, it is 1.4 miles back to Number One Road, and from there, it is 0.2 mile to your parked vehicle.

Allen Lake State Forest

Hiking distance: 5 miles
Hiking time: 2½ hours
Vertical rise: 85 feet
Map: USGS 7½' Fillmore; USGS 7½' Angelica

When you first meet Allen Lake State Forest, several things may strike you as unusual. The name may lead you to believe that the lake is large in relation to the forest, but actually, 2,420 acres of timberland make up the state forest, of which Allen Lake is only a small part. Much of the state forest sits on top of a high hill, one of the higher areas hereabouts. The hill may be a local high spot, but when you reach the top, it is more like a tabletop than a peak. The northern portion of Allen Lake State Forest around the lake is high but flat, providing a large expanse for level walking. A third surprise is that after you drive up from the Genesee River Valley below, you hardly expect to find a sizable body of water occupying the top of the hill—and not just a pond but a lake.

But these unusual features are really a bonus when you visit Allen Lake State Forest. You can picnic by the lake, launch a boat, canoe the lake, or do some serious fishing, spin casting, or fly casting from shore or from the top of the earthen dam if you lack a watercraft; and, of course, there are several miles of good hiking. Not bad for a day's outing.

Surrounding you is an environment that is similar to the Adirondacks. The thick forest around the lake is a mixture of hardwoods and evergreens, including a large stand of scotch pine along the access road.

A road circles the lake, but it is actually four intersecting roads, each with its own name, that form an almost-perfect square of 3.4 miles. Located in the center of the square is Allen Lake, reached by a 0.2-mile access road.

Circling the lake on these roads treats you to numerous vistas and overlooks; if there were a prize for a hill with the most vistas, the northern end of Allen Lake State Forest would win hands down.

The hilltop may be flat, but if you move a mile in any direction from the lake, the sides of the hill slope down, allowing a 360-degree view of the surrounding countryside as you circle the lake.

Why is this lake situated on top of a hill? The answer lies in the pitch of the land and the seepage. The lake itself is at an elevation of 1,899 feet, but to the east of the lake the land rises to an elevation of 1,984 feet. This 85-foot difference is enough to allow the water, which is given up slowly by the surrounding forest lands, to drain into the man-made lake, which sits in the middle of a saucerlike depression. At the lake's south

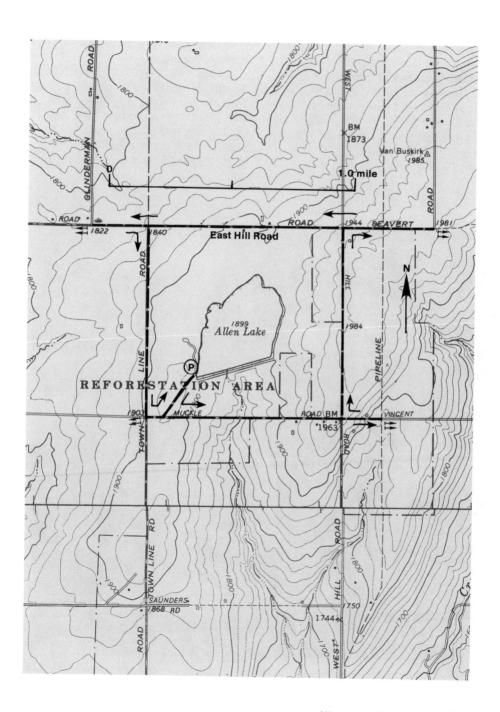

end is an earthen dam, 0.4 mile wide and ranging from 10 to 30 feet high, which backs up a lot of water in this most unlikely place. For those who like fishing, the lake contains pan fish, bullheads, and stocked brown trout.

There are no marked hiking trails in the state forest, but a number of roads run through it and over the hilltop to form a gridlike pattern. From this pattern, the hiker can choose hikes of various lengths and directions.

The state forest lies in northwestern Allegany County, just north of the village of Belfast and five miles east of Rushford Lake, one of the more prominent landmarks of the region.

Access. Allen Lake State Forest can be reached from the east or west by the Southern Tier Expressway (NY 17) or from the north or south by NY 19. If you use the Expressway, get off at Exit 30 and turn north onto NY 19. Drive north on NY 19 for 7.5 miles to Belfast. In the

Hiker looking over Allen Lake

center of the village, turn east onto County Route 16, which takes you in a half-mile past the village cemetery and across the Genesee River bridge. On the east side of the bridge, you cross Belfast Road and continue on a dirt road called Saunders Road. The elevation at the river's edge is 1,282 feet—702 feet below Allen Lake.

Saunders Road begins climbing immediately, and 0.4 mile brings you to the southern edge of Allen Lake State Forest. Another 0.8 mile takes you finally into the state forest itself. From here, it is 2.2 miles to an intersection with another dirt road; south of the intersection, this road is called Camp Road and north of the intersection, it is called Town Line Road.

Turn left onto Town Line Road, and drive 0.75 mile north to the intersection with Muckle Road. Turn right (east) here, and drive 0.1 mile on Muckle Road to the access road on the left. This access road brings you in 0.2 mile to a parking area on the west edge of Allen Lake. Park here.

Trail. You are now ready to try some of the walking routes on this hill. Follow the access road back to Muckle Road; turn left (east), and follow the dirt highway, Muckle Road, east through a stand of hardwood. At 0.7 mile, you cross another dirt road called West Hill Road. Once across, Muckle changes to Vincent Hill Road.

A short distance on Vincent Hill Road brings you to a downhill pitch and one of the many vistas found on this hilltop. The view includes Wigwam Creek, a mile away, and rolling hills across the valley. Retrace your steps back to West Hill Road. Turn right (north), and follow West Hill Road through a large stand of scotch pine; 0.75 mile brings you past more pine stands on the right and an open field on the left as you approach the intersection with East Hill Road.

At the intersection, turn right and walk a short distance to the pipeline right-of-way, running north and south. Here you find another overlook, with views like the ones you enjoyed before. Return to West Hill Road, cross it, and continue your hike, west now, along East Hill Road.

In 0.8 mile you pass stands of spruce on the left and young growth on the right. The growth is low enough to allow a nice view to the north, to Rush Creek valley and a series of hills beyond.

You now come to the intersection with Town Line Road, which runs north and south. A couple hundred feet west of Town Line Road, you have another nice view, this one looking north across Shongo Creek and west across the Genesee River valley. Return to Town Line Road, and turn south; here you follow a route lined with large stands of white pine.

When you get to Muckle Road after walking 0.7 mile from East Hill Road, you turn and look west down Muckle Road for more views of the landscape. Turn east on Muckle Road to the access road leading to Allen Lake; a few minutes on the access road bring you back to your parked vehicle.

Coyle Hill State Forest

Hiking distance: 5 miles
Hiking time: 2½ hours
Vertical rise: 576 feet
Map: USGS 7½' Angelica; USGS 7½' Belmont

Coyle Hill State Forest is located next to the Southern Tier Expressway (NY 17) about two miles west of the village of Belvidere and just slightly west of the midpoint of Allegany County. It has a commanding view of the county's central highlands.

The location of the Expressway makes the state forest easy to reach. A network of truck trails and dirt roads allows you not only to explore the attractive forest area but to put together whatever length hike you like—a short afternoon walk or a weekend jaunt of 15 miles round trip. Your big reward will be the many fine vistas you'll see when you reach the top of Coyle Hill and start your trip down.

The 2,343-acre Coyle Hill State Forest is relatively large, especially compared with the other state forests in Allegany County, including the tightly clustered state forests in the county's eastern section. But unlike these state forests, Coyle Hill stands isolated, like a sentinel guarding the southern flank.

The northern portion of the state forest is easily accessible by several dirt roads coming from the east, west, north, and south. The larger southern section, however, is without roads, although one truck trail manages to make its way

south along the western side for 2.5 miles.

Coyle Hill contains three knobs, the state forest's high spots. Two of these are located in the southern portion—one peaks at an elevation of 2,080 feet, and the other at 2,034 feet. They can be reached only by bushwacking south from one of the dirt roads with map and compass. The third high spot, at 2,038 feet, is located in the north; Coyle Hill Road passes over the top of this knob.

The state forest contains no marked hiking trails; you will hike on state truck trails and dirt roads, some single-laned, others double-laned. These roads will lead you to some of the best spots on Coyle Hill, which give you fine views of the Genesee River valley to the east and the hills beyond.

Coyle Hill drains mostly to the east, and the several streamlets eventually feed into the north-flowing Genesee River. This river cuts through the mid-section of Allegany County as it makes its way north from its origin in Pennsylvania to Lake Ontario.

Access. From the east or west, you can reach Coyle Hill State Forest by the Southern Tier Expressway (NY 17) or from the north or south by NY 19. The

Expressway touches the southern tip of the state forest, but take Exit 30, immediately north of the village of Belvidere. This village is a little over four miles southeast of Angelica and about two miles northwest of Belmont.

At Belvidere, you exit onto NY 19 and drive north about 0.1 mile to the intersection with Hess Road, which runs parallel to the Expressway. Follow Hess Road southwest for a mile, as the road curves north; continue for another 0.3 mile, to where it reaches Warner Road

intersecting on the left. Park here.

Trail. Your hike follows a loop that begins at Warner Road. It makes its way uphill in a northwestly direction for 2.6 miles, and there it intersects Coyle Hill Road. On your return the route follows Coyle Hill Road east to Kleinbeck Road and then to Hess Road, which takes you back to your parked vehicle for a round trip of 5 miles.

At the Warner Road starting point, walk west uphill past private land for 0.3 mile. At this point, you enter the state

View from Coyle Hill State Forest

forest. Here you find young tree growth on both sides of the road wiith pine and spruce on the right and hardwoods on the left.

The road evens out for a short distance. Trees and low vegetation have been cut back along both sides of the road, giving a feeling of openness as you continue your walk. Soon a streamlet appears on the left side of the road as you start to climb again. Your vertical rise up to this point has been a little over 200 feet.

The road now bends north, and your ascent is steeper for the next 0.4 mile. Then the road turns left and again heads west over more level ground. Another 0.4 mile brings you to a truck trail intersecting on the left.

This road runs southwest and then south for 2.5 miles. If you wish to make the prescribed loop, ignore this road; but once you become familiar with Coyle Hill, you may wish to return and include this truck trail in one of your hikes. It is also a route you can take if you wish to lengthen your hike by another 5 miles. This might be just right if you want a weekend outing; you can camp at the turnaround at the end of the truck trail and continue this loop hike the next day.

If you bypass the truck road, continue west over a streamlet for about 0.1 mile. There the road curves sharply to the right and heads north past a large stand of red oak. The road continues to climb for 0.3 mile, then levels out. You pass a stand of pine and larch on the right as you reach the southern edge of the northern section's high spot; locally it is identified as Coyle Hill itself. Another 0.5

mile brings you to the intersection of Coyle Hill Road at an elevation of 2,038 feet, the area's peak.

Looking to the left, you see that this section of Coyle Hill Road is only a narrow lane. The main route turns right onto Coyle Hill Road, which it descends as it heads east. Shortly, you reach the point where the road constitutes the boundary between the state land on the right and the private land on the left.

A little farther on, you reach a fork, where Middle Road goes left and Kleinbeck Road goes right. Both are two-lane dirt roads. This also is the point (elevation 1,907 feet) in your descent where you leave the state forest. Stay on Kleinbeck Road.

As you continue downhill, the area's openness allows you to enjoy fine views to the east and southeast. From the fork, it is 0.5 mile to the point where the road reenters the state forest. It continues for 0.2 mile before again leaving the state forest. The vistas here are just as impressive as they were earlier.

After leaving the state forest for the last time, continue your hike downhill for 0.4 mile, where you come to the intersection with Hess Road. Here you are at an elevation of 1,561 feet, a vertical drop of 477 feet from Coyle Hill's high point.

Turn right (south) onto Hess Road. You have found your way back to civilization as you pass houses and farms on both sides of the road. From the intersection, Hess Road runs first southeast for 0.35 mile and then south for another 0.35 mile, to intersect with Warner Road, where your vehicle is parked.

Rush Creek State Forest

Hiking distance: 5.2 miles
Hiking time: 3 hours
Vertical rise: 876 feet
Map: USGS 7½' Black Creek

Rush Creek State Forest is one of three natural areas in western Allegany County's heavily endowed state forest area. In fact, it is a next-door neighbor of Hanging Bog State Wildlife Management Area and of Crab Hollow State Forest to the southeast (see Hike 49).

Together these three state-owned tracts make a sizable area—7,128 acres over about 50 square miles, 7 miles long and 7 miles wide.

The most conspicuous landmark in the area is the elbow-shaped Rushford Lake, which at its southern end lies across the road from Rush Creek State Forest. The 8-mile-long Rushford Lake is fed by east-flowing Caneadea Creek; from the lake's dam, Caneadea Creek continues east for about 2 miles to the north-flowing Genesee River. Rush Creek, after which the state forest is named, flows north to the southern tip of Rushford Lake.

The state forest contains no marked hiking trails, but it does allow a hiker to walk through the entire length of the state forest from north to south by a state-maintained dirt road. But if you wish to hike a loop rather than retrace your steps, you can continue your hike on a network of dirt roads that will take you through the northeastern portion of Hanging Bog State Wildlife Management Area.

To avoid backtracking, the recommended hike takes you through the greater portion of Rush Creek State Forest for 3 miles and then 2.2 miles through the upper corner of the wildlife management area. On this route, you exit from the state land onto the paved Bellville–North Valley Road, which at the small community of McGrawville changes to Rush Creek Road. The distance from your exit point to your starting point on the paved highway is 1.6 miles. If you want to avoid walking the paved highway, bring a friend with a vehicle to arrange a car-shuttle between the two points.

Given the road network joining Rush Creek State Forest and Hanging Bog State Wildlife Management Area, you can make up a fair number of hiking routes, ranging from the short to the long. If you plan well, you can even make it a weekend camping venture.

Rush Creek State Forest, laid out in an elongated fashion from north to south, straddles the highlands situated narrowly between Rush Creek, to the northwest and Crawford Creek, two miles to the

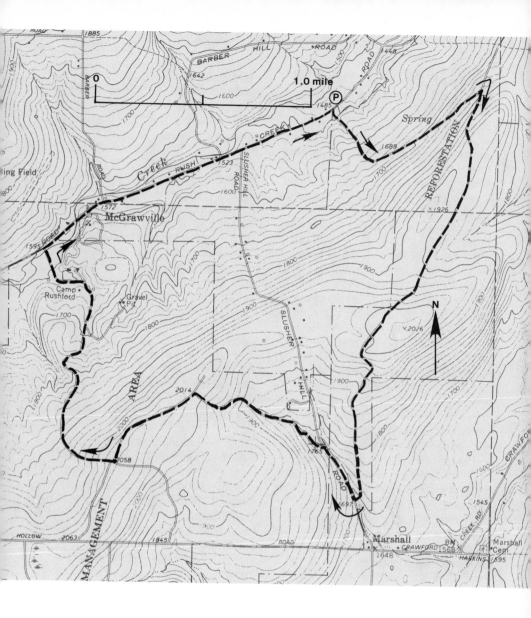

southeast. Between these two river valleys, the land rises 541 feet in about a mile to peak at an elevation of over 2,000 feet. The land may not be all that high, but it is high enough to make the hiker well aware of the area's hilliness.

The state forest contains several high points. The highest point, located in the state forest's southern portion, has an elevation of 2,026 feet. In the northern section, the area's single hill peaks at an elevation of 1,960 feet, while in the central section, the highest spot measures 1,858 feet. Hence, much of your hiking wil be done on the state forest's three-mile-long ridge. The land slopes off to the north into Rush Creek valley and to the south into Crawford Creek valley.

Access. You can reach Rush Creek State Forest from the east or west via the Southern Tier Expressway (NY 17). Get off at Exit 30, and drive north on NY 19 for 12 miles through Belfast to the intersection with County Route 49. The latter road is located a half-mile south of the village of Caneadea and about 0.1 mile south of the bridge crossing Caneadea Creek.

Turn onto County Route 49 and follow it west, then southwest, past Rushford Lake; the county route is called Hillcrest Road until it intersects Rush Creek Road at the southern tip of Rushford Lake. From this point, drive 0.35 mile to where the first dirt road intersects on the left. This is the trailhead leading into Rush Creek State Forest. Park here.

Trail. You begin your hike by following the dirt road that immediately heads uphill in an easterly direction. It is a steady climb for 0.3 mile, at which point the road turns left and begins to follow a more level route. You are still climbing, but not as steeply as before.

The next 0.6 mile brings you to an elevation of 1,800 feet, where you intersect a dirt truck road running in a north-south direction. Turn right (south) onto this truck road, which immediately heads uphill. The ascent is steep, and over the next 0.2 mile your vertical rise is 100 feet. The terrain levels for 0.7 mile, but soon the road becomes steeper. After a 0.2-mile climb, you reach the rounded hilltop; immediately to your left in 0.15 mile is the area's highest point, with an elevation of 2,026 feet.

From this point, you descend. The road winds south along the hill's slope for 0.8 mile, to where the truck road crosses a streamlet and intersects with north-south Slusher Hill Road.

Turn right (north) on Slusher Hill Road and follow it through a narrow, almost ravinelike valley for 0.3 miles, to where an unnamed dirt road intersects on the left (west) at the junction of intersecting streamlets. You now enter the Hanging Bog State Wildlife Management Area.

This road follows the west branch streamlet (on the right) to the stream's origin on the downside of the hill. Then the road goes uphill again and becomes steeper as it nears the top of the hill, where it turns left. Another 0.5 mile brings you to one of the high points in the north section of the Hanging Bog State Wildlife Management Area, at an elevation of 2,058 feet. Here you intersect a road running east and west.

Turn right onto this dirt road and follow it west; from here on, the route is all downhill. After running west for 0.2 mile, the road begins a slow turn to the north and continues downhill for a mile, making several sharp turns. A dirt road 0.3 mile long, leading to a gravel pit, intersects on the right.

Continue on the main route for another 0.25 mile, where you come to an area containing several wooden buildings and a sizable pond. This is Camp Rushford, the site of New York State's Environmental Education Camp. Another 0.2 mile brings you to a bridge over Rush Creek and then the paved Bellville–North Valley Road and the end of the wildlife management area.

Turn right onto the paved road, which, in 0.3 mile, brings you to a small cluster of homes—a community called McGrawville. At the intersection with Barber Road in McGrawville, the name of the paved road is now Rush Creek Road. From the intersection with Barber Road, it is 1.2 miles past Slusher Hill Road to your parked vehicle at the trailhead leading into Rush Creek State Forest.

Hanging Bog State Wildlife Management Area and Crab Hollow State Forest

Total hiking distance: 18.8 miles (3 hikes)
Total hiking time: 9 hours
Vertical rise: 691 feet
Map: USGS 7½' Black Creek; USGS 7½' Rawson

Astride the highlands of Allegany County are two interlocked parcels of state land, the 4,571-acre Hanging Bog State Wildlife Management Area and the 1,154-acre Crab Hollow State Forest. A bog pond is at the point where these tracts of state land join—the pond's southern half is located in Hanging Bog and its northern half is in Crab Hollow.

In Hanging Bog State Wildlife Management Area is a bog pond just over 0.3 mile long and 0.2 mile wide. It contains a score of small, grass-tufted islands that appear to be floating in formation on the surface.

This wildlife area is a bit unusual since the bog pond is situated literally on top of a hill—in fact, on a highland area that has an elevation of more than 2,000 feet. In these parts, this is high land indeed, and not exactly where you would normally expect to find a pond or a bog.

Its elevated location and the terrain explain how this is possible. Hanging Bog is located in a shallow depression in a relatively level area that is overlooked and dominated by four low-relief knolls. A little over a half-mile to the north is the area's highest point, 2,117 feet. A mile to the east is another hillock, at 2,073 feet. To the south is a third knoll, with an elevation of 2,062 feet; and to the west the land rises to 2,012 feet.

In the center of these four high spots is the bog pond, at an elevation of 1,960 feet—about 150 feet lower than the surrounding hilly landscape. This is low enough to allow drainage from the higher points to fill the shallow depression with water year-round.

The highland area with its four knobs is 5 miles wide and 4 miles long. It rises out of four valleys—Rush Creek valley in the north, Genesee River valley in the east, Black Creek valley in the south, and Rawson Valley in the west, through which flows Oil Creek.

Four miles southwest of Hanging Bog is Cuba Lake, and a little farther south is the village of Cuba. Here Rawson Valley and Black Creek valley come together to form a wide, flat valley. During the deglaciation period some 11,000 years ago, this valley served as the main south-flowing drainage area for waters coming from the melting Wisconsin glacier.

The Oil Creek–Black Creek valley is also the route of the old Genesee Valley Canal. Completed in 1861, this canal linked Lake Ontario at Rochester with the Allegheny River at the Pennsylvania border; 112 locks were required for canal boats to cover this distance.

Here, too, is the location of the famous Seneca Oil Spring, the so-called "burning spring," where oil was first discovered in America in 1627 (more than 230 years before the first successful oil well was drilled in Titusville, Pennsylvania); the spring is now protected in a small park in Oil Spring Indian Reservation, 2 miles north of Cuba. Seneca Indians once lived on the reservation, but have since moved to other reservations farther west in the state, leaving the Oil Spring Reservation unoccupied.

In spring, when the water in Hanging Bog is high, the pond drains to the south a short distance to a small man-made impoundment. From here the water flows to the northeast to form the headwaters of Crawford Creek. By the time Crawford Creek reaches the hamlet of Oramel, 8 miles to the northeast, it has become a respectable stream; an additional 0.5 mile farther north brings the creek to its confluence with the Genesee River.

Both parcels of state land are located in the Town of New Hudson in northwestern Allegany County. Together they cover 5,725 acres of rolling hills, extensive forestlands, scrublands, and marshlands. The largest portion of the Hanging Bog State Wildlife Management Area was acquired from private owners by the U.S. government in the 1930s and transferred to New York State in 1962 for wildlife management.

Since 1984, this wildlife area has been managed to provide nesting, feeding, and cover habitat for a wide assortment of wildlife. Common to the area are the white-tailed deer, cottontail rabbit, gray squirrel, wild turkey, ruffed grouse, woodcock, raccoon, red and gray fox, opossum, and several species of waterfowl that use the many ponds for resting, feeding, and nesting.

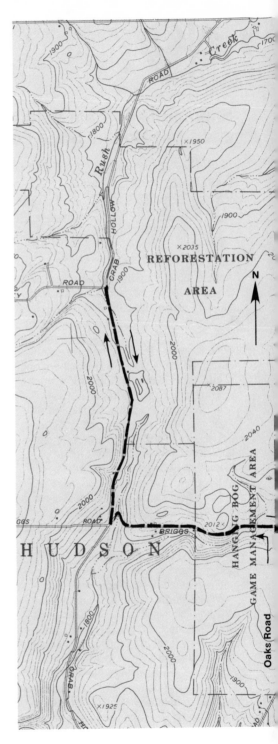

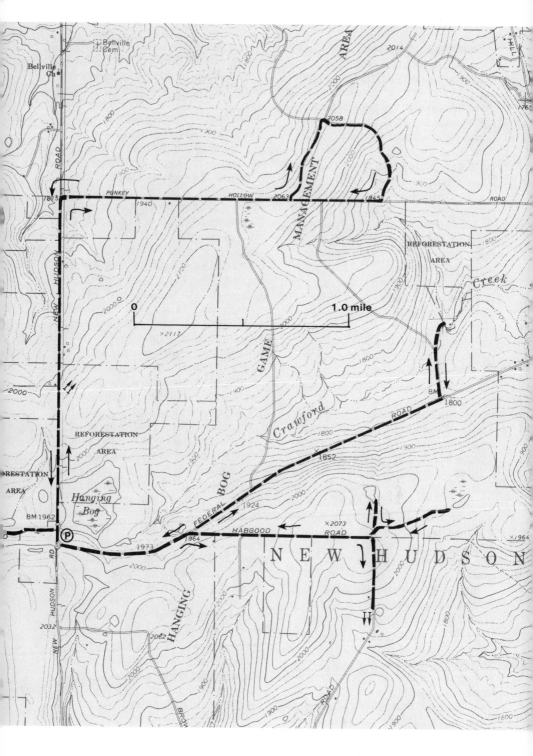

Land management practices include the establishment and care of conifer plantations, as well as the thinning and selected lumbering of hardwoods. In addition, abandoned pastures and fields are mowed, and small marshes and ponds are developed and maintained. As a result, the Hanging Bog tract provides a varied but attractive landscape. It has a mix of open fields and large stands of evergreens and hardwoods, ponds, marshes, and streams.

Crab Hollow State Forest, in turn, is managed primarily to grow and harvest trees. Hence, this land is heavily forested. Although most of the state forest is located outside and to the west of the wildlife area, a sizable chunk of the state forest is also found within the wildlife area.

The combination of these two state parcels provides an ideal environment for either leisure strolling or serious hiking. An extensive interconnected road system covers both parcels, but no marked hiking trails are found in either parcel. Nonetheless, the road network allows you to reach virtually any part of the combined 5,725-acre area.

By combining several of the roads and truck trails, three hiking routes suggest themselves, for a total of 18 miles. You can hike all these routes during a weekend backpack outing with camping near Hanging Bog, or you can hike them one at a time during several visits to the area.

There are no designated camping or bivouac sites either in Hanging Bog State Wildlife Management Area or in Crab Hollow State Forest. It is just a matter of finding a good spot and pitching your tent for the night. If you are planning to stay at one spot for more than three days, a permit is required. Such a permit can be obtained from the regional office of the state's Department of Environmental Conservation, located in Olean (716-372-0888).

The recommended hiking routes include the Federal Road–Habgood Road route (6.6 miles), the New Hudson Road–Punkey Hollow Road route (7 miles), and the Briggs Road–Crab Hollow Road route (5.2 miles). These mileages cover the round-trip distances.

Access. The wildlife area and the state forest can be easily reached. From the east or west, take the Southern Tier Expressway (NY 17) to Cuba; from the north or south, take NY 305 to the same village. From Cuba, drive north 5 miles on NY 305 past Cuba Lake (on the left) and through a crossroad called Lyons Corners to New Hudson Road, which intersects from the north. From the intersection, it is 2.6 miles uphill on Hudson Road to Hanging Bog.

In the east, the departure point is the village of Belfast which sits astride NY 19. Follow NY 19 south out of Belfast for just over a mile to the intersection with NY 305 coming from the right; take NY 305 southwest for 8.5 miles to the intersection with New Hudson Road, and then turn north on the latter road for 2.6 miles to Hanging Bog.

In the north the departure point is the hamlet of Rushford, through which NY 243 passes. A little more than a mile south and then east on NY 243 brings you to County Route 49; follow this road south for about 3 miles to the end of Rushford Lake, where the road is intersected by Rush Creek Road. Turn here, and drive southwest on Rush Creek Road (which later turns into Bellville–North Valley Road) for 3 miles, where it is intersected from the south by New Hudson Road; 2.6 miles uphill on New Hudson Road is Hanging Bog. None of these roads is marked; hence, you will need a USGS topographic map to tell you where you are going.

When you reach the bog, you have also come to a point where three roads almost intersect: the north-south New Hudson Road is intersected from the east by Federal Road, and a short distance north of this intersection, New Hudson Road is intersected from the west by Briggs Road. The bog lies adjacent to New Hudson Road, immediately east of the spot where all the roads intersect. Park your vehicle here.

Trails. All the recommended hiking routes radiate from Hanging Bog pond, with one route going east, one north, and the third west. For openers, try first going east on unmarked Federal Road.

Day One (Federal Road–Habgood Road, 6.6 miles). This route takes you through the south-central portion of Hanging Bog State Wildlife Management Area and to one of the several high spots surrounding the bog pond. At the intersection of New Hudson Road and Federal Road, turn onto Federal Road, and walk east on level terrain; Federal Road passes along the southern edge of the bog pond and the pond's outlet stream.

From your starting point, continue on Federal Road, a flat, tree-lined route, for 0.4 mile; on your left through the trees and tall grass, you can see a small man-made impoundment. It receives water from Hanging Bog and then releases it to the east into the beginnings of Crawford Creek. An additional 0.3 mile brings you to a dirt road, Habgood Road, intersecting from the east and a small pond on the road's west side; the pond flows north a short distance to Crawford Creek.

At the intersection, turn right onto the unmarked Habgood Road; 0.2 mile brings you to a road intersecting from the south, where private land is found. Continue on Habgood Road, and soon

the land on your right becomes state land; all the land on the left side of the road is part of the Hanging Bog wildlife area. However, in 0.2 mile, the land on the right again reverts to private holdings, although state land continues on the left side of the road.

An additional 0.3 mile uphill brings you to level land and the top of an unnamed hill with an elevation of 2,073 feet, as well as the place where Habgood Road turns south. When you reach the 90-degree turn, walk south a short distance where the land pitches downward; here you have a spectacular view overlooking Black Creek valley to the south and the high rolling hills beyond separating Black Creek valley from White Creek valley.

At the road's turn you also find footpaths running north and northeast to two small ponds. At the beginning of the footpaths there is a sign stating that motor vehicles are prohibited on these paths.

From Habgood Road, there is initially only one footpath heading north. About 200 feet down this path, however, you come to a fork, with one path heading north and the other angling to the right in an easterly direction. The north-bound path is a short one, and in less than 0.2 mile it leads to an attractive pond. The other path takes you in a little over 0.3 mile to the other, smaller pond, which is located in a boggier area. Even though both ponds are located on this flat hilltop, they sit in just enough of a depression that water can collect in the ponds easily.

After visiting both ponds, retrace your steps to Habgood Road and then back to the intersection with Federal Road. Turn right onto Federal Road, and continue your hike on this road in a northeasterly direction; a little over 0.3 mile brings you to a road intersecting on the left. Continue past this road, downhill on Federal Road for a mile, to where a truck road intersects on the left. Turn here and walk downhill and over Crawford Creek for 0.4 mile, to where the truck road ends on the north side of Crawford Creek.

This is your turnaround point. Retrace your steps to Federal Road, and then back 2 miles to Hanging Bog.

Day Two (New Hudson Road–Punkey Hollow Road, 7 miles). This hike starts you off in Hanging Bog State Wildlife Management Area, takes you north through a square inholding of Crab Hollow State Forest, and then back into Hanging Bog by way of Punkey Hollow Road. As before, start your hike at the bog pond; but this time, head north on the tree-lined New Hudson Road.

As you leave Hanging Bog, you begin a gradual but barely noticeable ascent as you proceed north. At the 0.6-mile mark, you reach the road's highest spot, at 2,000 feet, where you have a fine view to the north overlooking Rush Creek valley (1.5 miles away) and of the hills lying beyond.

For the next 0.5 mile, you walk on high but level terrain; the road then pitches gradually downward, and an additional 0.3 mile brings you to another dirt road, Punkey Hollow Road, intersecting on the right. The elevation here is 1,815 feet, for a vertical drop in the last 0.8 mile of 285 feet.

Turn here, and walk east on Punkey Hollow Road. The road climbs gradually uphill for the next 0.7 mile, where the land then levels off. A little to the south from this point is an elongated knoll (elevation 2,117 feet), one of the several high spots surrounding Hanging Bog. Drainage here is to the east, and a small streamlet 0.2 miles south of Punkey Hollow Road feeds into Crawford Creek.

An additional 0.2 mile brings you to an unnamed dirt road intersecting on the left. The elevation here is 2,063 feet, giving you a vertical rise from New Hudson Road of 248 feet—a fair climb. Turn here, and walk north over level terrain; you are on the beginning of a loop that after 1.6 miles brings you back to the intersection. The next 0.4 mile takes you to another intersection. Turn right onto an unnamed dirt road. Walk east and gradually downhill for 0.2 mile; there the road turns south, and the descent becomes steeper until, after walking 0.8 mile, you intersect the east-west Punkey Hollow Road at an elevation of 1,845 feet. Your vertical drop to this point has been 213 feet.

Turn right (west) on Punkey Hollow Road. From here, it is an uphill climb for 0.4 mile where you encounter the unnamed road intersecting from the north—the one you took earlier when you started the loop you now are completing. From here, retrace your steps a mile back to New Hudson Road and then south to Hanging Bog.

Day Three (Briggs Road–Crab Hollow Road, 5.2 miles). On the west side of Hanging Bog is the intersection of north-south New Hudson Road and east-west Briggs Road. Begin your hike by heading west on Briggs Road. This route takes you through a small portion of Crab Hollow State Forest, then through Hanging Bog State Wildlife Management Area, and finally along the western edge of Crab Hollow State Forest.

At the start, you pass a small private inholding on your left, then a 0.4-mile long inholding of Crab Hollow State Forest. From your starting point, it is 0.2 mile to a sizable pond on the north side of the road in the Crab Hollow portion of this forested area. The pond is 0.2 mile long. As you reach the western edge of the pond, you encounter a dirt road, Oaks Road, intersecting from the south. The road runs south over a level portion of a hilltop, one of the several high spots found here.

Walk south on Oaks Road for 0.4 mile, to where the land pitches down; here you have an excellent view of Black Creek valley and the high hills to the south and west. After you have enjoyed the vista, return to Briggs Road and continue hiking west; 0.4 mile brings you to the western boundary of Hanging Bog State Wildlife Management Area.

From here, the land pitches down, and the road passes private land; in 0.5 mile, you reach the headwaters of the south-flowing Black Creek. Once over the bridge, Briggs Road intersects north-south Crab Hollow Road.

Turn right (north), and follow Crab Hollow Road north as it makes its way through a narrow but attractive valley running between thickly forested hillsides. From the intersection, it is 0.4 mile to the southern boundary of Crab Hollow

State Forest on the right side of the road.

From the boundary line, it is 0.2 mile to a sizable pond almost 0.2 mile long. In the middle of the pond is a tree-covered island. This unnamed pond sits on a divide from which water drains to the south into the beginnings of Black Creek and to the north into the beginnings of Rush Creek.

All of the land on the east side of the road for the next 0.6 mile belongs to Crab Hollow State Forest, and beyond that for an additional 0.5 mile, the state forest occupies land on both sides of the road.

Continue north on Crab Hollow Road; 0.3 mile brings you to where the headwaters of Rush Creek pass under the road, switching from the right to the left side. A short distance from this point takes you to the intersection of Dewey Road from the west.

This is your turnaround point. From here, retrace your steps south to Briggs Road and then east to Hanging Bog.

50

Swift Hill State Forest

Hiking distance: 7 miles
Hiking time: 3½ hours
Vertical rise: 510 feet
Map: USGS 7½' Houghton

Swift Hill State Forest is tucked away in the northwest corner of Allegany County, well off the beaten path and away from major highways. Foot traffic and just about any other kind of traffic are at a minimum. To come to this area is to experience a kind of tranquillity that only a remote, forested hilltop can provide.

Not surprisingly, the 1,568-acre state forest has several assets that make it ideal for hiking. High ground overlooks countryside where the scenery is a pleasant mix of fields and forests, the terrain a varying blend of high but level hills, and signs of civilization are at a distance. Yet it is not all that difficult to get to the state forest if you know what backroads to take.

Running through the state forest's northern portion is a small section of the Finger Lakes Trail (FLT), which originated 40 miles back in Allegany State Park. This white-blazed trail runs for 1.6 miles through Swift Hill State Forest and continues east over private land for 2.2 miles to the hamlet of Higgins, situated in a narrow valley through which flows Sixtown Creek. From Higgins the FLT continues its easterly route toward-Portageville and into the southern tip of Letchworth State Park. Here a spur trail runs north off the FLT through the park's east side to Mount Morris; the main FLT continues eastward.

Going the other way from Swift Hill State Forest, the FLT follows county roads west for 5 miles through Farmersville State Forest (see Hike 34). A few miles farther south, the FLT passes through the northern section of Bush Hill State Forest (see Hike 33).

Although the FLT runs only a short stretch in Swift Hill State Forest, it nonetheless provides for a most pleasant—and even in midsummer, a cool—hike through plantations of tall hardwoods that shade the foot-trail. The FLT takes you over the high ground of Swift Hill, after which the state forest is named. Here the hills look as if they had been pressed together and their tops flattened to provide for a wide, level ridge two miles long and a mile wide.

The area's elevations reach respectable heights, ranging from 1,900 feet to over 2,000 feet. But from the valleys below, the vertical rise is only about 400 feet. Nonetheless, the sides of Swift Hill are steep, except in the west, where Swift Hill blends evenly with the plateau-like land at an elevation of around 2,000 feet.

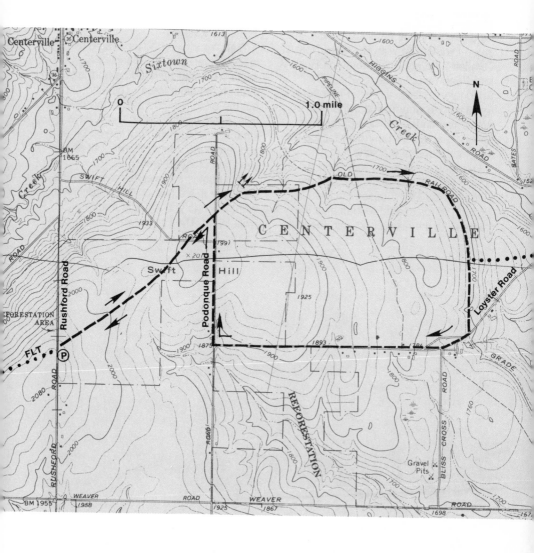

Nature has given this land a quality that appeals not only to the eye but to the heart as well. To be sure, there is high ground to climb; but once on top, the terrain is level, making for easy walking. The hilltops also provide eye-arresting vistas to the north, east, and south from the various overlooks you will find on the hiking route.

Access. The easiest approach to Swift Hill is to find NY 19, which runs in a north-south direction in western Allegany County. In the county's northwestern part is the village of Fillmore, and little over a mile north on NY 19 is the hamlet of Hume. From Hume drive 0.7 mile north on NY 19 to where County Route 3 (also called Buffalo Road) intersects on the left.

This road runs west in a straight line

for 5.6 miles to the hamlet of Centerville at the intersection wiith Rushford Road. Turn left here and drive south on Rushford Road for 0.7 mile, to where Swift Hill Road intersects on the left. From here, it is 0.3 mile to where Swift Hill State Forest begins on the left side of the road. The road acts as a boundary for the 0.8-mile-long edge of the state forest.

From the intersection with Swift Hill Road, it is 0.8 mile to the point where the Finger Lakes Trail crosses the road. A sign at the forest's edge indicates the trailhead to the hiking path into the state forest. Park here.

Trail. Your hike begins at an elevation of 2,080 feet, one of Swift Hill's high spots. You start by heading northeast through the state forest. The land slopes, but the pitch is moderate for the next 0.3 mile, to where the terrain levels for a stretch; the footpath now rises a bit as you reach the center of Swift Hill at an elevation of 2,010 feet.

This spot is so level that you are unaware that it is a hilltop. A short distance farther brings you to a dirt truck trail, Swift Road. The FLT crosses it and con-

View from Swift Hill

tinues over level terrain for little over 0.1 mile to the north-south Podonque Road. If you want a fine view looking north, turn north on Podonque Road and walk through the forest to its northern edge.

On the right side of the road is a large open area, allowing a view down the steep hill to Sixtown Creek valley and across to the rolling hills beyond.

Retrace your steps back to the FLT, and follow it as it runs northeast through the state forest. Here you find the land sloping downhill, at first gradually, then more steeply. You pass over a gully where a streamlet has its beginning, and then you reach the end of the state forest.

The FLT continues downhill for 0.2 mile, where it enters what was once a railroad right-of-way (the tracks were removed years ago). Then it passes over a pipeline right-of-way. The FLT continues on the level railroad grade as it follows the hill's contour, running first eastward for a little over 0.5 mile, then curving southward. After 0.4 mile, it turns east again for 0.3 mile to intersect Loyster Road.

The FLT crosses this road and goes east, bypassing the hamlet of Higgins, located a short distance to the north. Your route, however, goes in the other direction. Turn west on Loyster Road; 1.3 miles brings you past a number of homes along the road in a gradual climb to where the state forest begins on the left. A short distance beyond, the land on the right changes from private to state forest.

In little over 0.3 mile from the eastern edge of the state forest, you reach the intersection with Podonque Road. Turn right here, and walk north for 0.5 mile to the intersection with Swift Hill Road. Turn onto Swift Hill Road, and walk west to intersect the FLT. A distance of 0.7 mile in a southwesterly direction on the FLT brings you to Rushford Road and your parked vehicle.

Also from The Countryman Press
and Backcountry Publications

The Countryman Press and Backcountry Publications, long known for fine books on travel and outdoor recreation, offer a range of practical and readable manuals.

Hiking Series:

50 Hikes in the Adirondacks, $11.95
50 Hikes in Central New York, $11.95
50 Hikes in Central Pennsylvania, $10.95
50 Hikes in Connecticut, $11.95
50 Hikes in Eastern Pennsylvania, $10.95
50 Hikes in the Hudson Valley, $10.95
50 Hikes in Lower Michigan, $12.95
50 Hikes in Massachusetts, $11.95
50 More Hikes in New Hampshire, $12.95
50 Hikes in New Jersey, $11.95
50 Hikes in Northern Maine, $10.95
50 Hikes in Ohio, $12.95
50 Hikes in Southern Maine, $10.95
50 Hikes in Vermont, $11.95
50 Hikes in West Virginia, $9.95
50 Hikes in Western Pennsylvania, $11.95
50 Hikes in the White Mountains, $12.95

Other Outdoor Recreation Guides

25 Bicycle Tours in Eastern Pennsylvania, $8.95
20 Bicycle Tours in the Finger Lakes, $8.95
25 Bicycle Tours in the Hudson Valley, $9.95
25 Bicycle Tours in Ohio's Western Reserve, $11.95
Canoeing Central New York, $10.95
Discover the Adirondack High Peaks, $14.95
Discover the West Central Adirondacks, $13.95
Walks & Rambles in Dutchess and Putnam Counties, $9.95

Other Books of Interest:

Maine: An Explorer's Guide, $16.95
New Hampshire: An Explorer's Guide, $16.95
Vermont: An Explorer's Guide, $16.95
New England's Special Places, $12.95
New York State's Special Places, $12.95
Family Resorts of the Northeast, $12.95
Pennsylvania Trout Streams and Their Hatches, $14.95

We offer many more books on hiking, walking, fishing and canoeing in New York State, New England, the Midwest, and the Mid-Atlantic states—plus books on travel, nature, and many other subjects.

Our titles are available in bookshops and in many sporting goods stores, or they may be ordered directly from the publisher. When ordering by mail, please add $2.50 per order for shipping and handling. To order or obtain a complete catalog, write The Countryman Press, Inc., P.O. Box 175, Woodstock, Vermont 05091.